The Melbourne Portraits Project: A Photographic Ode
by Paul Tocatlian

Published by Kisau Press
All photography by Paul Tocatlian
San Jose, CA, USA
www.kisau.com

ISBN (Print): 979-8-218-18684-5
ISBN (eBook): 979-8-218-18685-2

First Edition

The **Melbourne Portraits** Project

A Photographic Ode

Paul Tocatlian

Contents

Acknowledgments

I'd like to begin by acknowledging the Traditional Owners and Custodians of the land on which the photos in this book were taken, the Wurundjeri people of the Kulin Nation. Sovereignty was never ceded. I also pay my respects to their Elders, past, present, and emerging.

Creating this book was both harder than I expected and more rewarding than I could have imagined. None of it would have been possible without my partner, Hannah Do. She encouraged me to pursue this project and supported me during my two-year stay in Melbourne, even while we were 7,875 miles apart. When I returned to the San Francisco Bay Area, Hannah continued to help, spending countless hours selecting photos, organizing chapters, and shaping the visual narrative.

I'm eternally grateful to my daughter, Jenna Tocatlian, who I love to the moon and back. I didn't see her for over two years, and during that time, she graduated from college, started her career in Public Relations, moved into her first apartment, contracted COVID-19, got a puppy, bought her first car, and so much more. I wish I could have been there for every milestone. Still, that distance brought us closer and strengthened our connection. Her editorial guidance and advice were essential in shaping this book.

Finally, to all the creatives who contributed to making this book a reality—whether you were in front of or behind the camera—your support, collaboration, and artistry have elevated this project beyond what I could have imagined. I'm also deeply grateful to those who have guided me along the way, including Ted Forbes from The Art of Photography, whose invaluable advice during the 'Photo Zines—Concept to Creation' workshop helped me truly grasp how to bring this book to life from an initial idea to a finished work. This book is better because of all of you.

Dedication

This book is the sum of the creative influences and experiences that unfolded during my two years in Melbourne. It is dedicated to the photographers, models, hair and makeup artists, writers, street artists, and other creatives who joined me on this photographic journey.

Foreward

Dear Stranger,

Everybody has their way of feeling alive. For me, it's my pen. For Paul, it's his camera.

When I first saw Paul taking photos on the streets of Melbourne in between COVID-19 lockdowns, I knew photography was his lifeline. When he shot, his eyes burned electric-bright, full of light. He clicked-clicked-clicked his shutter with the intensity of a madman determined to burn the darkness away from the subject's eyes.

Taking photos of real people with real stories nearly every day, Paul got to know Melbourne better than most Melbournians. He wanted to ensure every person he collaborated with could tell their tale. In one frame. In a city of five million. He wanted his photos to make them feel less like an extra and more like a star. By doing this.

His mind-blowing experiences and countless encounters were not down to luck but to his pure, unbridled kindness and openness to meeting new people. Paul never charged a cent for his photos, no matter who he shot or where he went. To him, happiness was compensation, which makes this book and his work the charm it is. Pure. Raw. Unfiltered. Giving. Like Paul himself.

I hope you enjoy this book as much as I did getting to know Paul, getting photographed by him, and befriending him. I wouldn't even call this thing you are holding a book, but an open window into the life of a man who wanted to understand the world for what it is and make every stranger he encountered along the way feel special.

For Paul, his camera was his cure to the pandemic when he was isolated in a city far from home. He started with something quite personal. Then made it universal. I hope he inspires you to pick up your cure and shoot your heartache away too.

Jay Ventress

Introduction

Introduction

The Backstory

This book was born on the streets of Melbourne during the COVID-19 pandemic. Despite spending 262 days in lockdown during my two-year stay, I fell in love with the city's eclectic mix of empty streets, Victorian-era skyscrapers, Art Deco buildings, and post-modern landmarks. For me, Melbourne became more than a place—it became my studio.

What truly sets Melbourne apart, though, is its people. It's a city where people from every walk of life and every corner of the world come together. This melting pot of cultures encouraged me to unlock my passions and fuel my creativity, leading to numerous collaborations with photographers, models, hair and makeup artists, writers, and street artists.

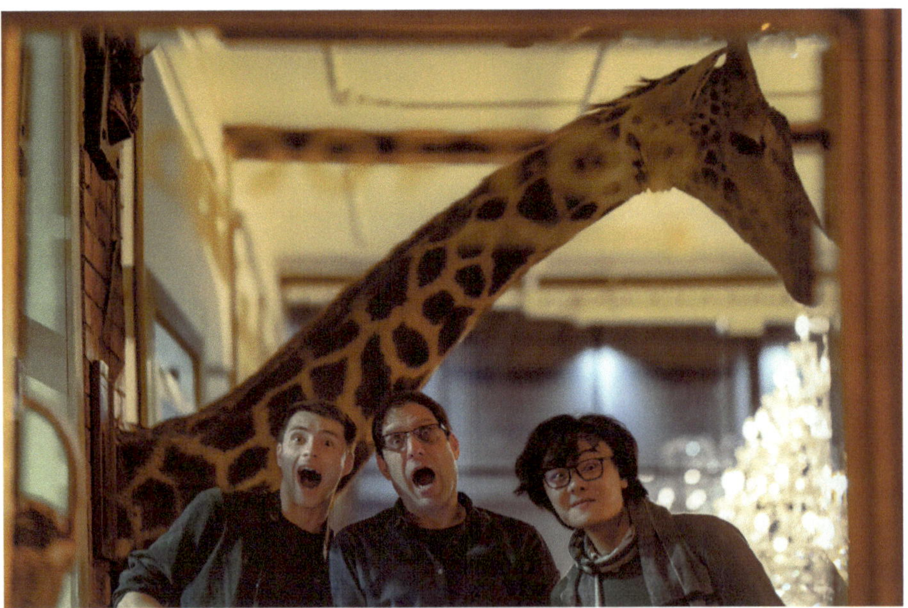

In a world where over 50,000 photos are taken every second and 100 million are uploaded daily, why publish a curated collection of portraits? The answer lies in the profound impact these images, and the stories behind them, had on me, the creative individuals who collaborated on this project, and hopefully those who will discover these photos in this book.

Finding Healing Through Art

The pandemic affected us all in different ways. It claimed millions of lives and turned economies upside down. On a personal level, many of us faced mental and emotional struggles, and I was no exception. Being so far from my loved ones—half a world away—was heartbreaking, frustrating, and at times, felt pointless.

I reached a turning point: to move from surviving to thriving, I had to create. Armed with my camera, I connected with other creatives, and together we brought purpose and joy back into our lives by capturing moments in the streets of Melbourne.

This book is a curated collection of portraits that showcase the resilience and creativity of this city and the people I encountered. Through these photographs, I hope to show the transformative power of photography as a means of breathing new life into our everyday lives.

Part of a Journey

Like many photographers, I remember my first camera and the thrill of capturing my first image. It was intoxicating and addictive. My first camera was a Kodak Pocket Instamatic. In the 1970s, I had been gifted a superpower—the ability to freeze time.

As time went on, my prized possession became a Canon A-1, and I found myself drawn to photographing people, capturing their stories in a single frame.

Decades later, with a digital mirrorless camera in hand, I organized my first photo shoot in the streets of Saigon. What began as creative chaos soon turned into something magical. The models, the surroundings, the light—it all came together in a way that told a story.

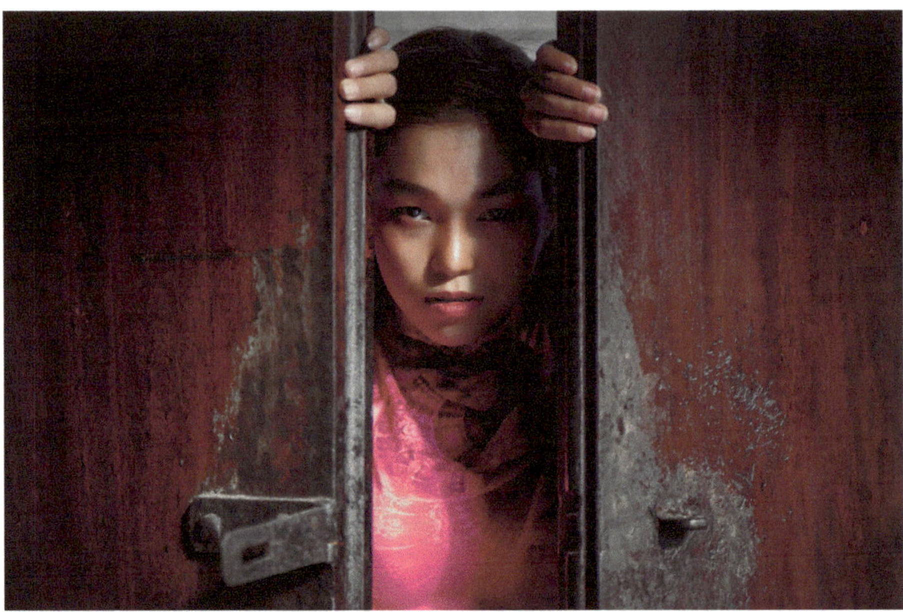

The icing on the cake came when one of my photos of Vân Nguyễn, taken at the Bà Thiên Hậu Pagoda, won the 500px Takeover March 2020 Edition Quest. Despite its technical flaws, the image resonated with the 500px community of 15 million photographers, proving that a photo's true value lies not just in its technical merits but in the story it tells.

With every photo shoot, I realized there were infinite possibilities I hadn't yet imagined. I discovered that collaborating on photo shoots could bring people together in ways I hadn't anticipated. The camera became a tool for connection, growth, and shared creativity.

This book represents the next stage in that journey—capturing portraits in the streets of Melbourne during a pandemic. It's a journey that empowers people to be bolder, dream bigger, and constantly strive for improvement.

Let's Do It!

"How's your afternoon looking?" Jay, a street writer I met through his 'Dear Stranger' poems scattered across Melbourne, would often ask. His energy was infectious, and suddenly, "afternoon" started at 5 pm, just as I'd be winding down for the evening.

From that point on, my days stretched into 5-to-9 adventures, and whenever I asked Jay about hitting the streets of Melbourne, his answer was always, "Let's do it!"

What started as an unlikely friendship turned into a bond rooted in our shared passion for storytelling—Jay with his pen and me with my camera. This camaraderie carried into every collaboration I was part of, inspiring me at every turn. Whether I met someone once or many times, each encounter was memorable.

This book is for anyone seeking creativity in their life. Whoever you are, whatever you create—here's to the positive energy that comes from embracing our passions and working together. I hope these pages inspire you to be bolder and dream bigger.

About This Book

This book isn't a tutorial on how to take great portraits, and it's not a how-to guide for street photography. Instead, it's a curated collection of portraits inspired by my time in Melbourne, celebrating the extraordinary people I met along the way.

Traditionally, the word 'portrait' brings to mind an image of someone sitting in front of an artificial backdrop. While that kind of portraiture can be powerful, it's not the only way to tell a story through photography.

In this book, you'll find backdrops that might seem unremarkable on their own—a grungy alleyway, a brick wall, a faded building, a dirty window, or even a shadowy underpass. But each setting adds its own character, helping convey a mood that brings the subject's story to life.

The portraits in this book aren't meant to be viewed in isolation but rather as part of a larger visual narrative. They're divided into distinct chapters, each with its own theme, exploring different approaches to natural light portraiture. Together, these images take you on a journey that I hope will transport you from the first page to the last.

Companion Website

Creativity often comes from knowing what to leave out, focusing only on what truly matters. When creating this book, I had to make tough choices about which photos and stories to include, knowing that some of my favorite moments wouldn't make it to the final pages. But the journey doesn't end here.

To explore more, including additional standout shots, behind-the-scenes stories, and insights into the process, I invite you to visit www.kisau.com. The website is an extension of this book, offering readers a deeper dive into the world behind the images. There, you can leave a comment, engage in conversation, and connect with a broader creative community.

This project is as much about the ongoing journey as it is about what's captured in the pages. I encourage you to explore, join the conversation, and find inspiration through the extended world we're creating together online.

Chapter 1

The Street Is My Studio

"Fine painters from academies will
one day be bedazzled by nature,
driving them to forsake their studies
before moving their canvases
outdoors. Fine photographers will
one day tune into the whispers from
the hidden alleys, submitting the
urge to move their studios into the
streets."

R.C. Waldun

The Street Is My Studio

The streets of Melbourne became more than just a backdrop—they became an integral part of the stories I wanted to tell. In their quiet stillness, I found a different kind of energy, one that brought out something unique in each moment. Every alley, every staircase carried its own character, shaping the way I captured what unfolded in front of me.

There's something powerful about letting the environment speak for itself. The worn bricks, industrial steel, and graffiti-covered walls became part of a conversation between the style, the personality, and the world around them. The contrast between what was worn and weathered, and the vibrancy brought into those spaces, created moments that felt genuine and full of life.

Embracing the imperfections in our surroundings allowed me to explore Melbourne in a new light. The natural light falling through buildings, the play of shadows across streets—these elements gave me the chance to capture something real. The city didn't need to be perfect or polished to add to the energy of the experience. It just needed to be seen for what it was, full of character and potential.

This chapter is a reminder that the streets around us are filled with possibilities. They don't need to be bustling or glamorous to create something meaningful. Wherever you are, whether in a quiet alley or a busy square, there's a story waiting to be told. It's in the textures of the city, the light falling on someone, and the moments we create when we embrace our surroundings for what they are.

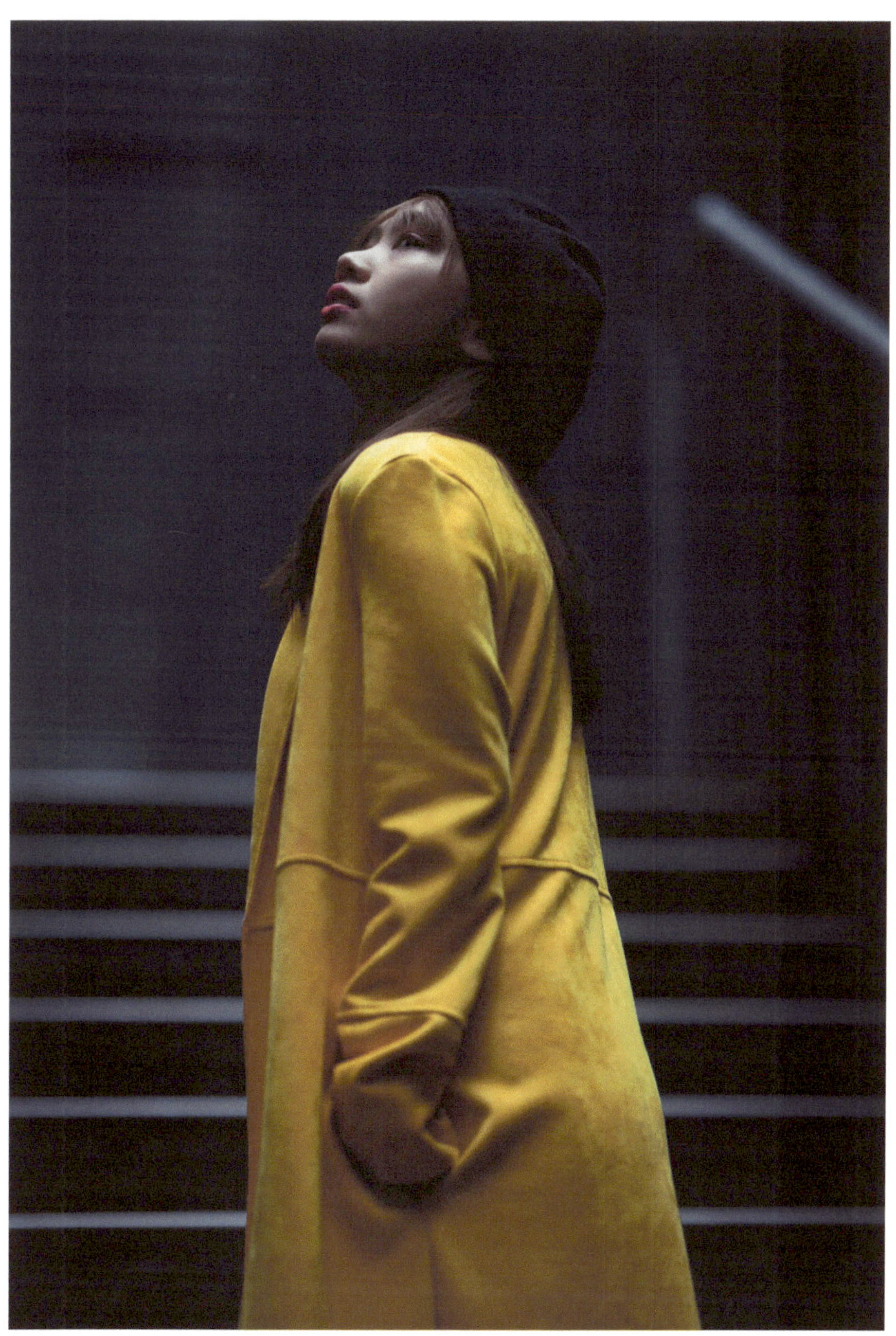

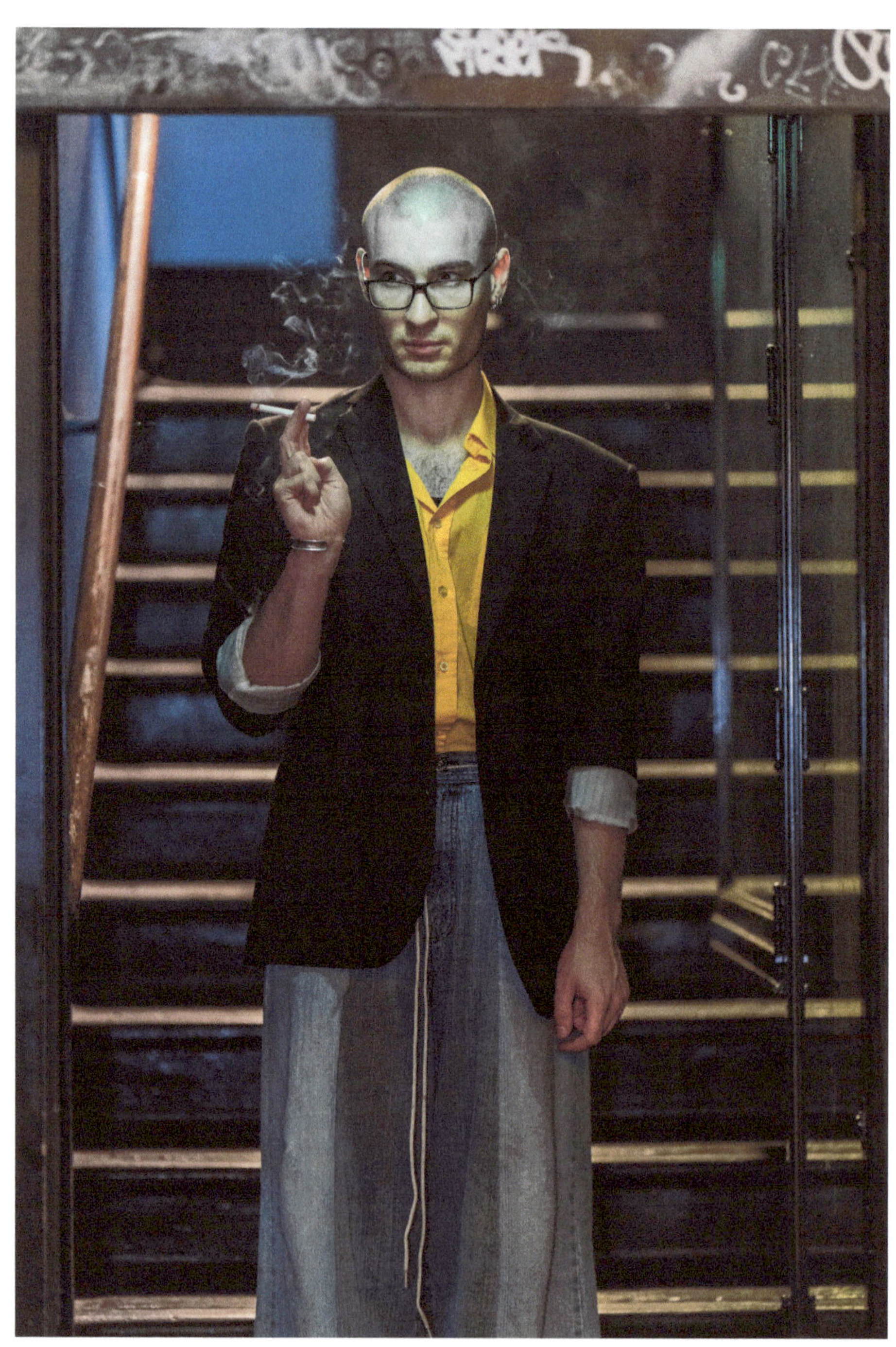

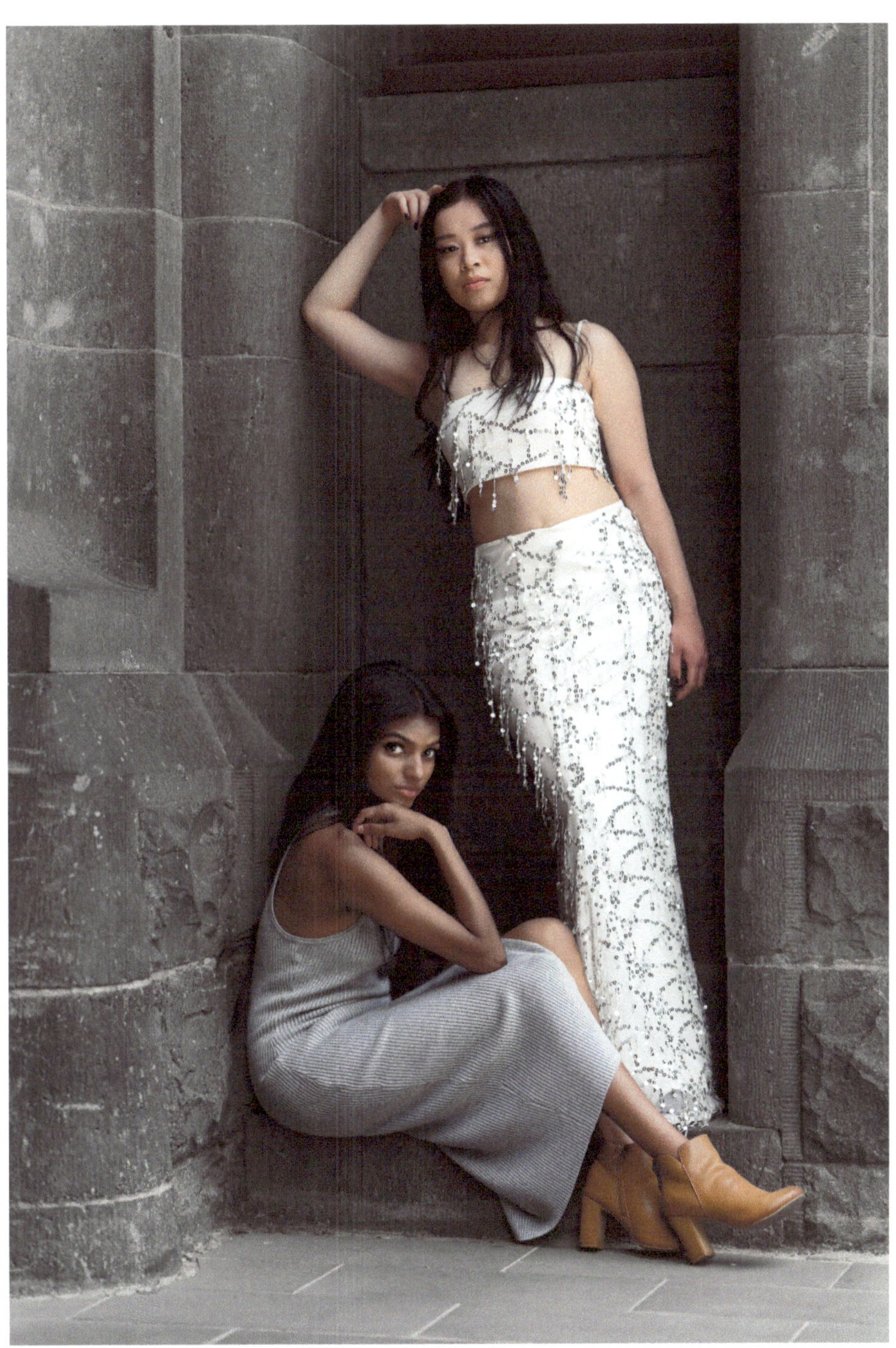

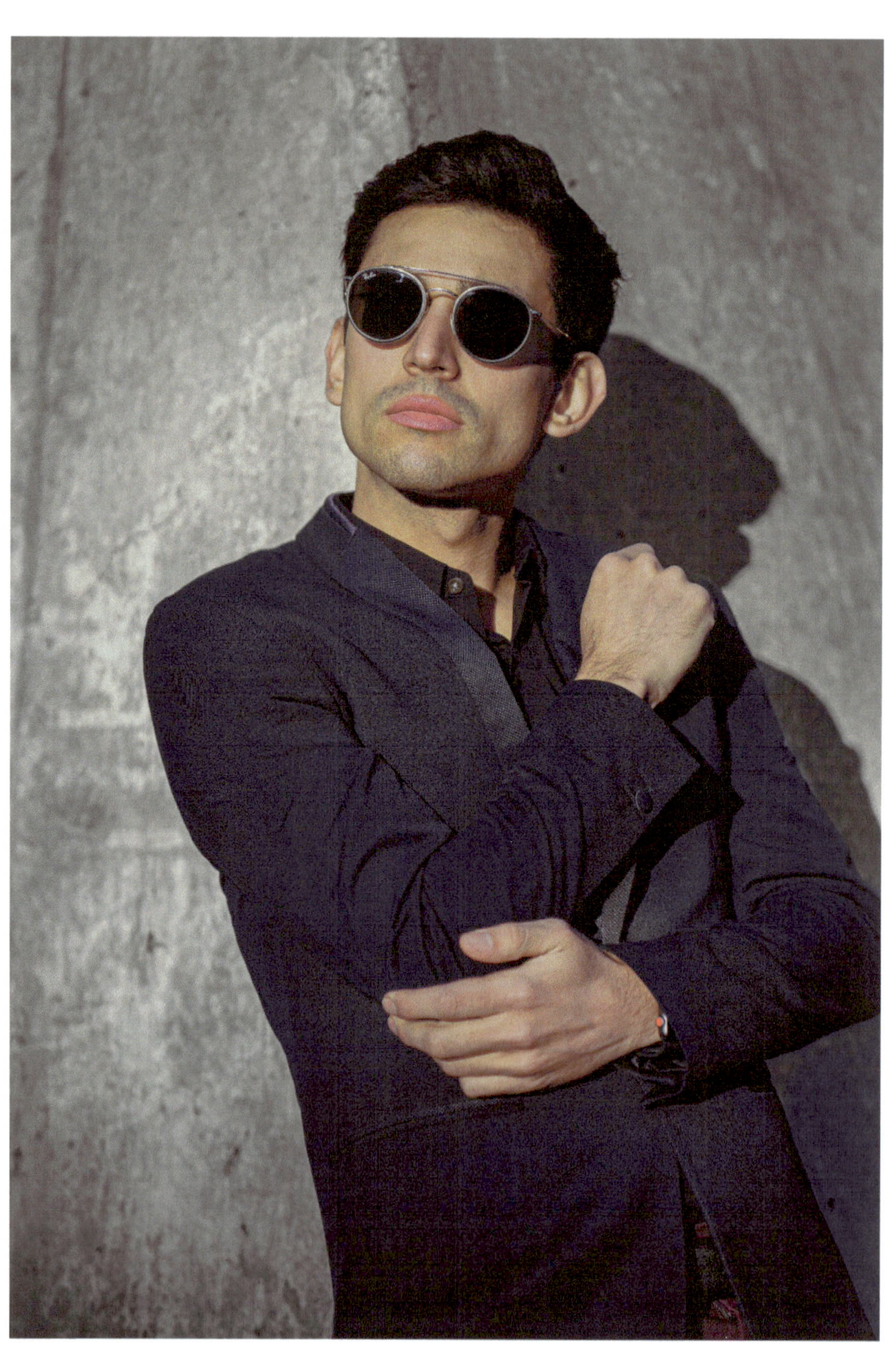

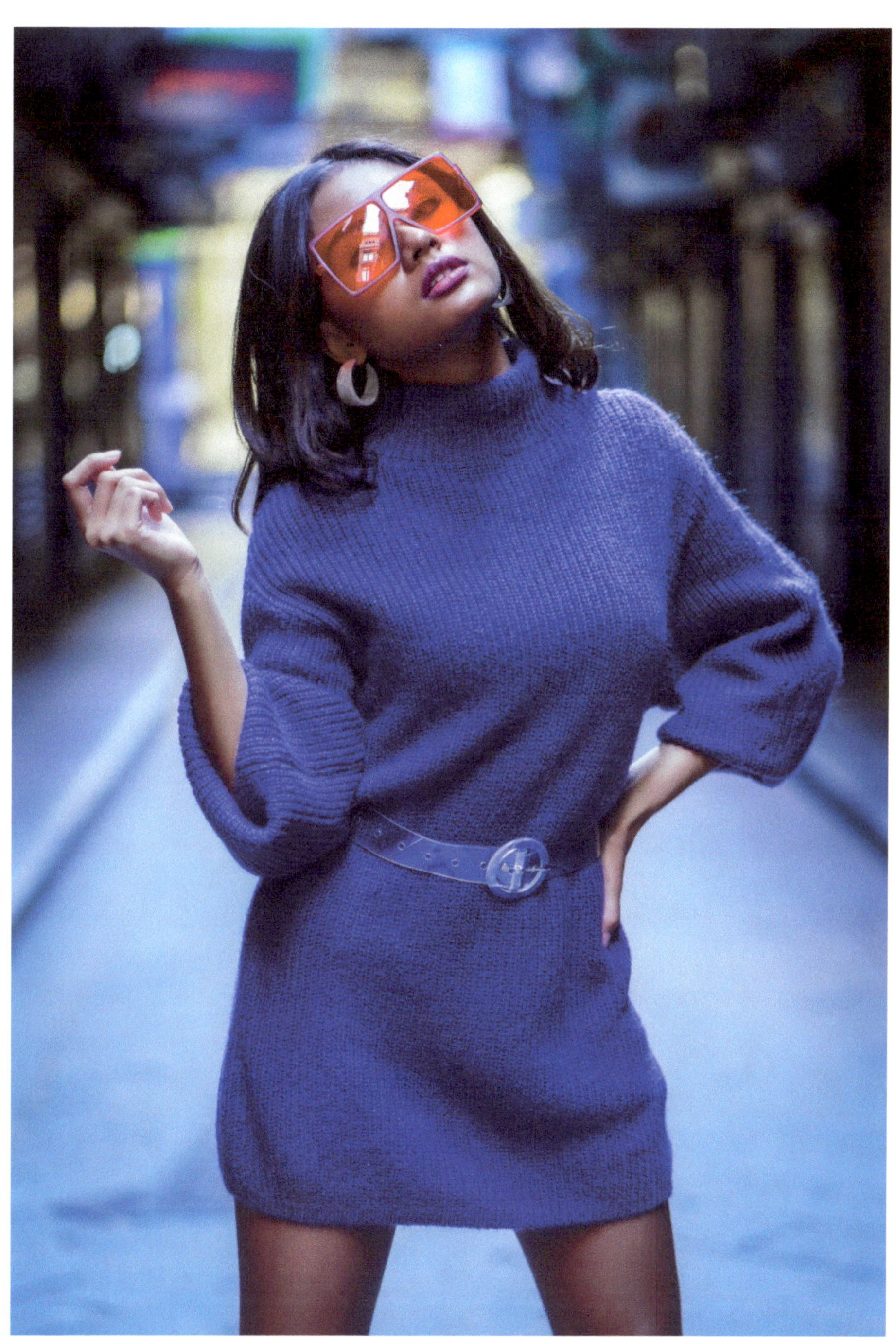

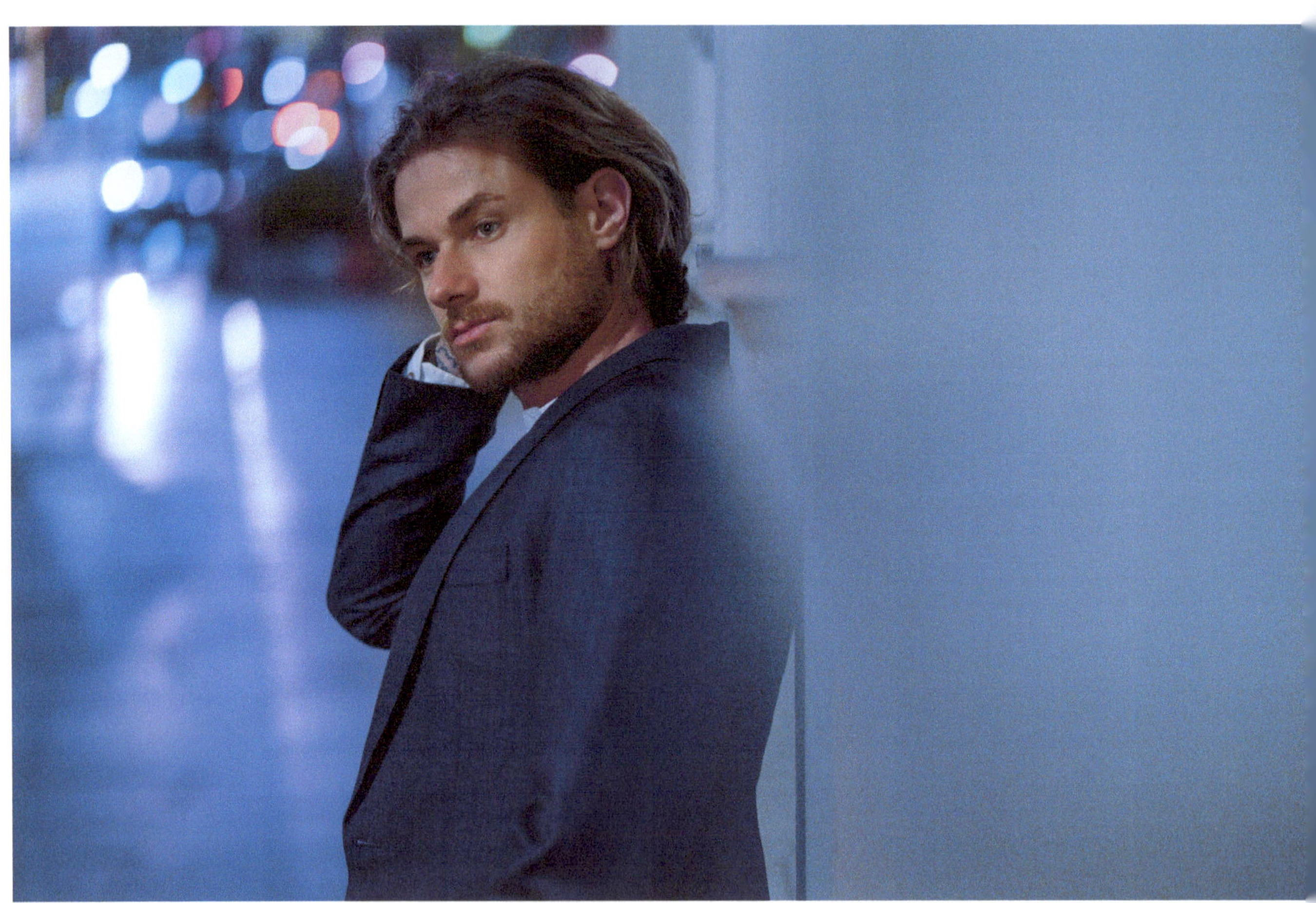

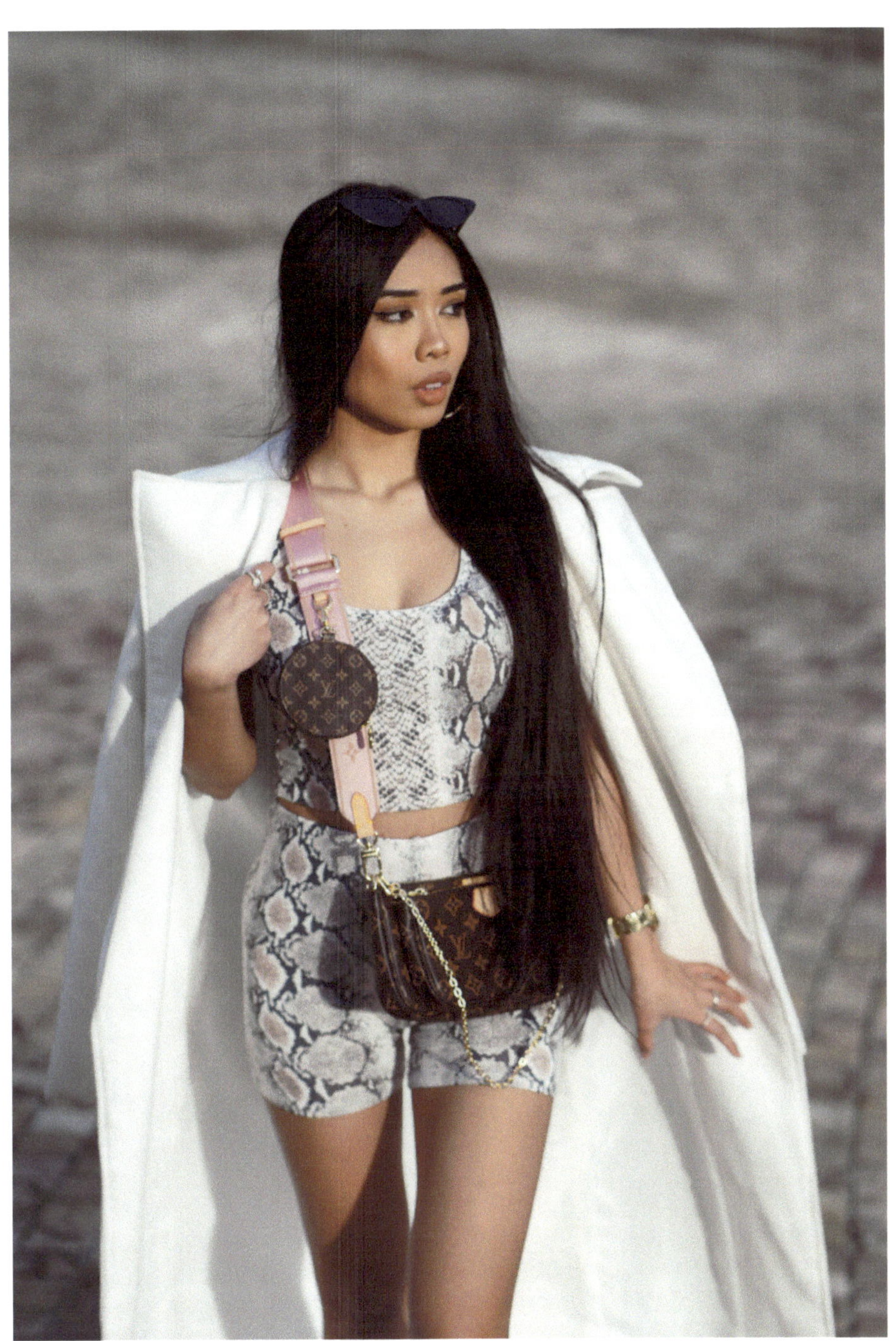

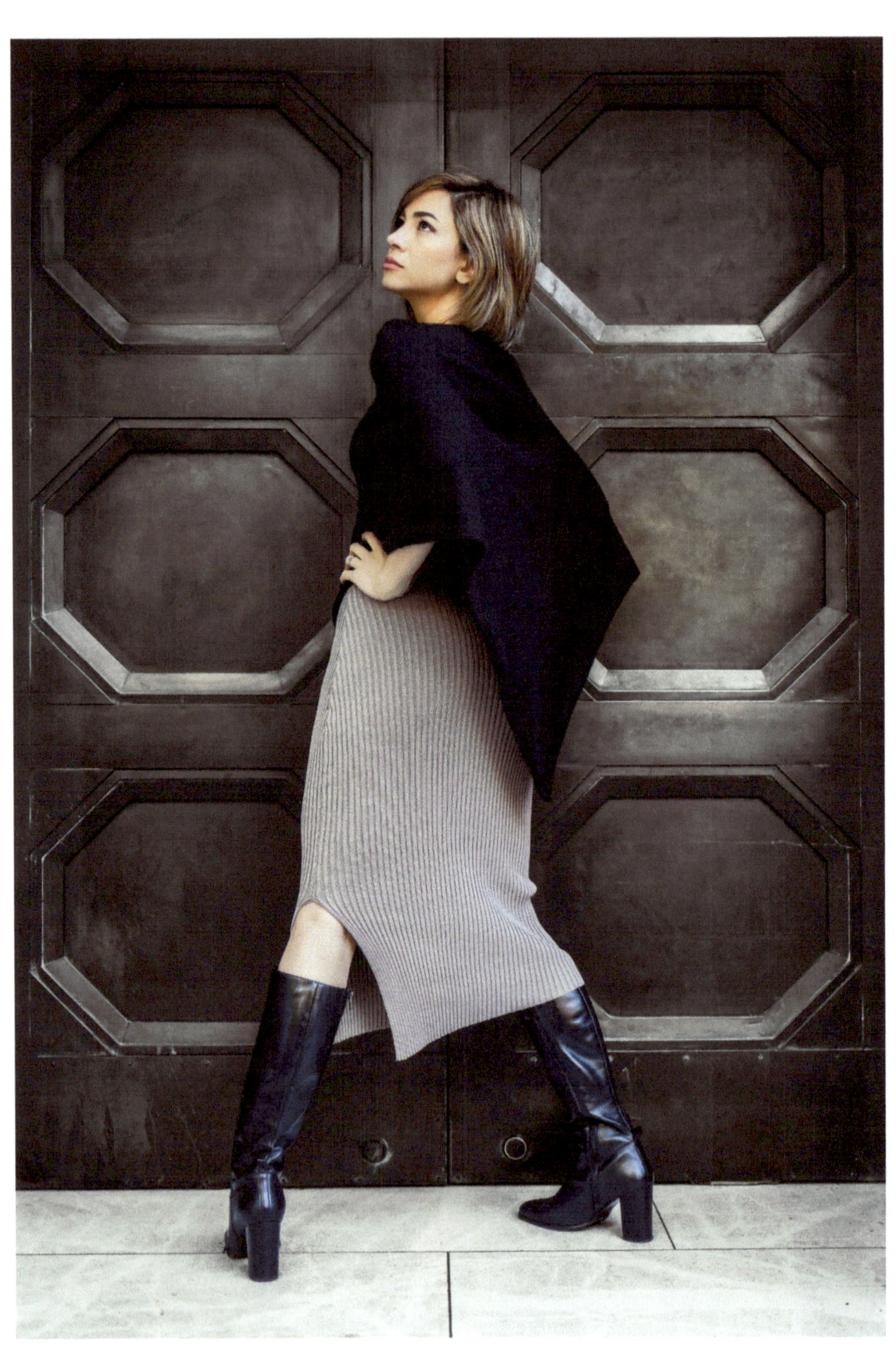

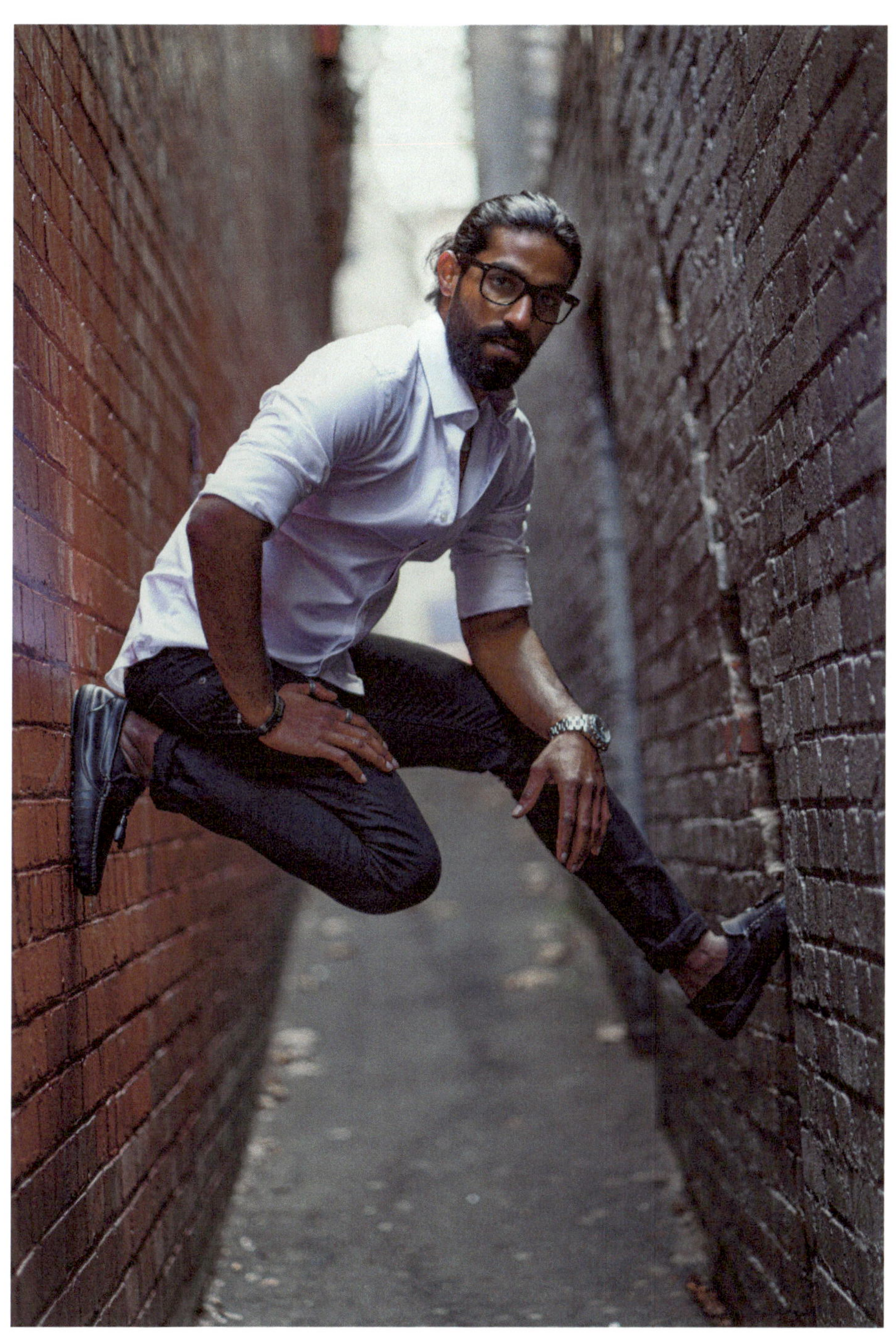

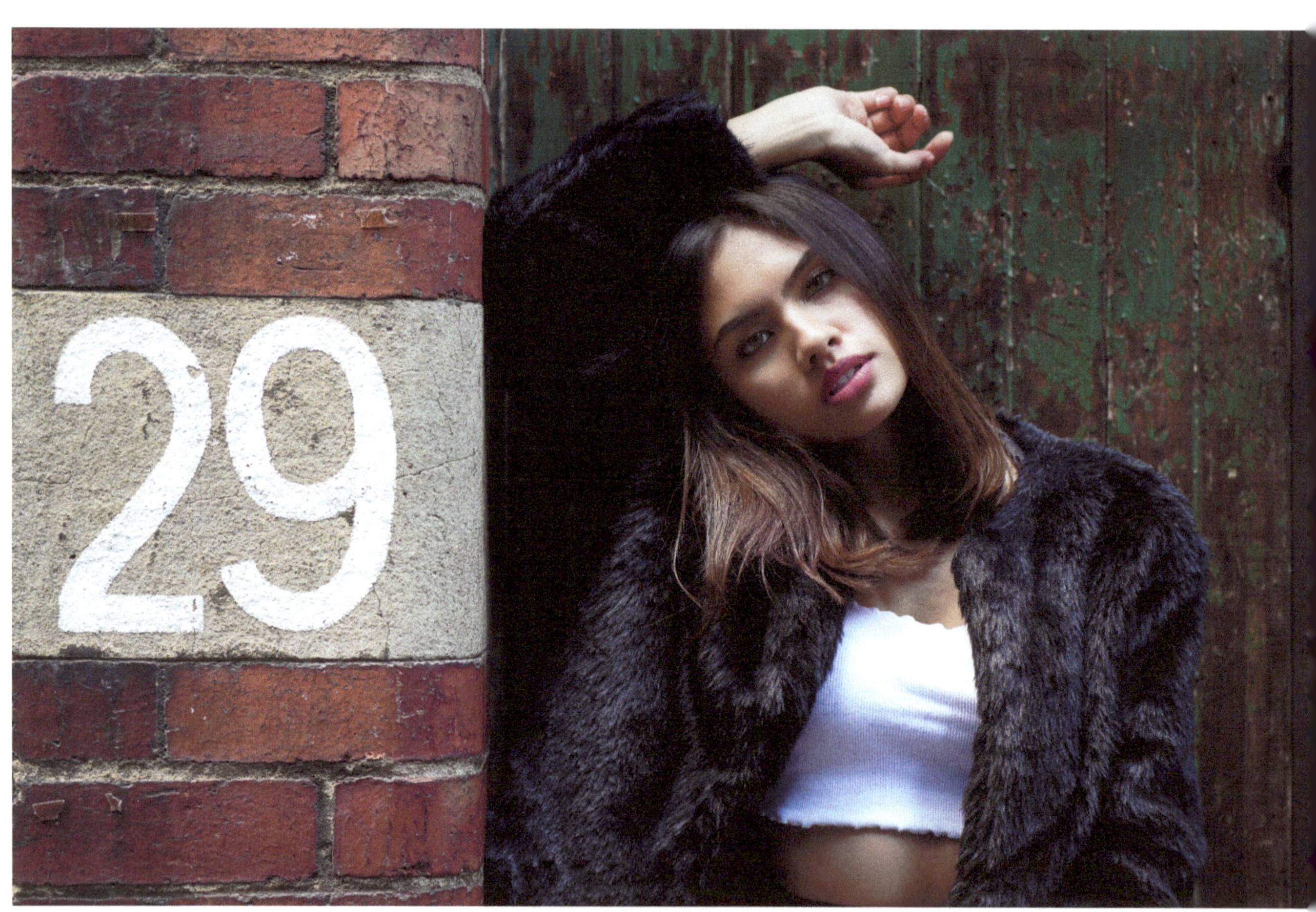

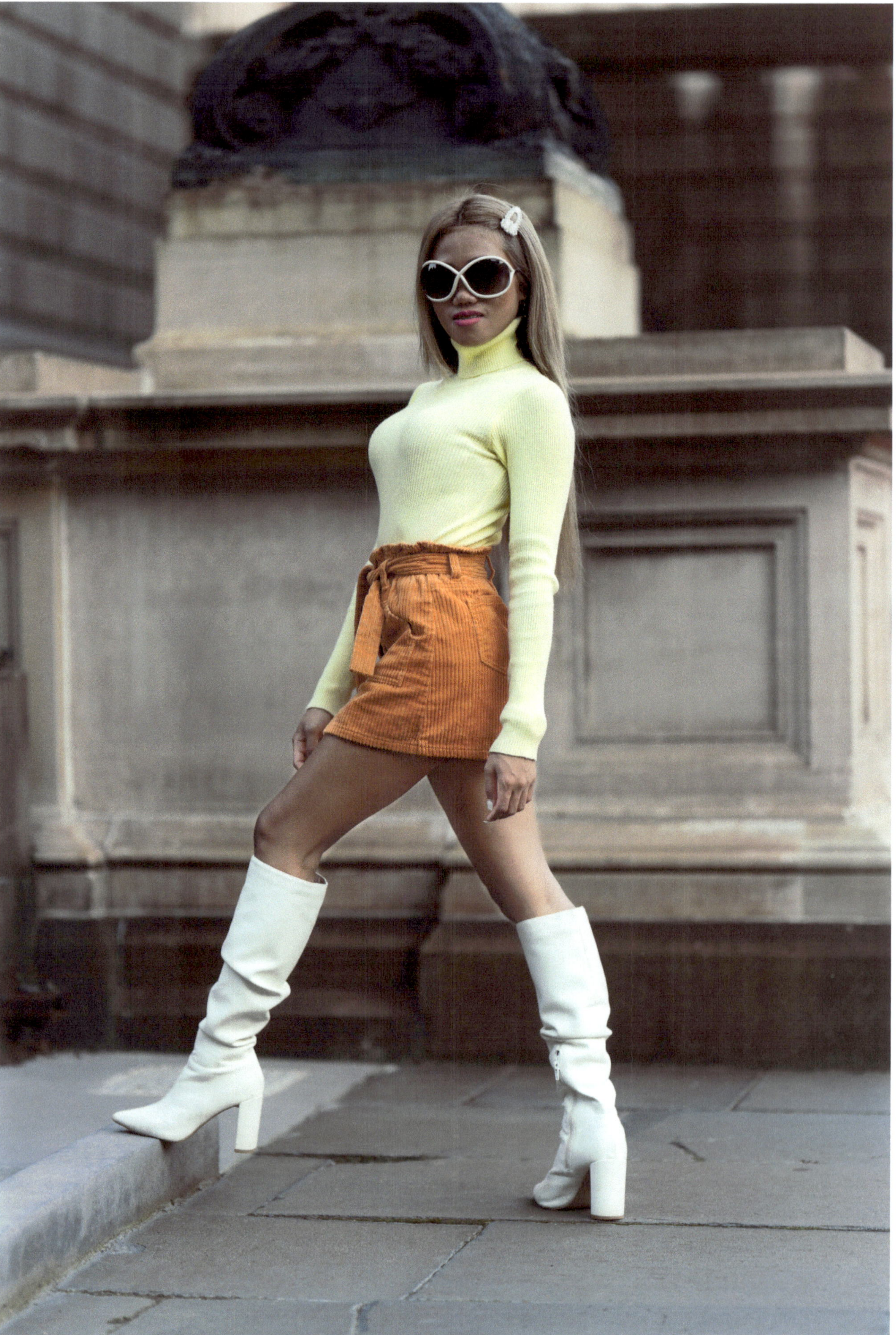

Chapter 2

Chiaroscuro

"We were standing in one of the alleyways of Melbourne when Paul pulled me aside and directed me to stand in the darkest corner of the lane. I shuffled my feet from side to side. 'Come forward,' he said. I leaned an inch toward his lens. 'There! Hold right there.' He directed me to lower my eyes, to stare right at the lens. I stood there in awe of his ability to manipulate light and shadow, to blend foreground with background to create a sense of both atmosphere and nothingness. Seeing that photo of myself against the darkness, noticing my every pore and strand, every imperfection against the black – I loved myself."

Jaidyn Luke Attard

Chiaroscuro

Light and shadow became my tools for storytelling in this chapter. There's something about the way natural light cuts through the darkness that brings a scene to life, creating a sense of depth and quiet intensity. All of these portraits were taken on location, using only available light, which gave each shot an authentic feel. The minimal lighting, often spilling through a window or creeping into narrow alleys, allowed for a delicate balance between what's revealed and what remains hidden in the shadows.

The mood here is contemplative and intimate, inspired by the chiaroscuro technique used by painters like Caravaggio and Rembrandt. The dark backdrops keep the focus sharp, pulling the eye toward what the light chooses to highlight—a glance, a gesture, or a detail. These strong contrasts between light and dark create a soft tension, making every moment feel deliberate yet effortless. There's a quiet strength in the simplicity, as though the light itself is shaping the narrative in subtle, painterly ways.

These portraits aren't just about highlighting physical features—they're about evoking emotion through restraint. Less becomes more when you strip away distractions and focus on what the light touches. The natural shadows wrap around the scene, while the glow of light adds an atmosphere that feels intimate. It's about finding beauty in the balance, in the contrasts, and in what the darkness leaves to the imagination.

This chapter is a reminder that light and shadow are powerful storytelling elements, no matter where you are. Using natural light on location, you can find that balance and create a mood that's as much about what isn't shown as it is about what is. The interplay of light and dark invites you to look closer, to feel the subtle tension between the seen and unseen.

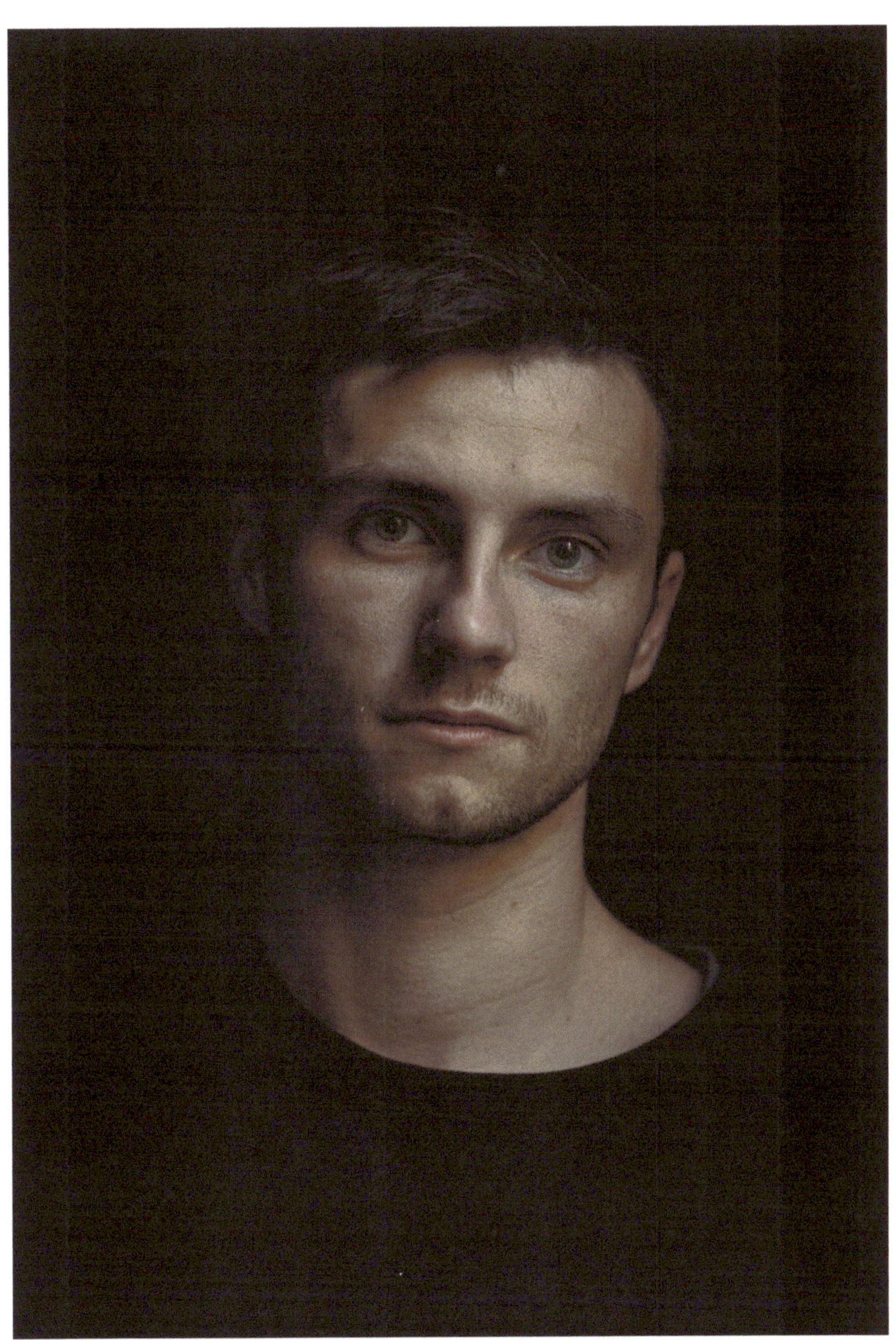

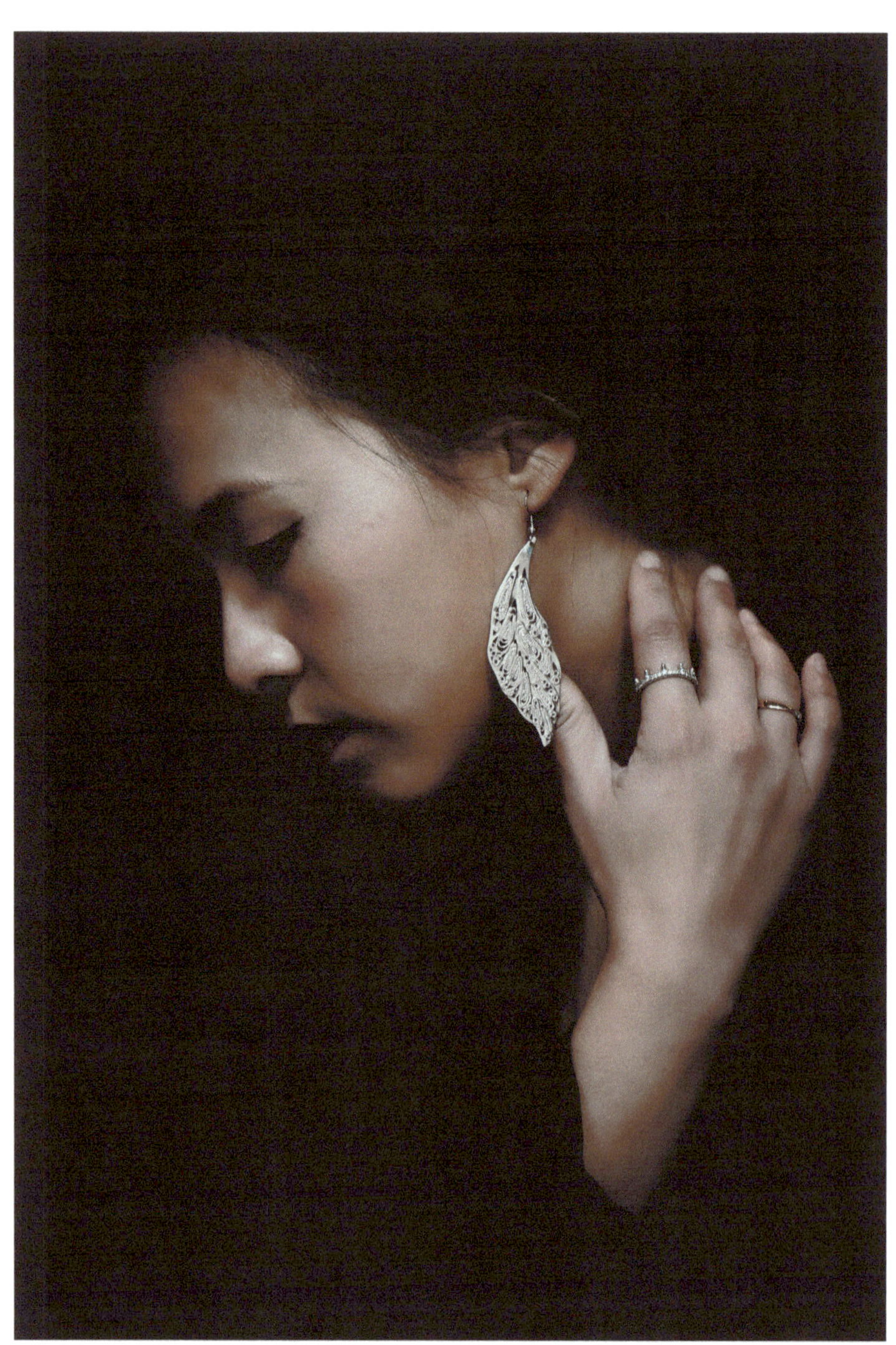

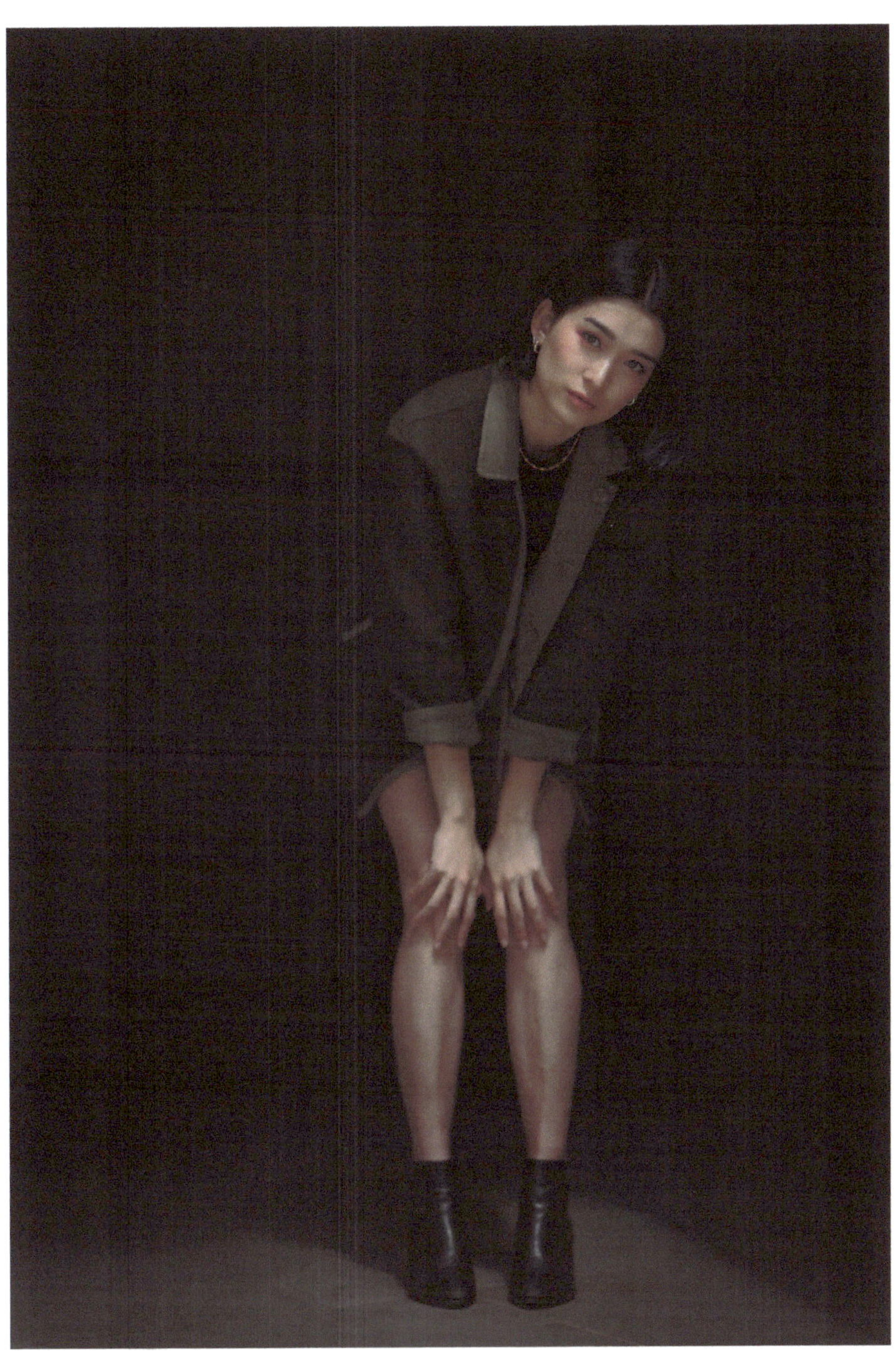

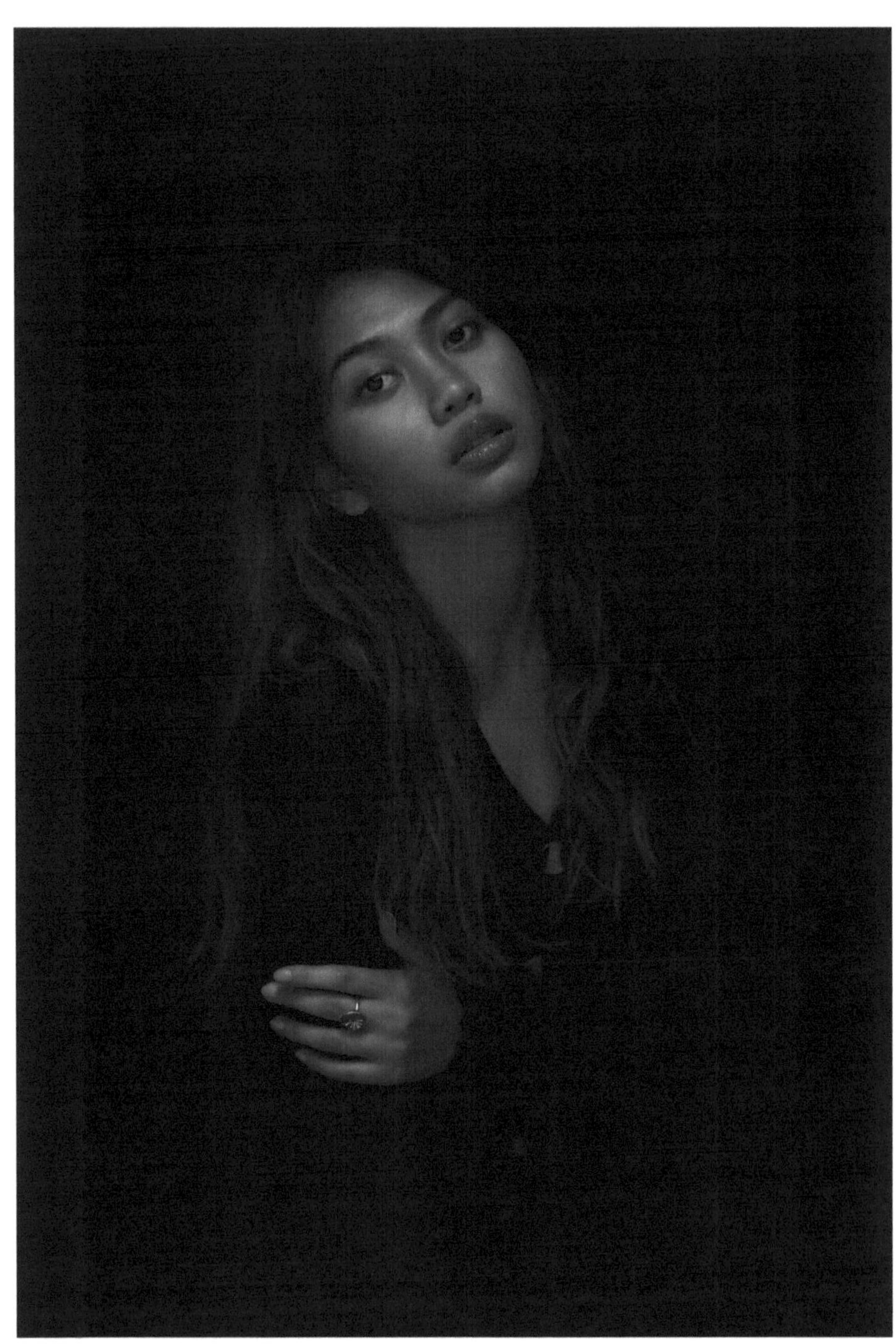

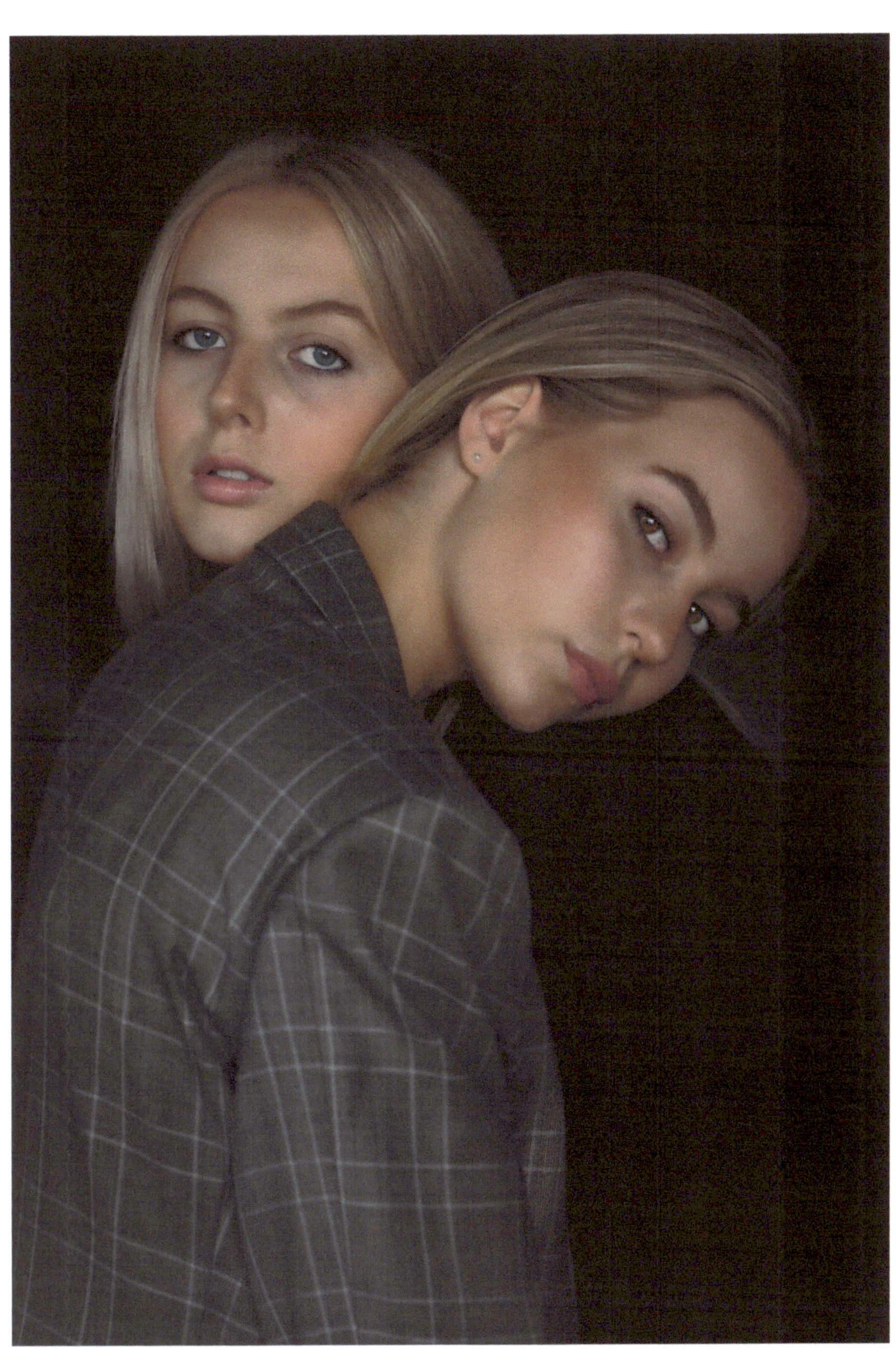

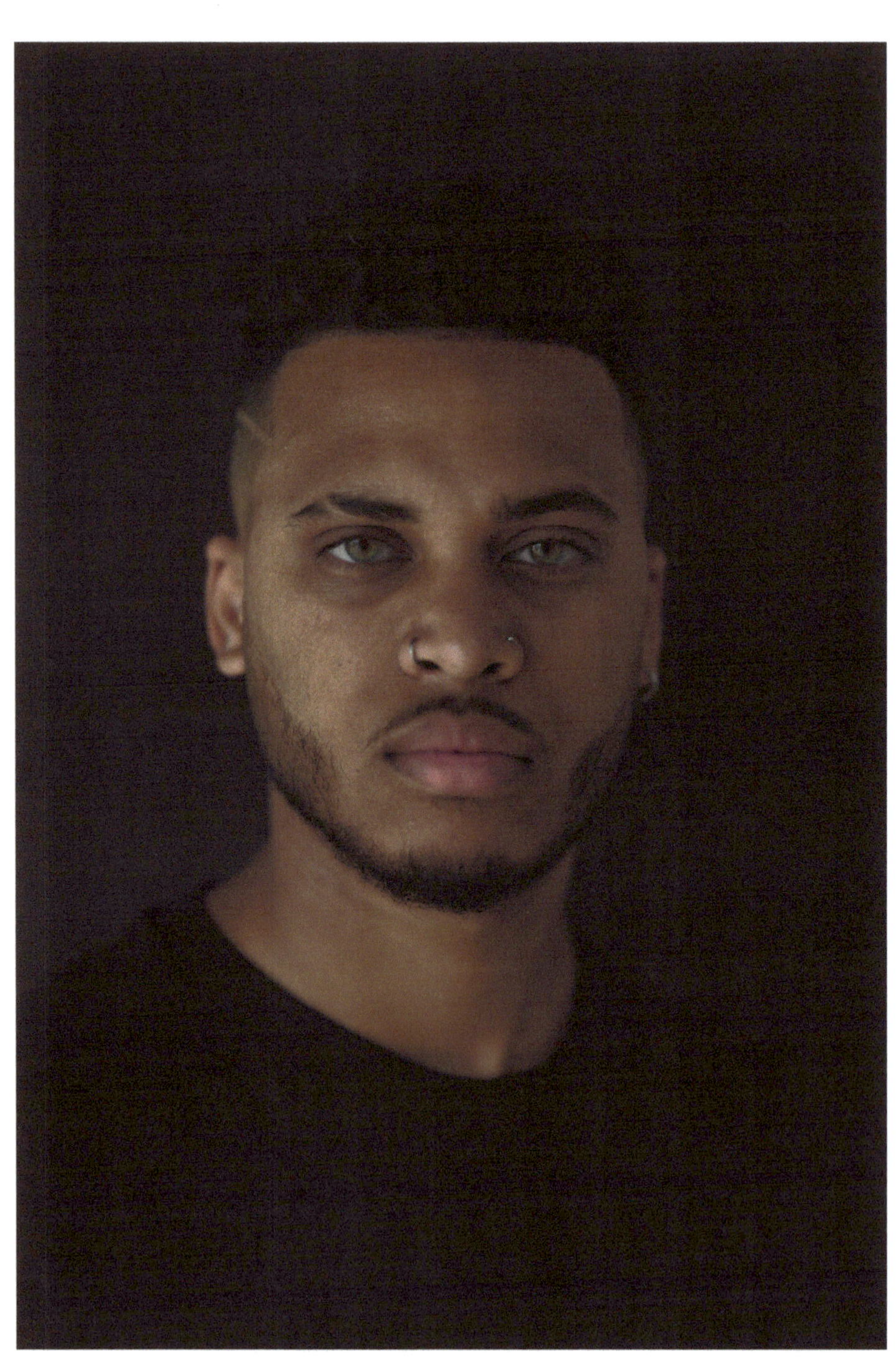

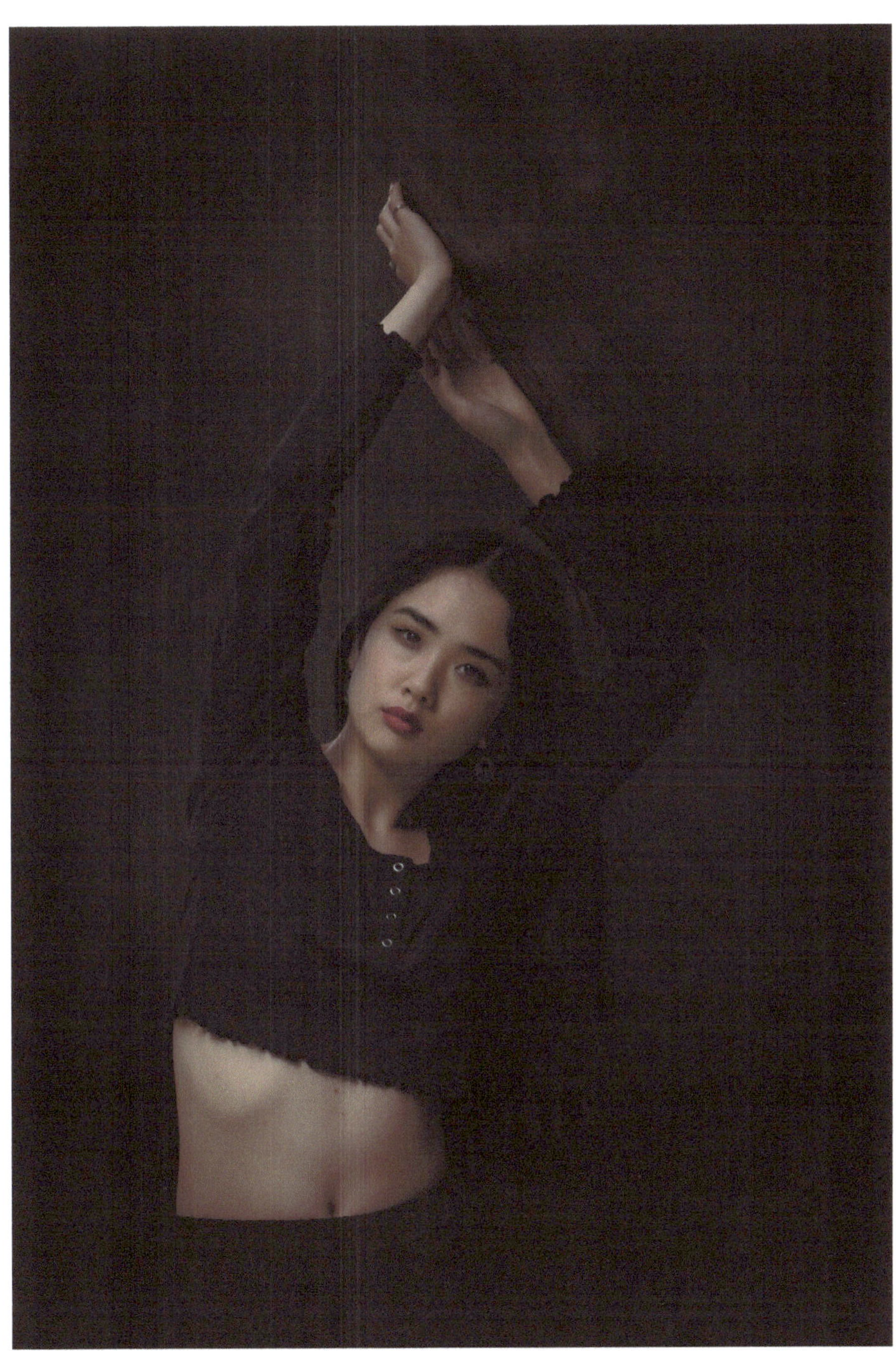

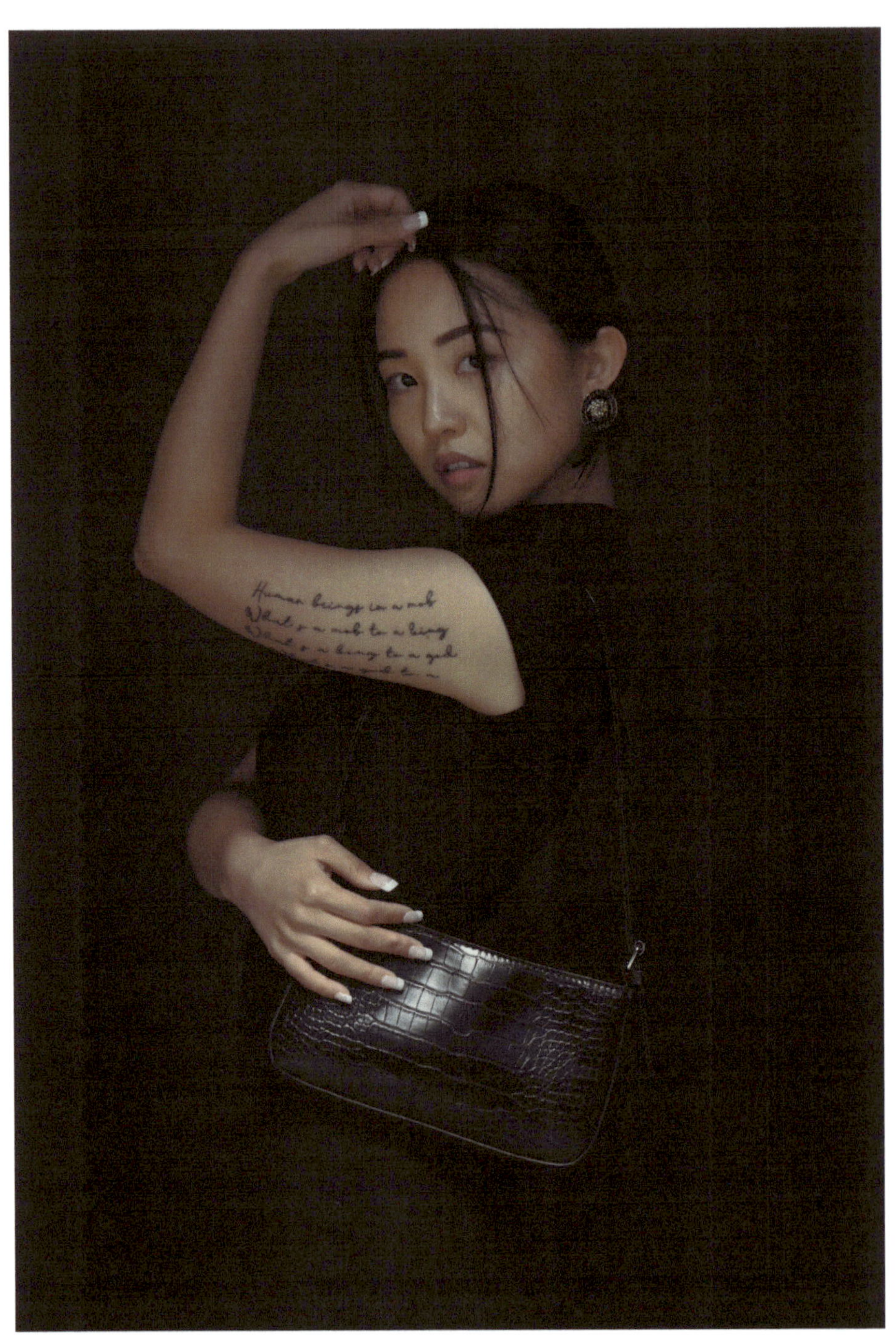

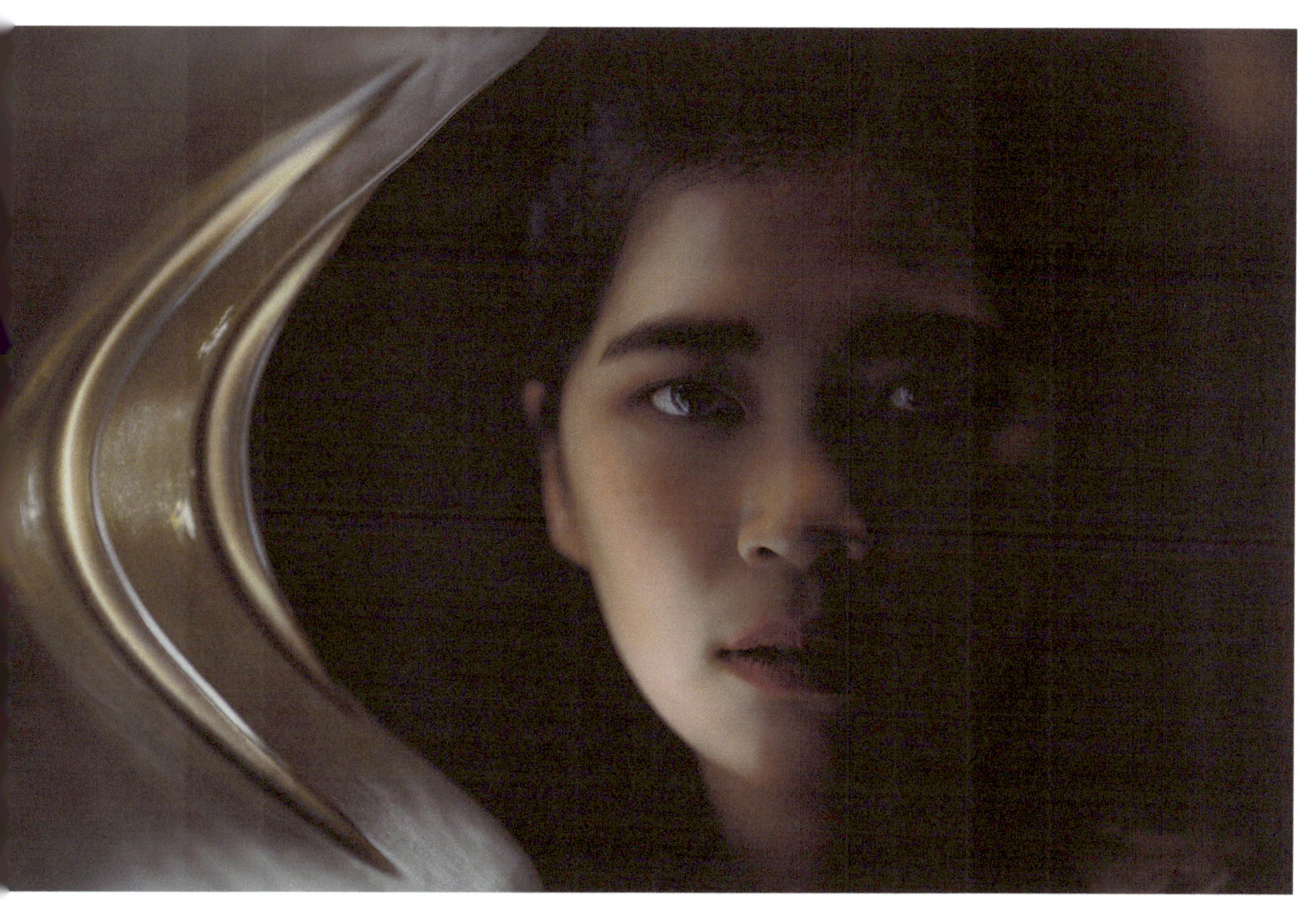

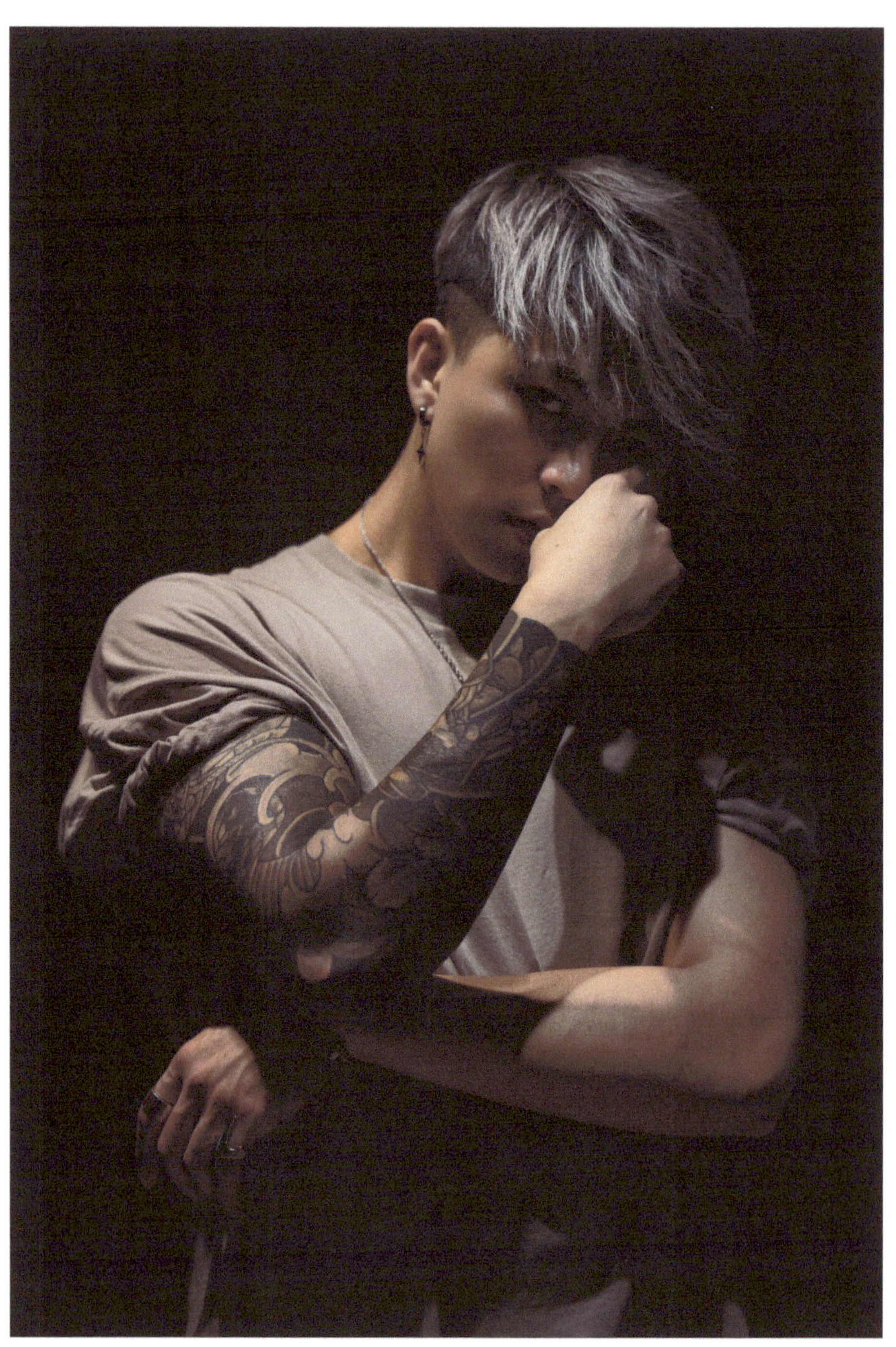

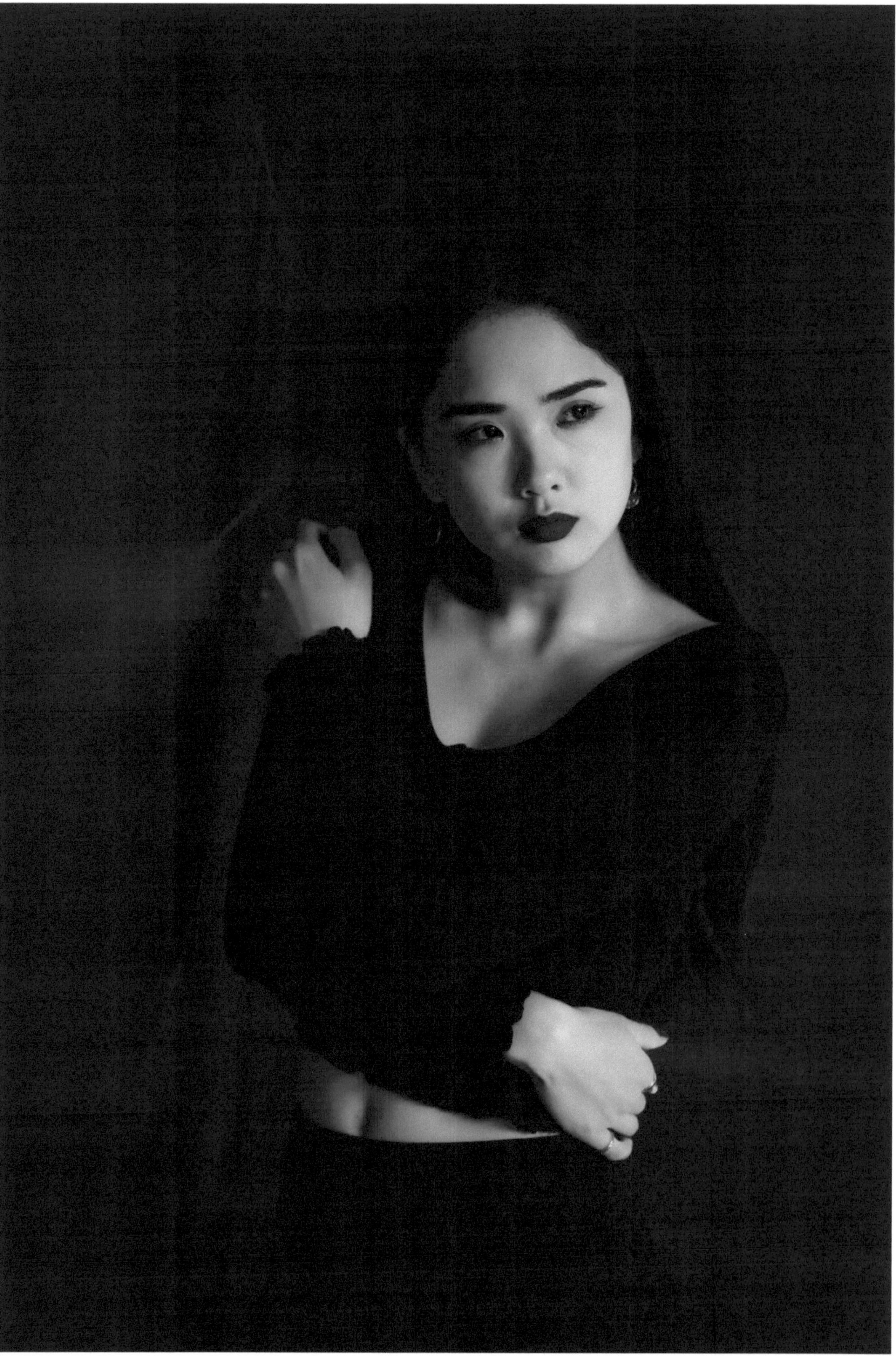

Chapter 3

Creative Freedom

"The magic happens
when you let go
and let your imagination take over."

Jessie Nguyen

Creative Freedom

Breaking away from the norm invites a chance to explore the more whimsical side of photography. The vibrant, quirky images in this chapter are filled with imaginative staging that encourages embracing a playful approach to creativity. Whether it's adding unexpected props or pops of color that make the scene feel dreamlike, the focus is on letting go of usual boundaries and allowing creativity to lead without constraint.

The backdrops are anything but traditional. In these settings, neon signs glow in soft hues, playful props like vintage telephones or plush decor enhance the atmosphere, and the overall ambiance is rich in fantasy. There's a deliberate clash between modern aesthetic and retro vibes that transforms ordinary objects into something extraordinary. By using vivid colors and eclectic compositions, each image becomes a statement of its own—one that doesn't take itself too seriously, but instead invites you into a world where anything feels possible.

Natural light is still a key player here, though its use is more playful. The glow of artificial neon mixes with the soft natural light, creating a dynamic interplay that shifts the mood from soft and introspective to bright and energetic. The result is images that feel fresh and full of life, capturing that fleeting feeling of youthful spontaneity. Every element in the frame adds to this sense of freedom and experimentation.

Our goal is to inspire you to step outside of your usual creative comfort zone. With the right amount of imagination and bold choices, you can turn any space into a canvas for your next great idea. It's a reminder to be daring, to think outside the box, and most importantly, to enjoy the process of creating something truly unique. After all, this chapter is about celebrating the fun side of photography, where the rules are made to be broken and every shot feels like an adventure in itself.

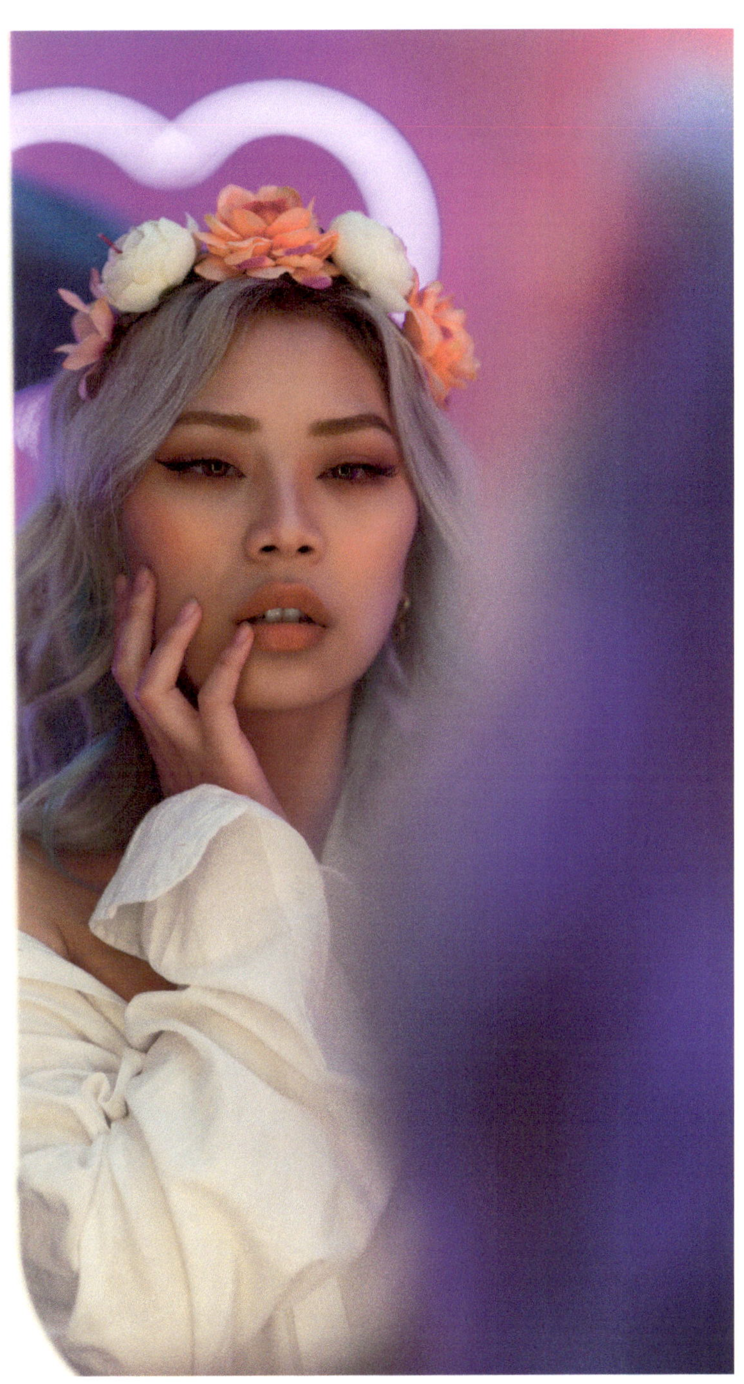

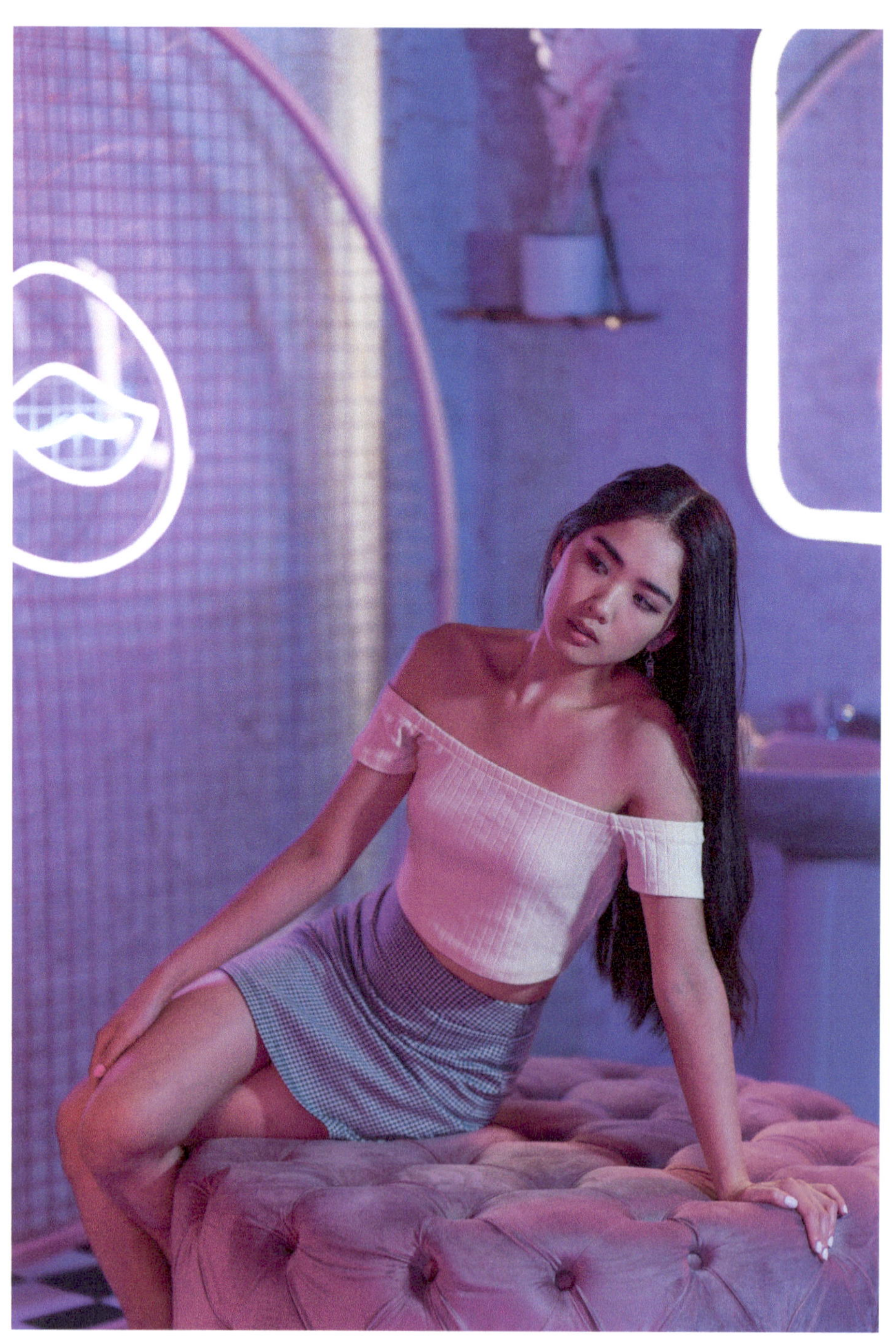

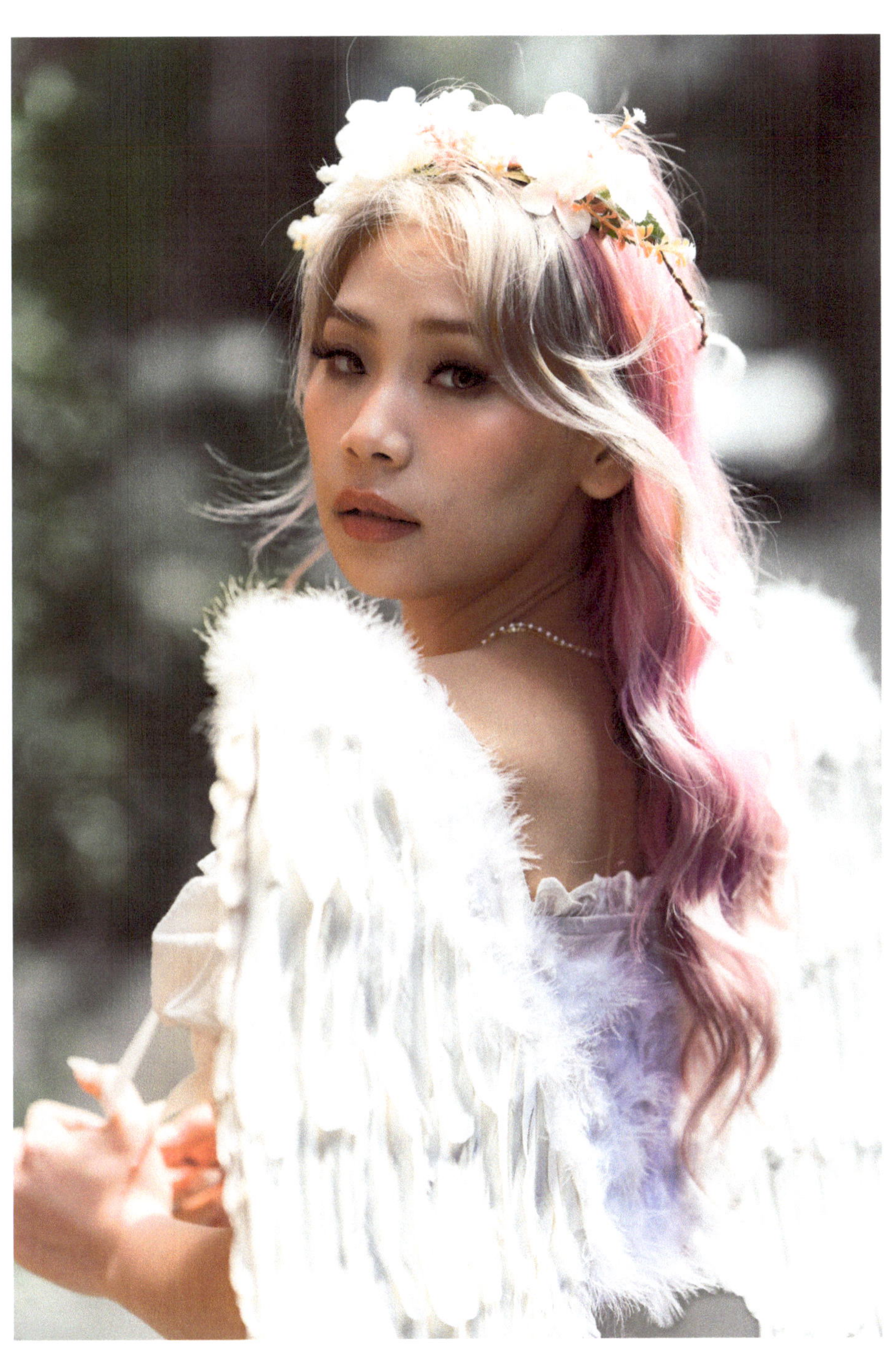

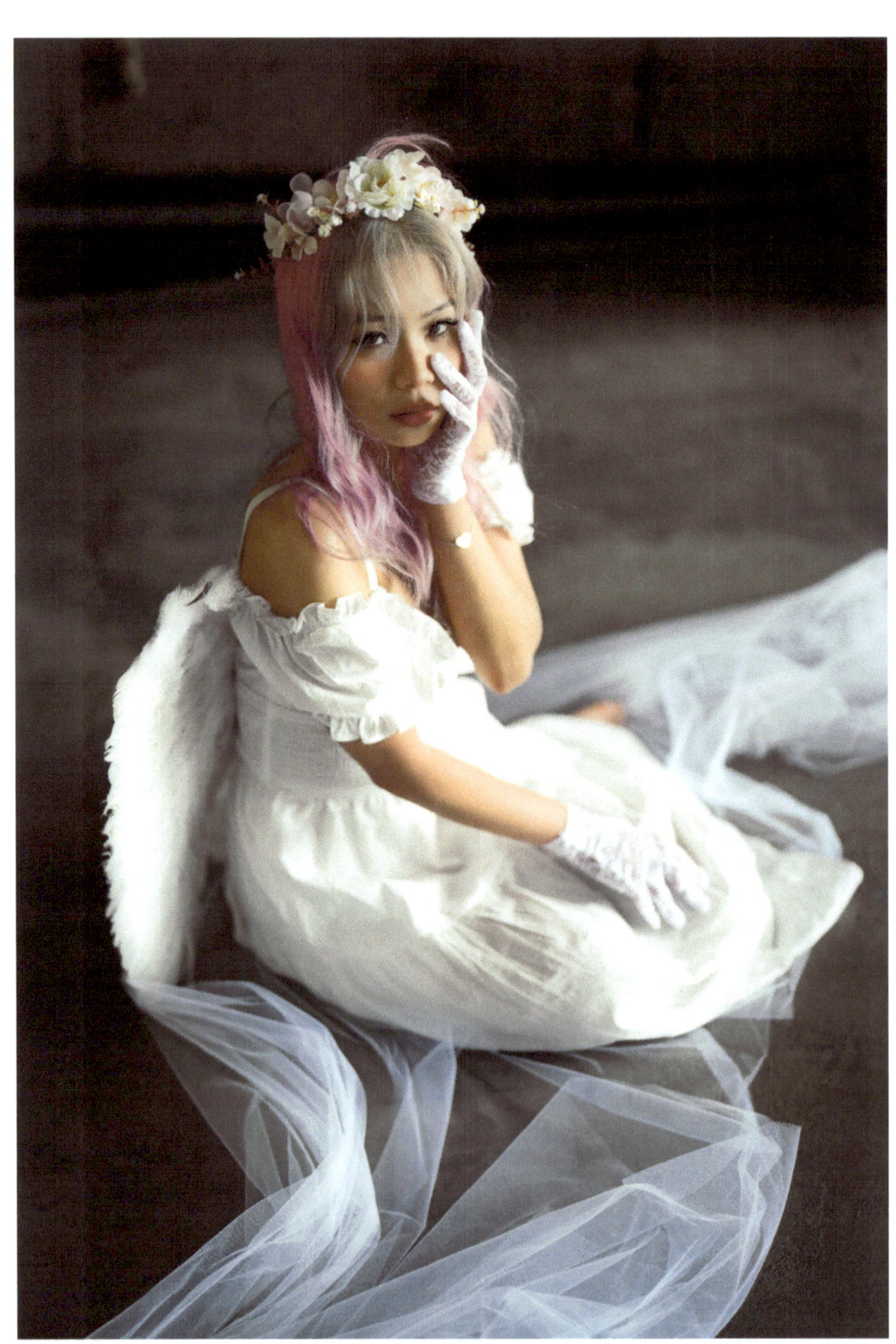

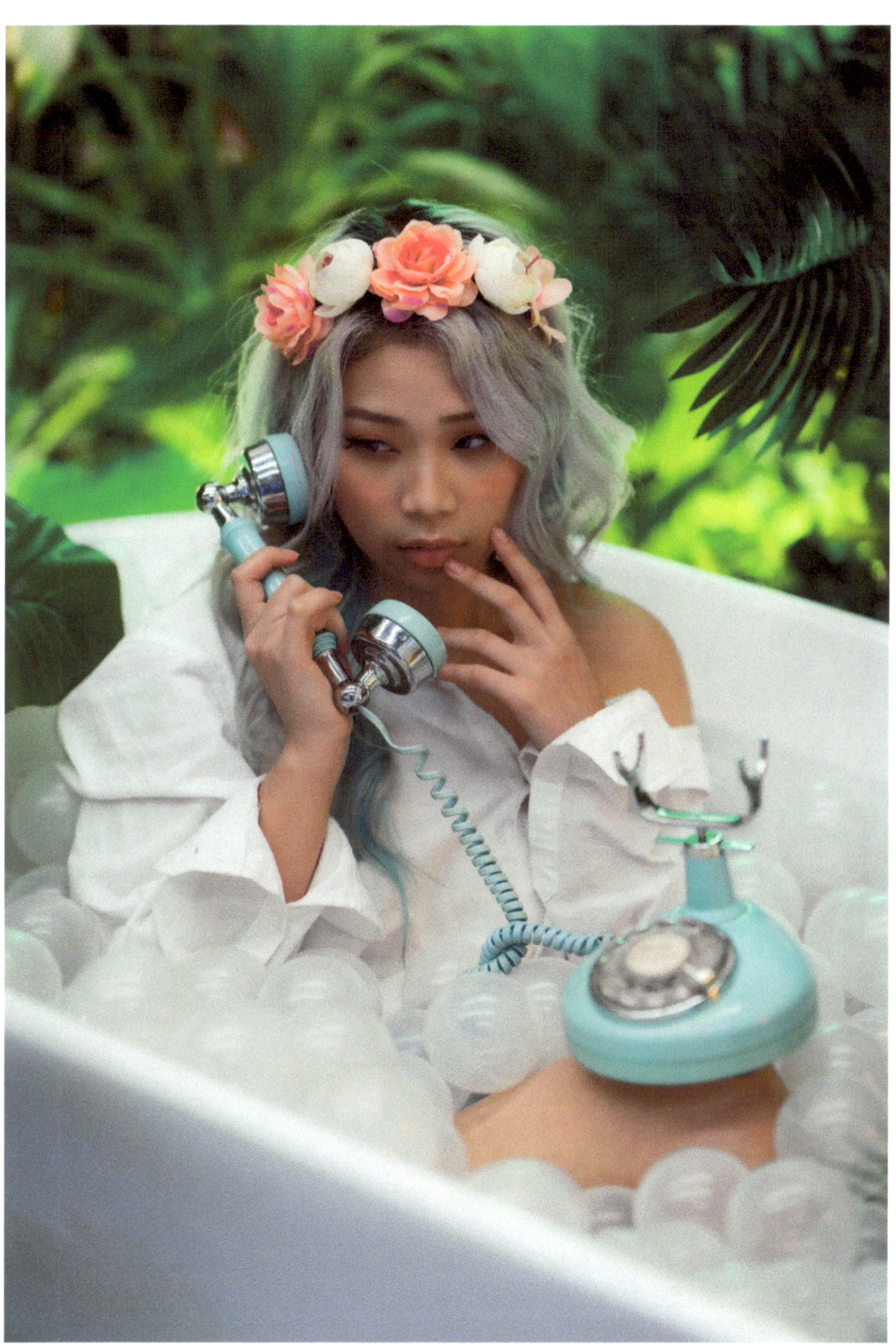

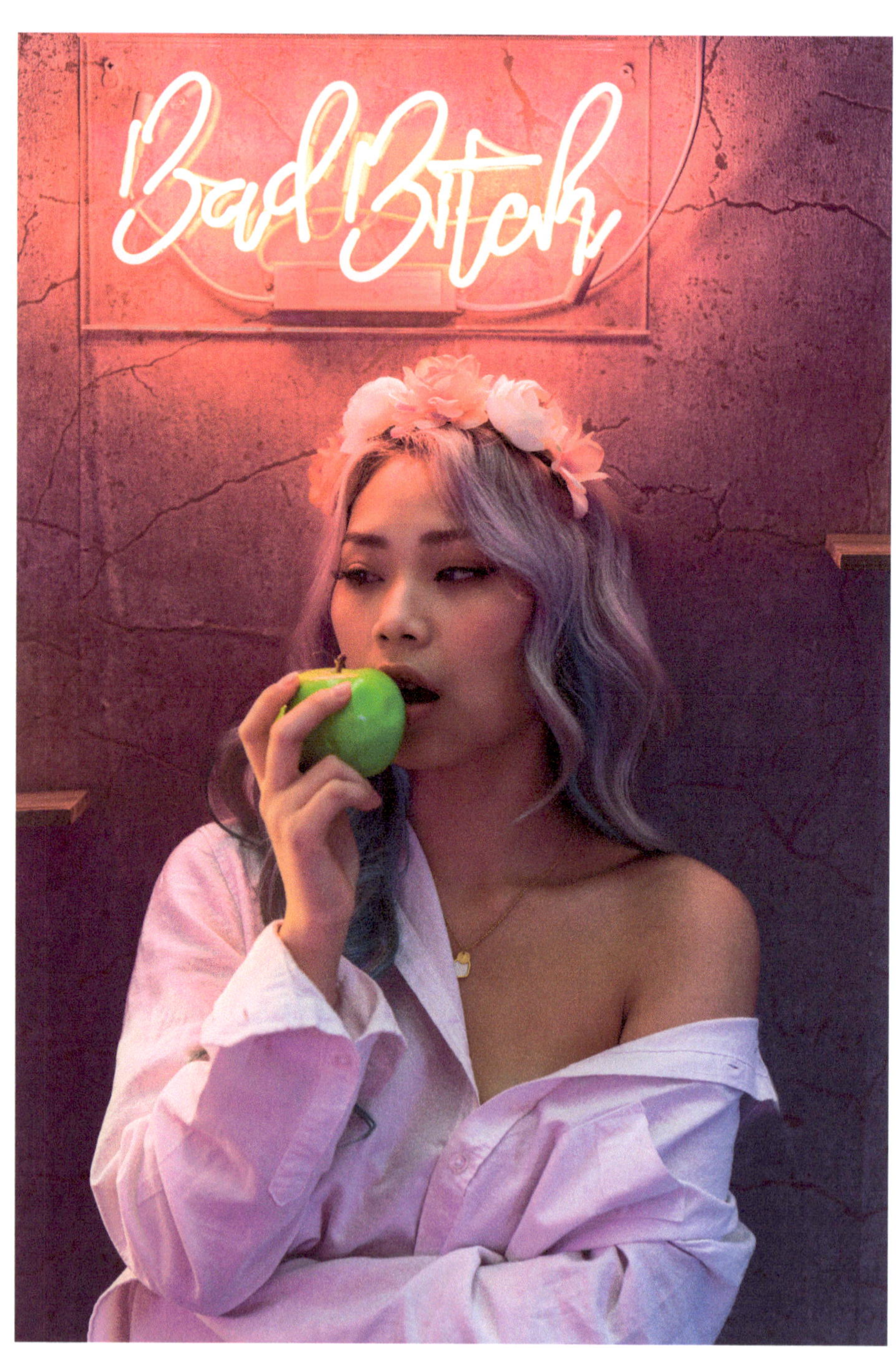

Bad Bitch

Chapter 4

Concrete Jungle

"When the noise fades,
what's left is the truth.
Raw.
Deliberate.
Powerful."

Jay Ventress

Concrete Jungle

What happens when the background fades, and all that's left is a striking expression or a bold stance? In this chapter, the desaturated backgrounds allow those moments to stand out with clarity, giving the focus entirely to the person in front of the lens. The contrast between their vivid energy and the muted surroundings creates a powerful dynamic, where every glance, every movement becomes more deliberate and captivating.

Desaturating the environment goes beyond aesthetics—it creates space.. The muted tones allow for an even stronger presence, highlighting the boldness of an outfit, the intensity of a pose, or the quiet confidence in a look. The result creates a mood where each image tells a story without distraction.

There's a simplicity to this approach that brings out something deeper. With the environment taking a step back, the focus shifts fully to the expression and emotion, making every detail feel more intentional. It's a reminder that sometimes less is more—that you don't always need a busy background to make a moment feel significant.

For creatives, this chapter offers inspiration on how to harness contrast and minimalism to amplify storytelling. It's an invitation to play with visual dynamics, showing how paring back can lead to images that are bold, impactful, and truly memorable.

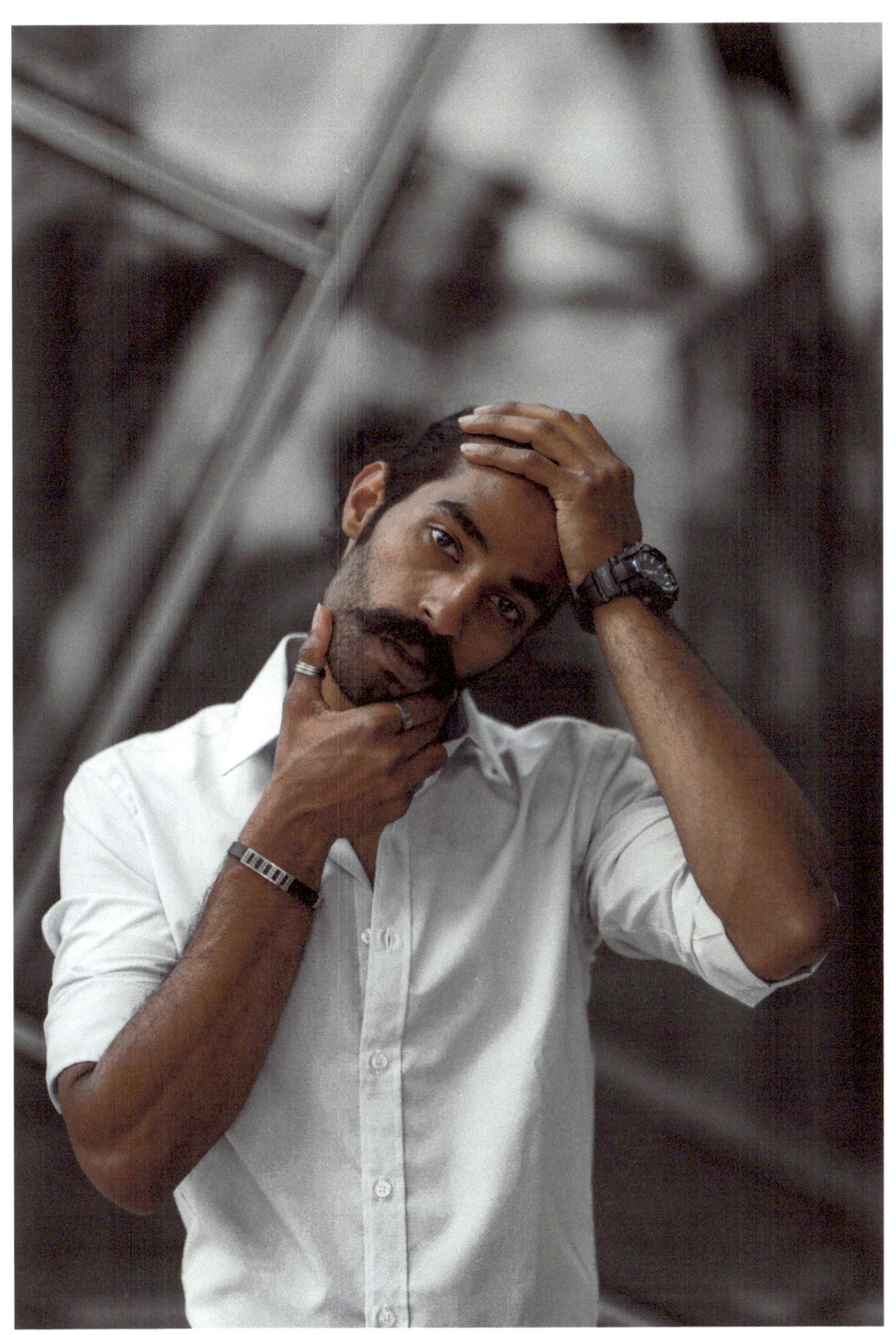

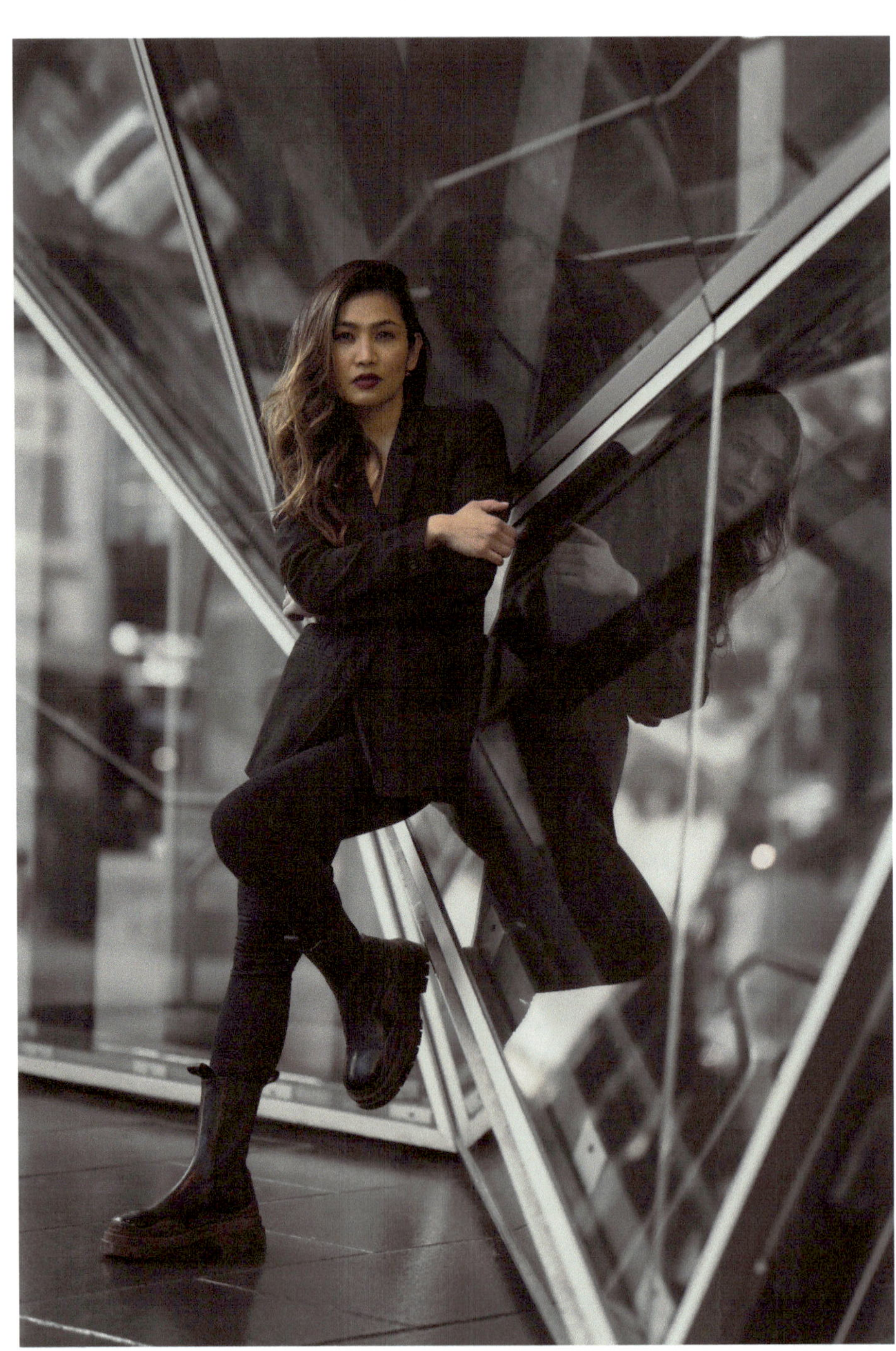

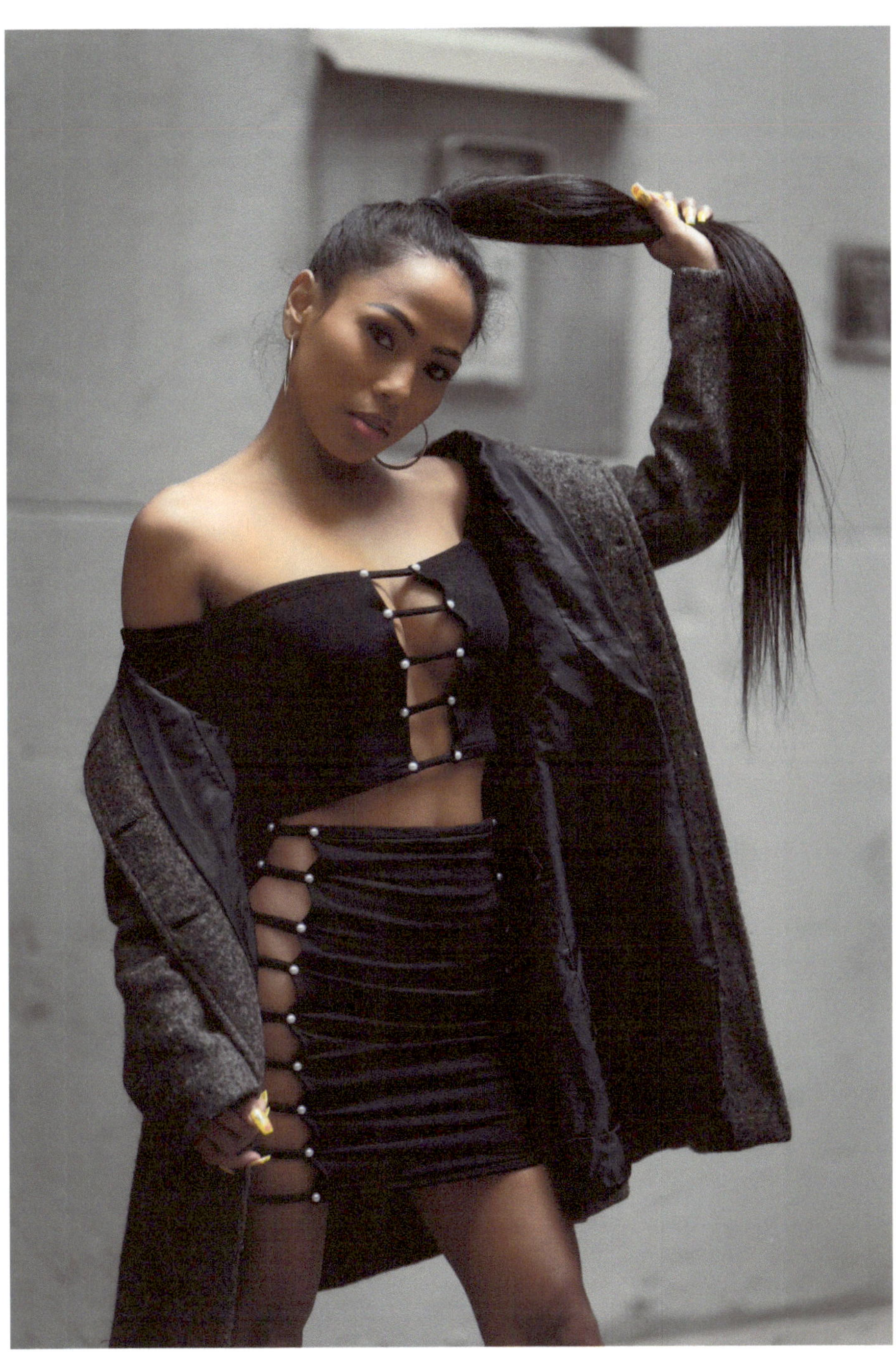

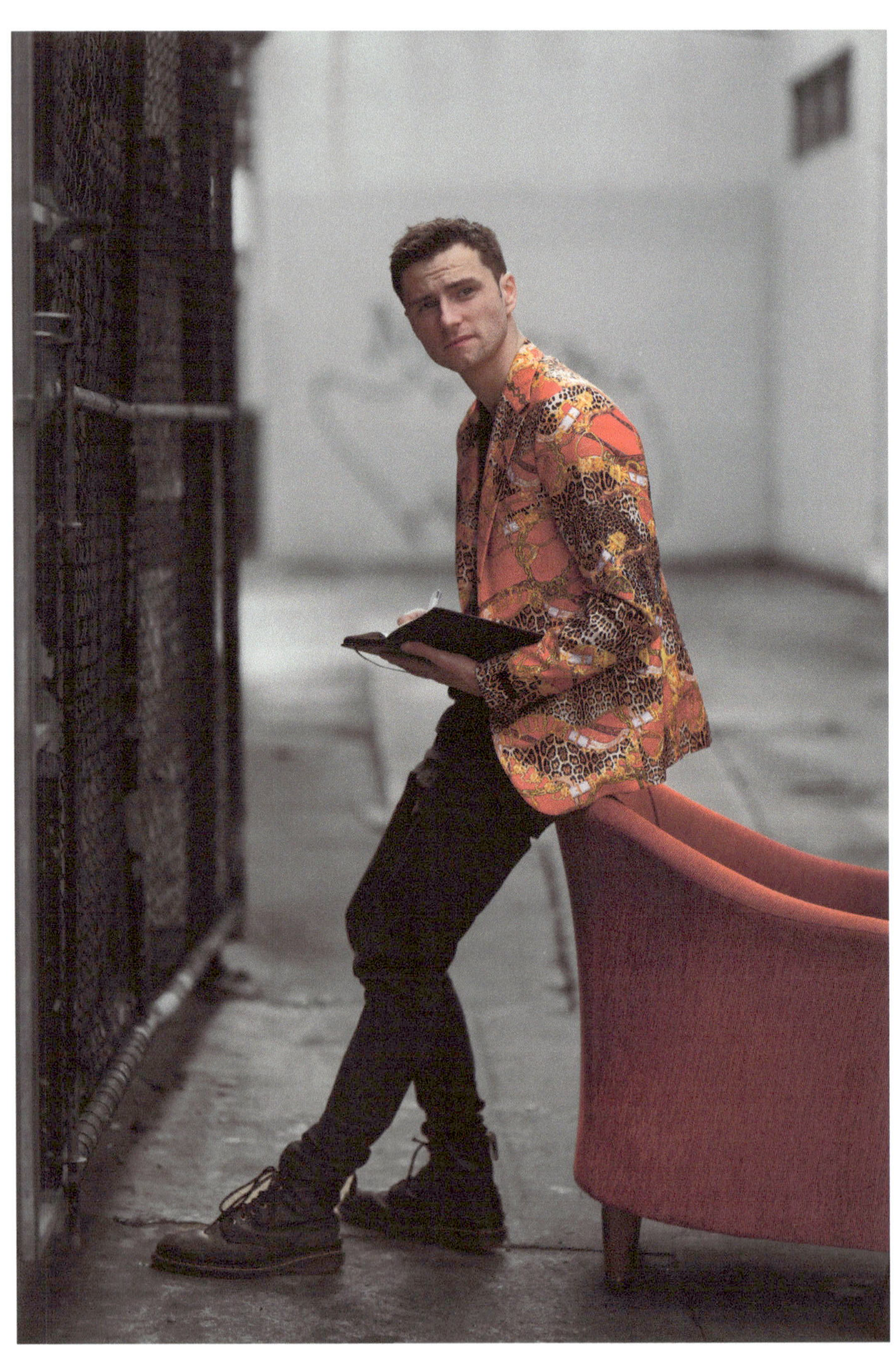

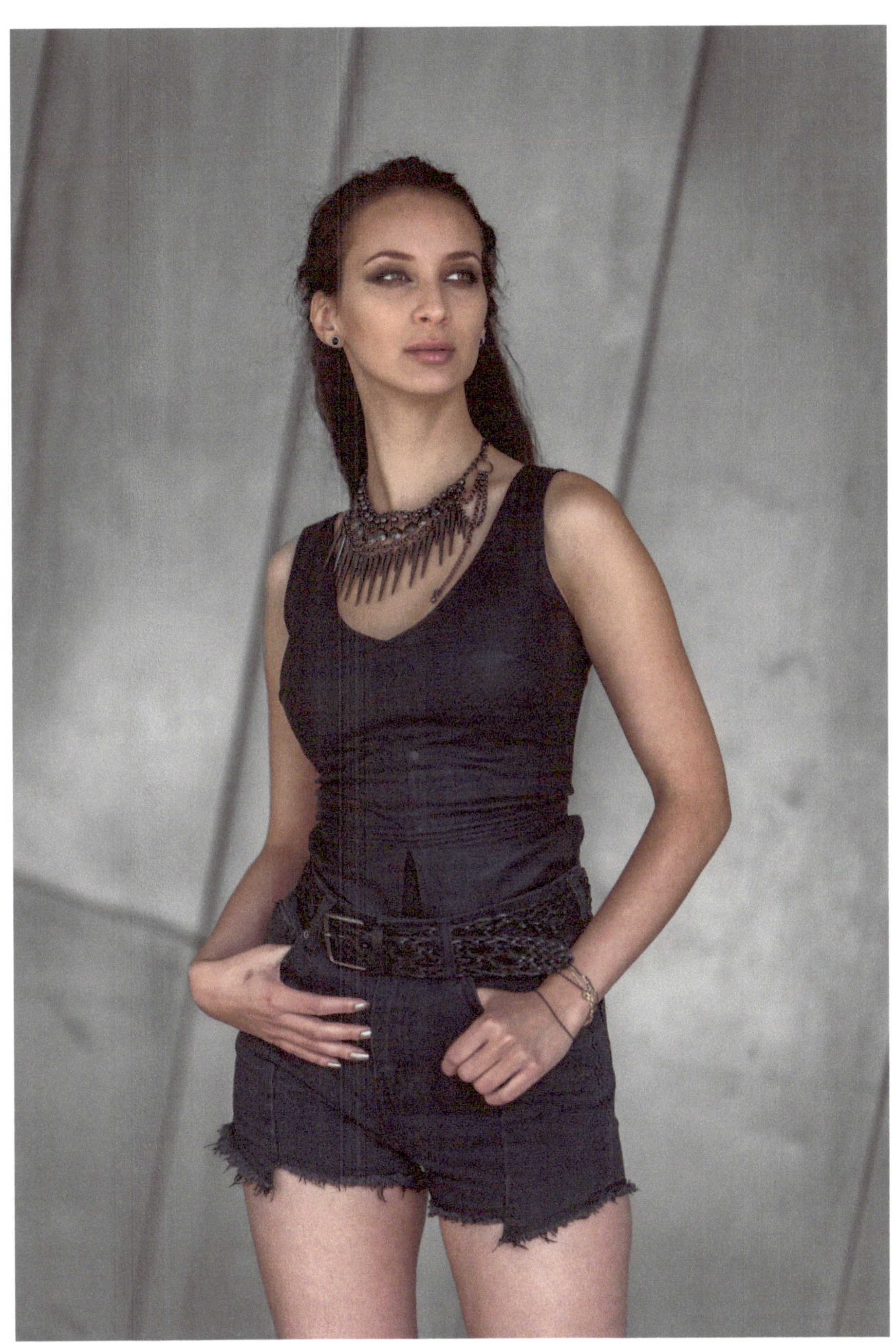

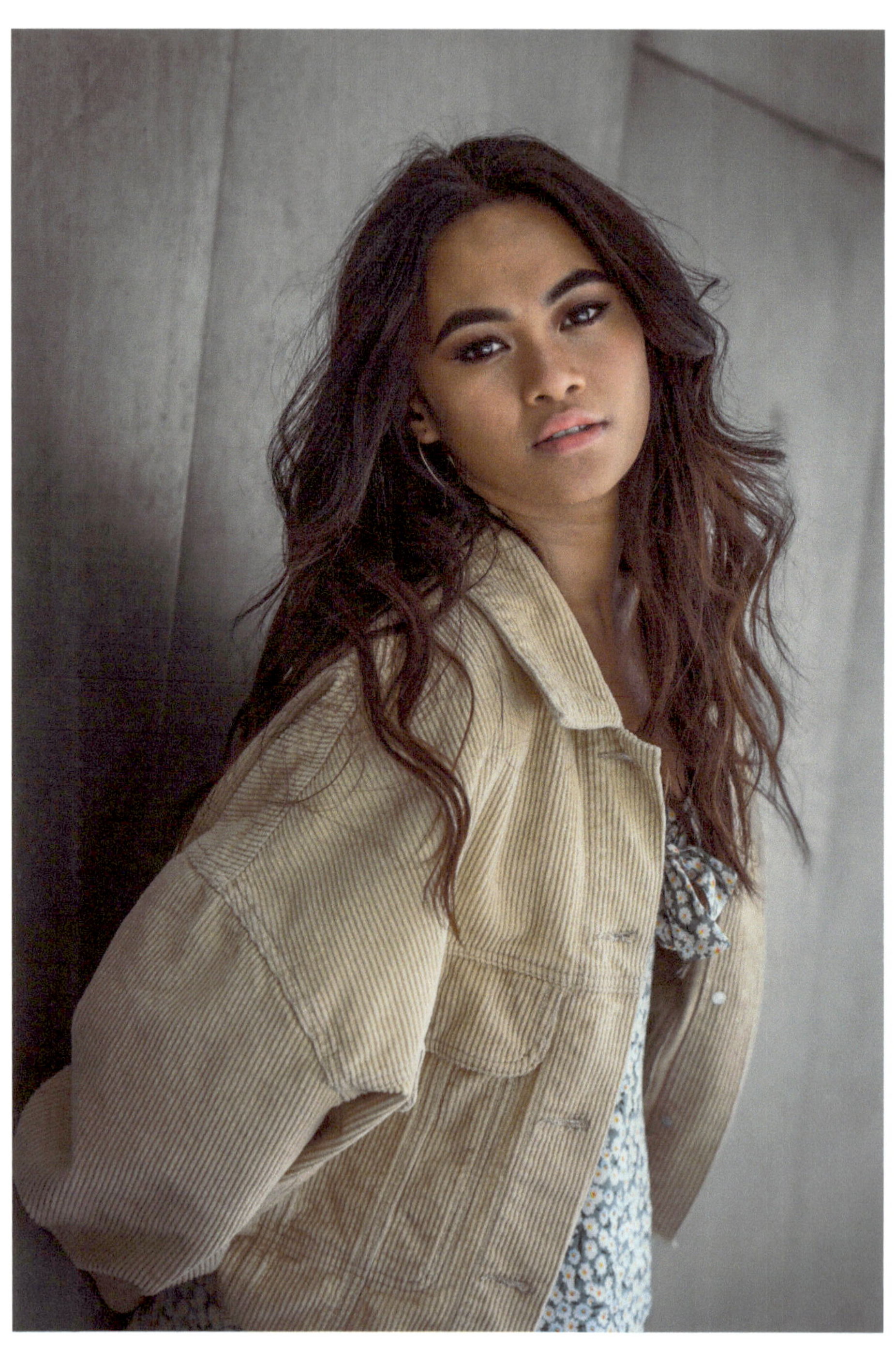

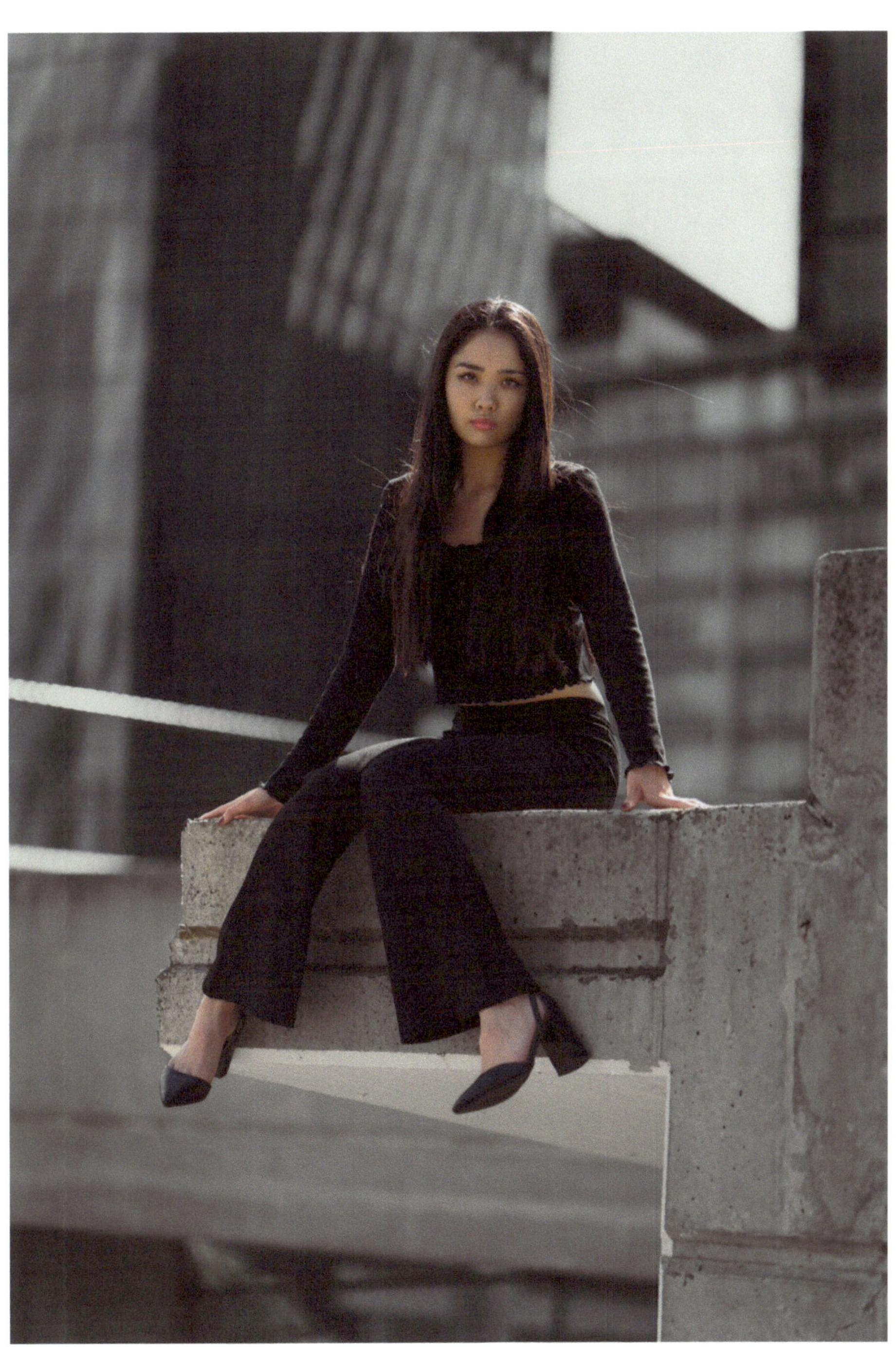

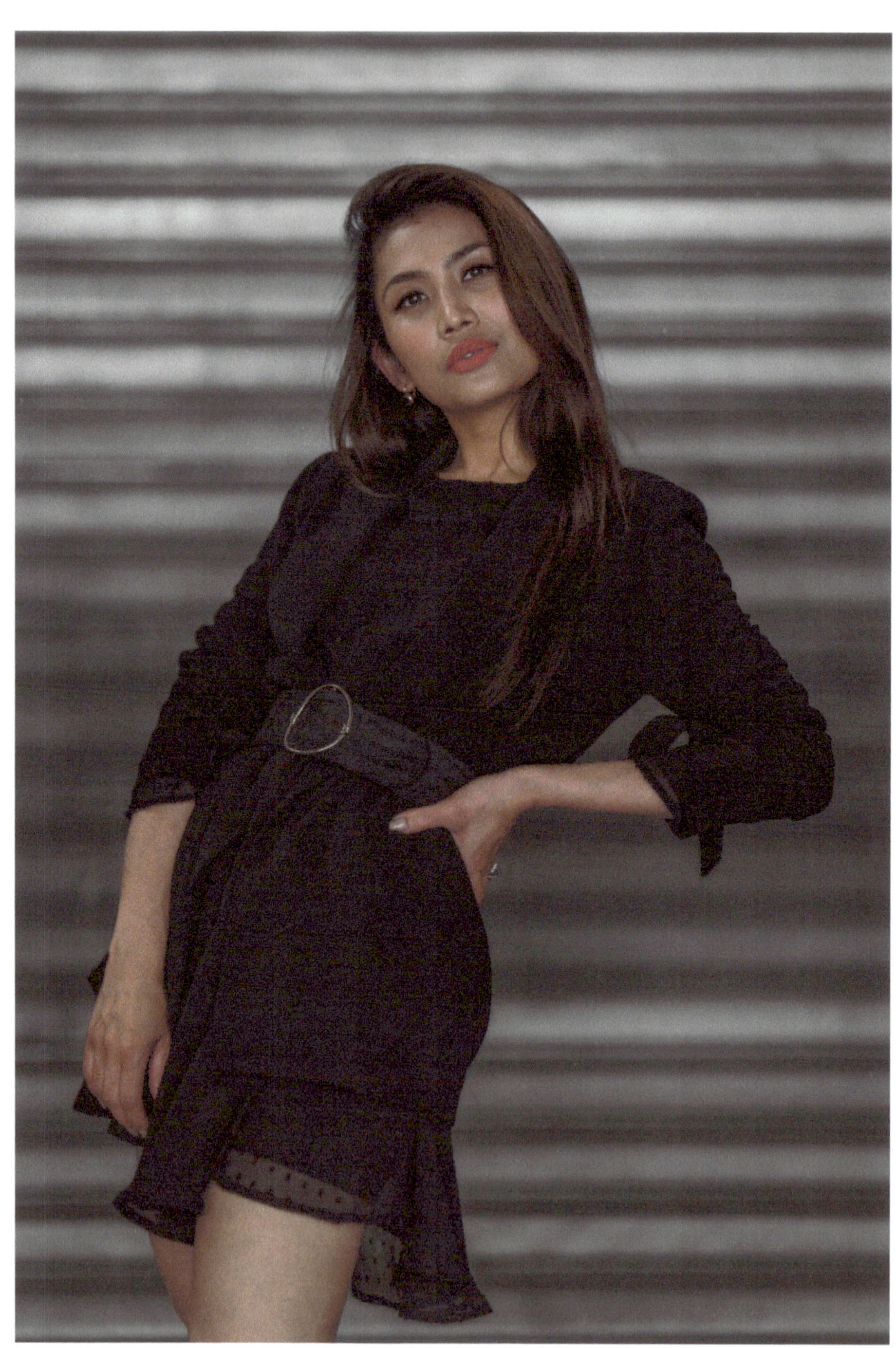

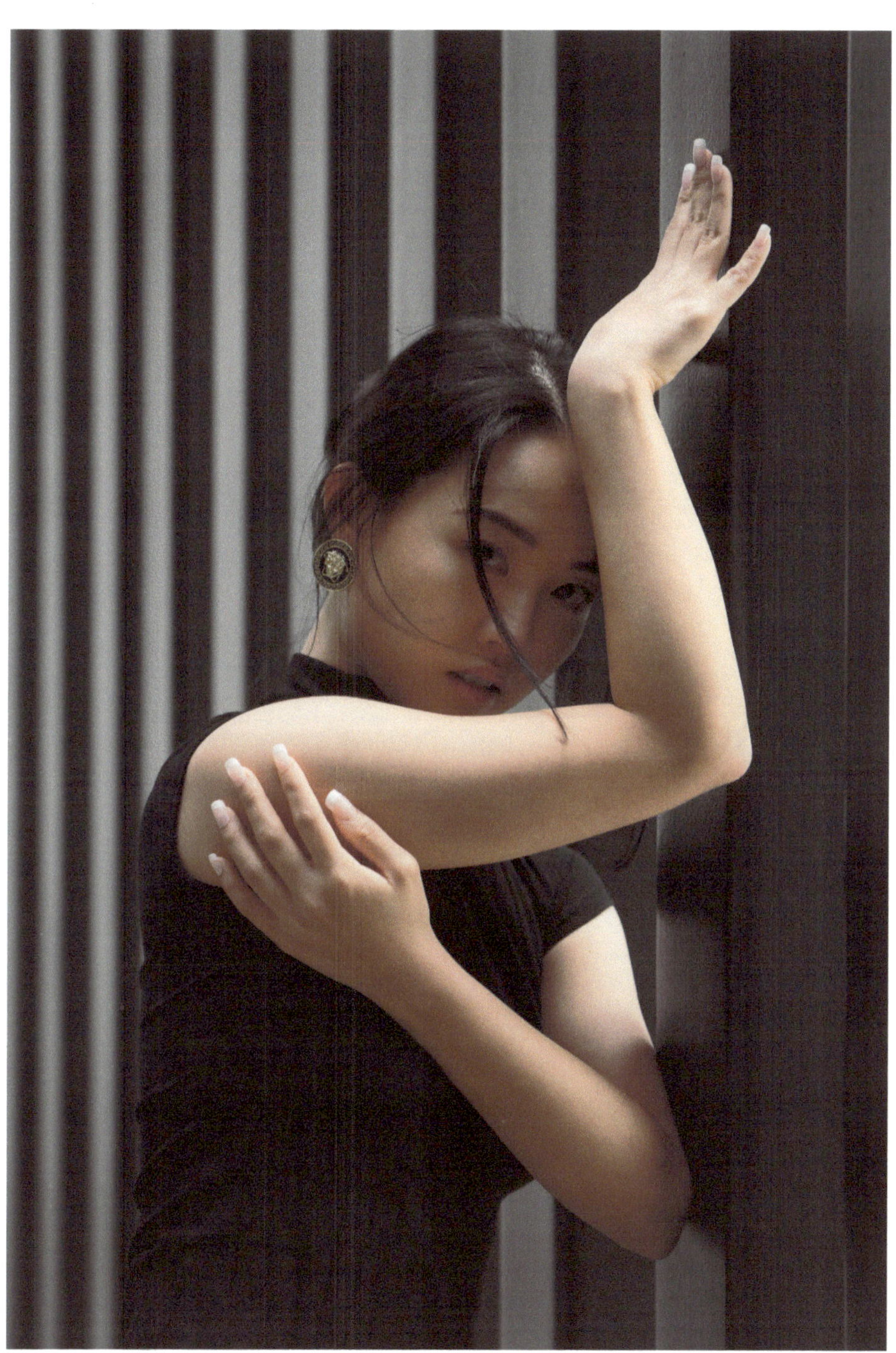

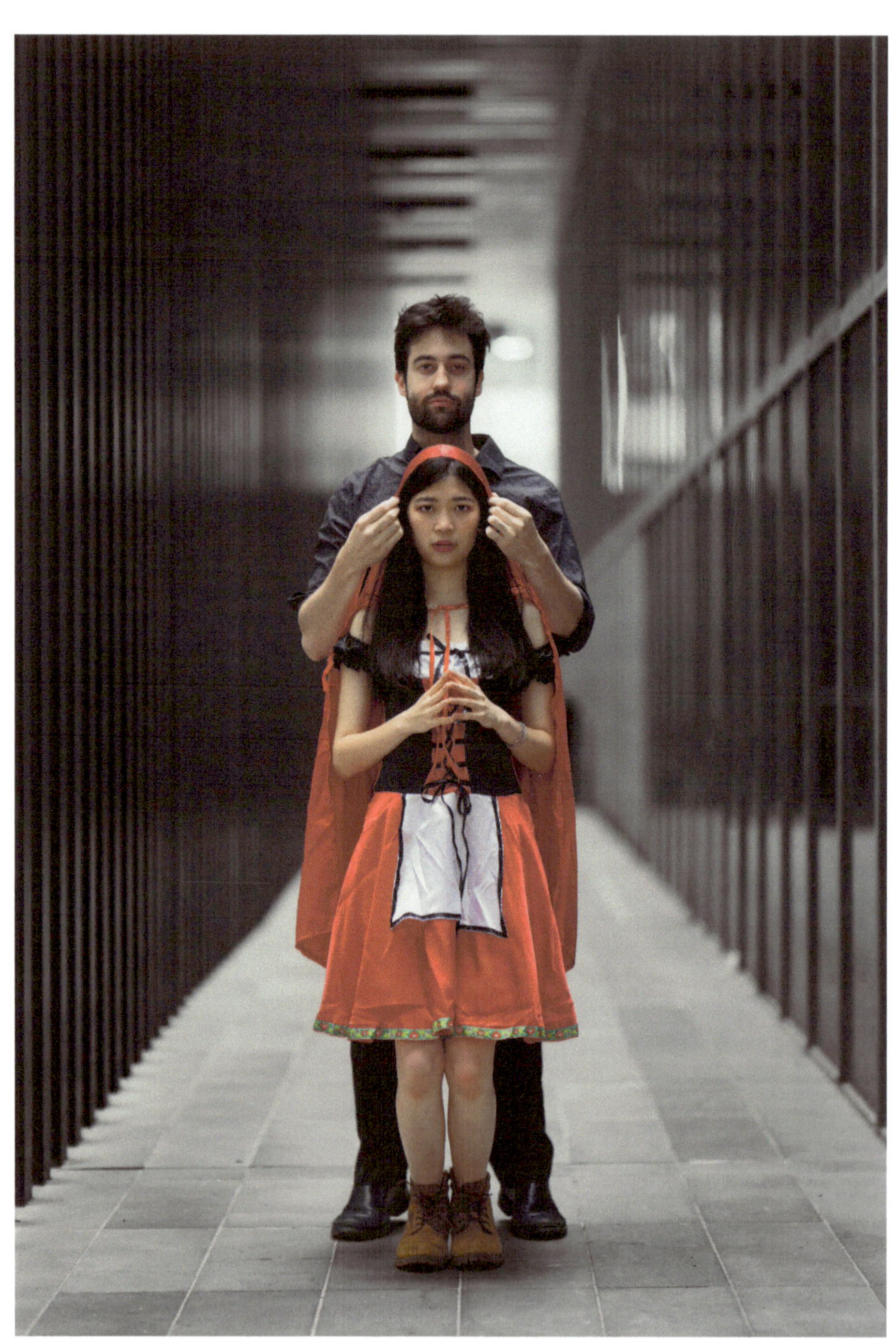

Chapter 5

Visual Echo

"Looking past the surface
takes effort,
but that's where
the truth really comes to light."

Irfan Amin

Visual Echo

Reflections and layers shape how we perceive the world, adding depth and meaning beyond the surface. Glass, mirrors, and light play together in these images, creating moments where what's reflected speaks as much as what's directly seen.

The soft haze of reflections invites a sense of mystery, blurring the line between reality and its mirrored counterpart. Each portrait offers a glimpse into another dimension, not just capturing a face, but hinting at something elusive and profound. It's a subtle dance between clarity and obscurity, where the reflections hold their own stories.

Through transparent layers and fogged surfaces, these images explore both concealment and revelation. The visual barriers become part of the narrative, asking you to look beyond the obvious and discover hidden depths. Every reflection, every layer adds a new element to the story, enhancing the complexity of what's being portrayed.

For creatives, this chapter is an invitation to embrace unpredictability. Reflections and layers offer endless opportunities to see things differently, to find beauty in what's partially hidden or distorted. It's a reminder that sometimes the most compelling stories are told not through direct sight but through the echoes that appear when you look closer.

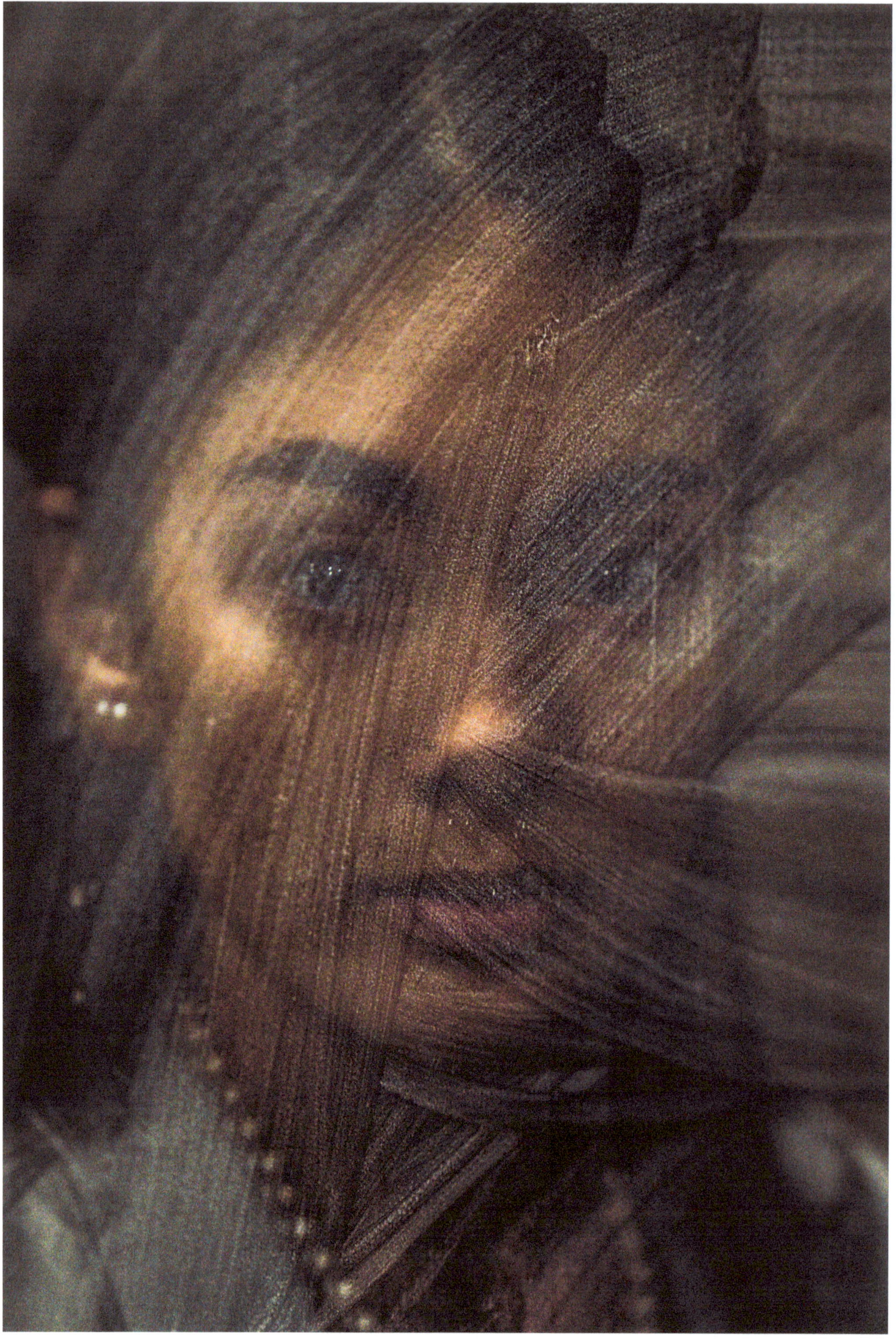

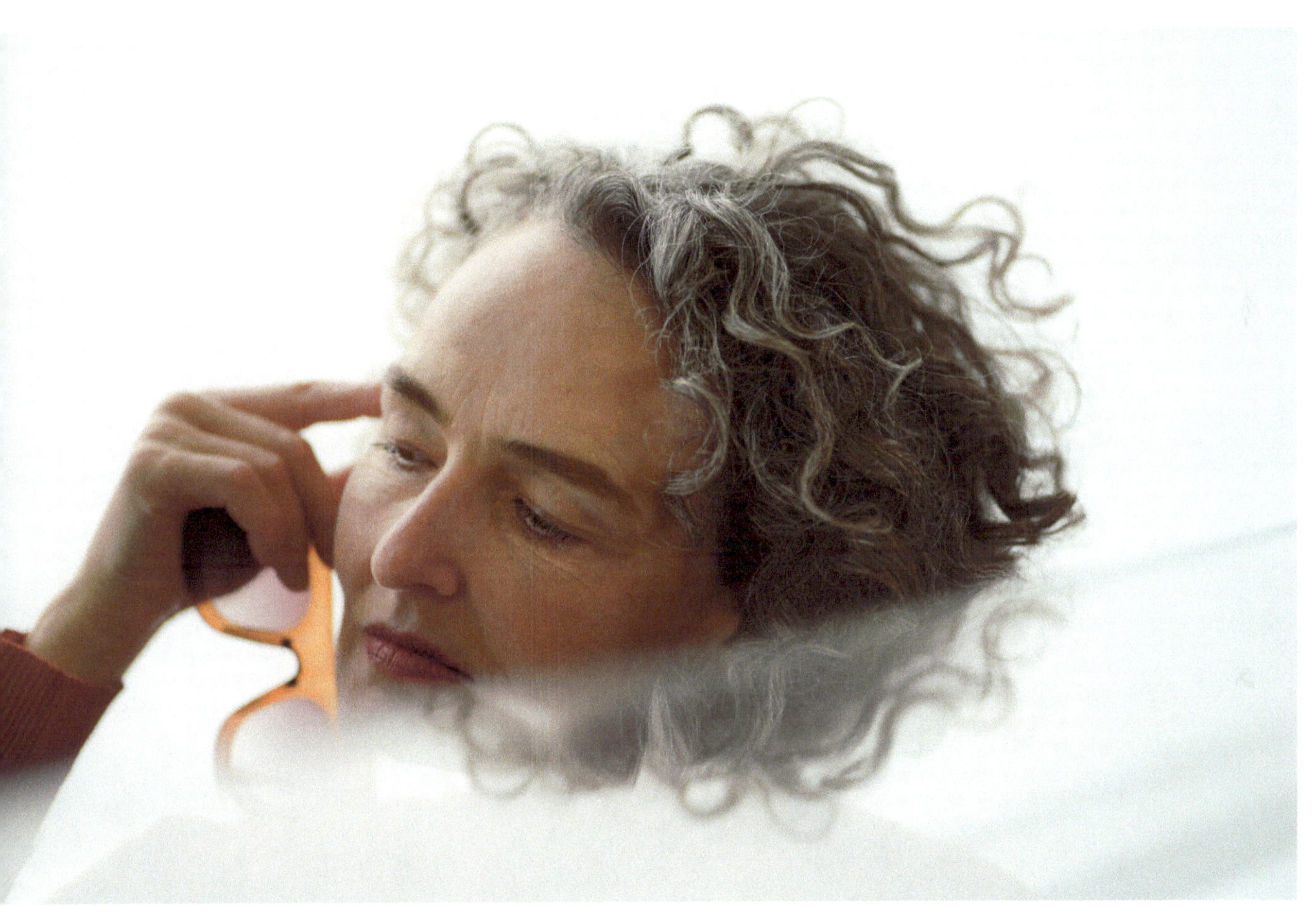

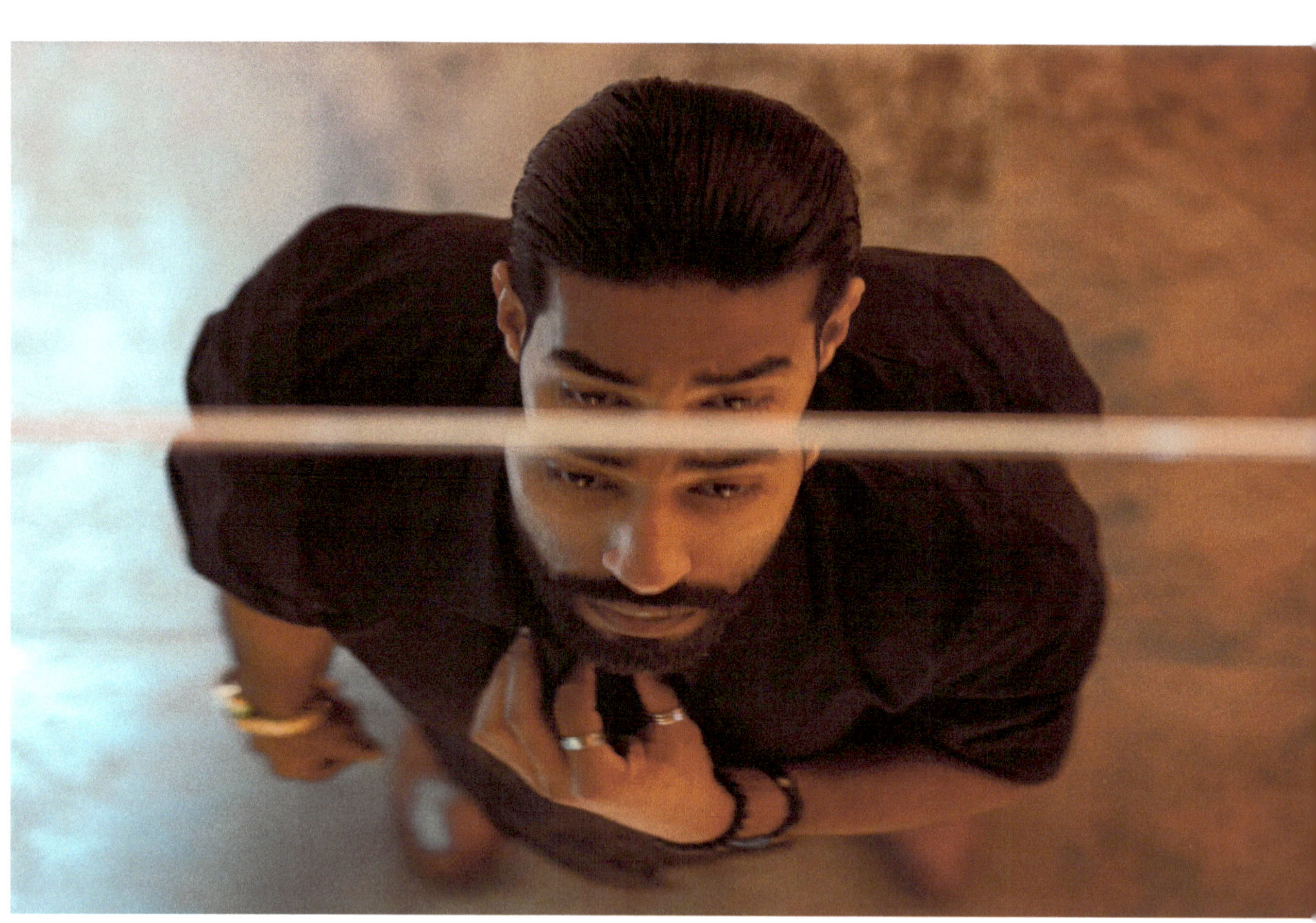

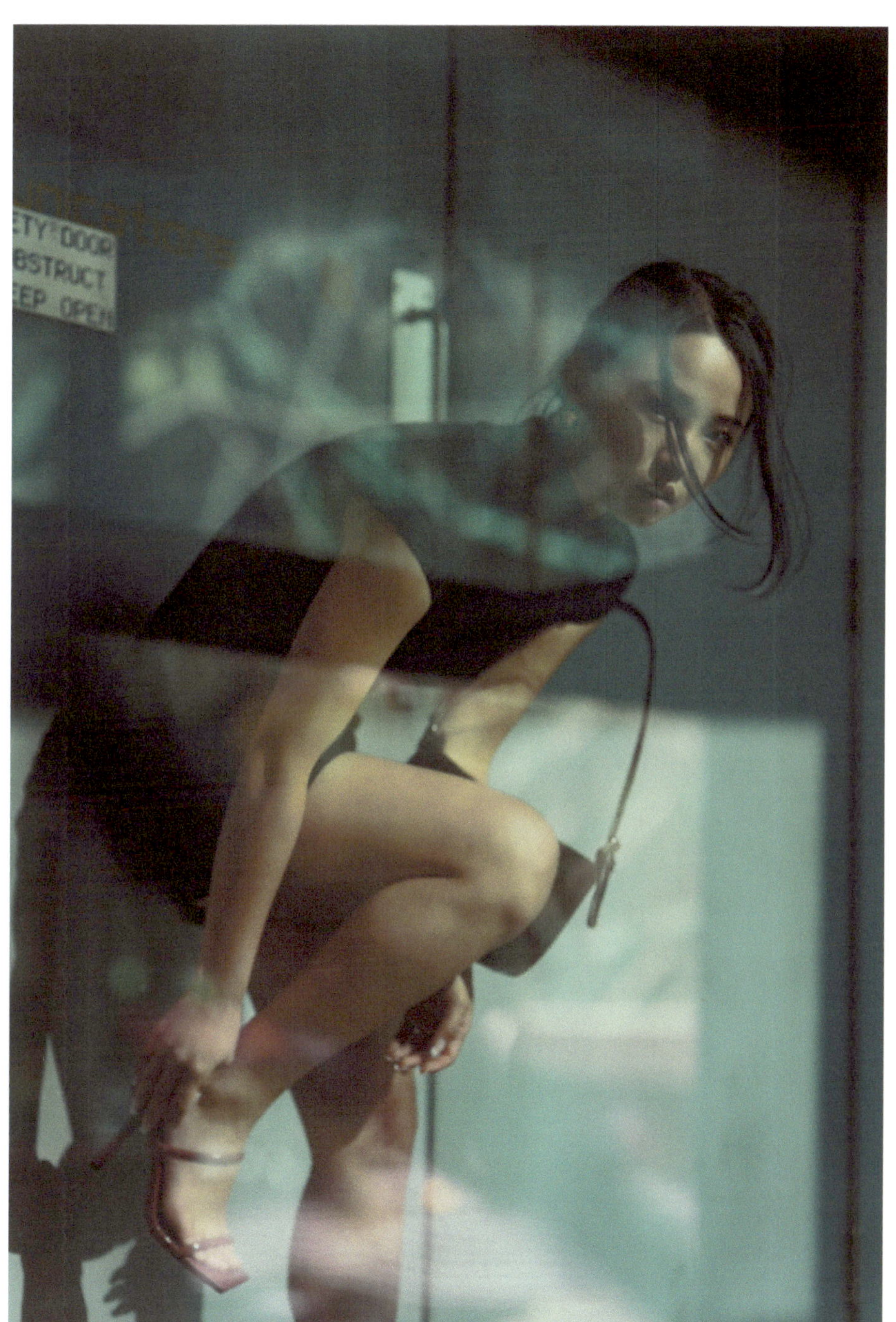
ETY DOOR
BSTRUCT
EEP OPEN

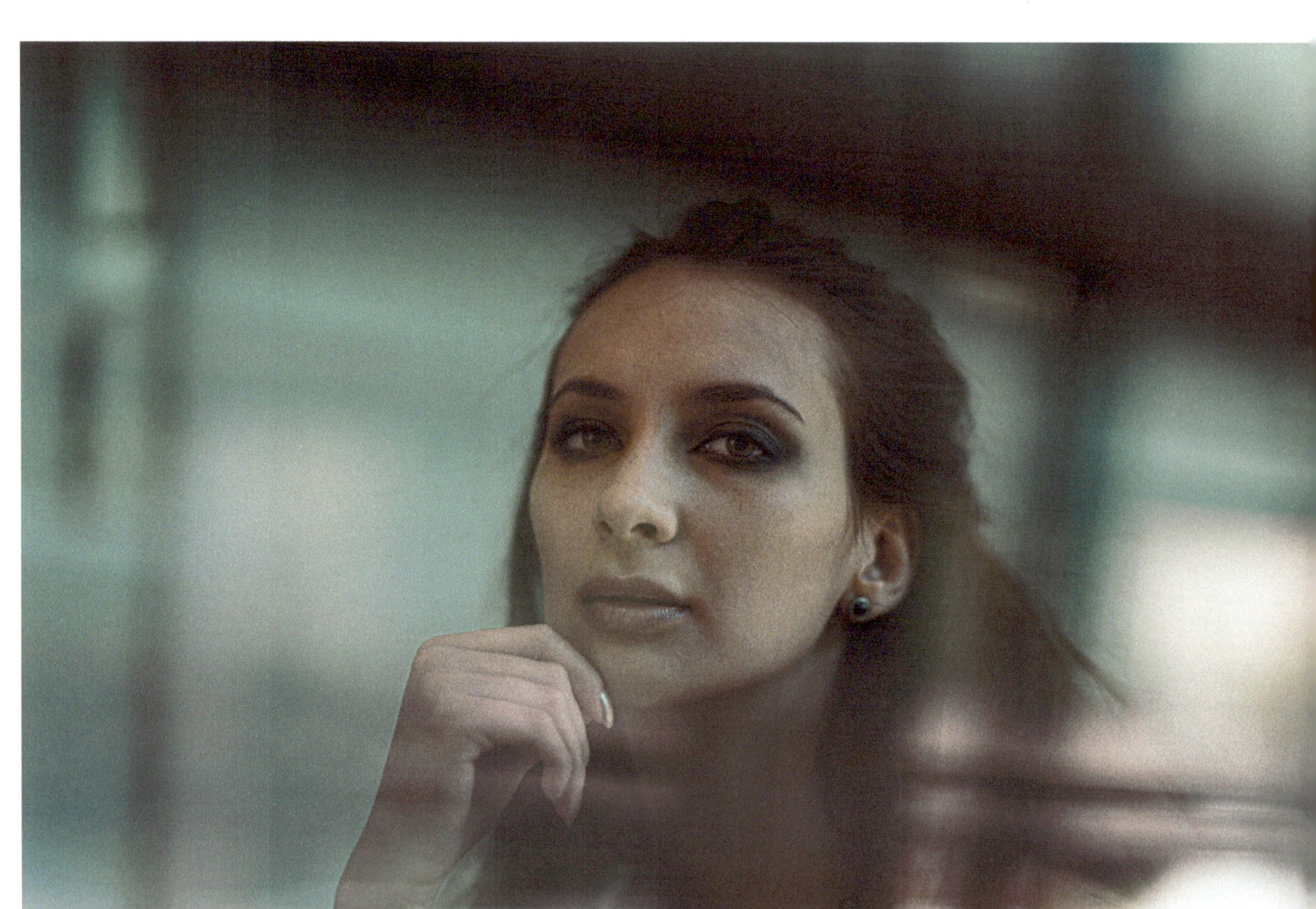

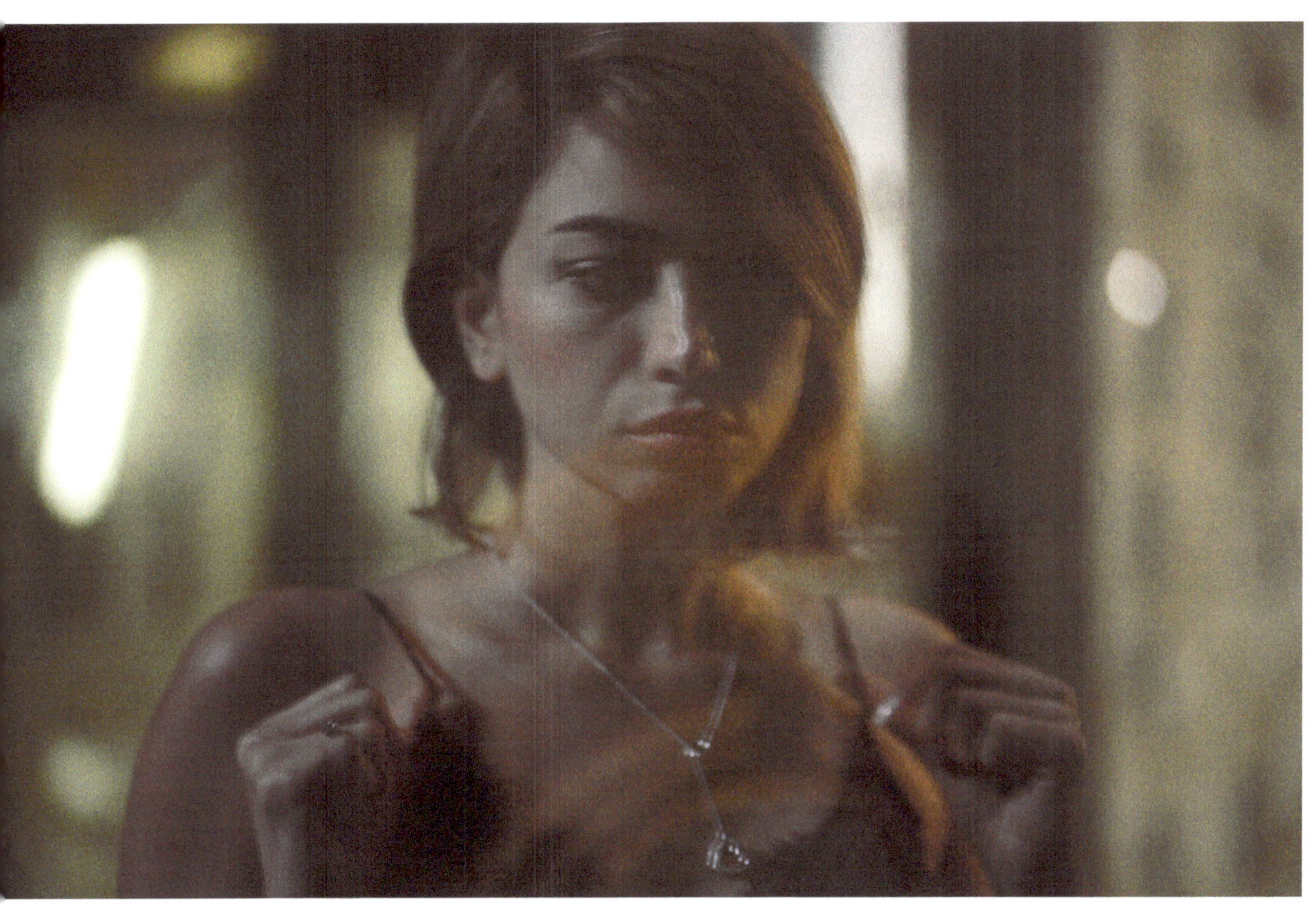

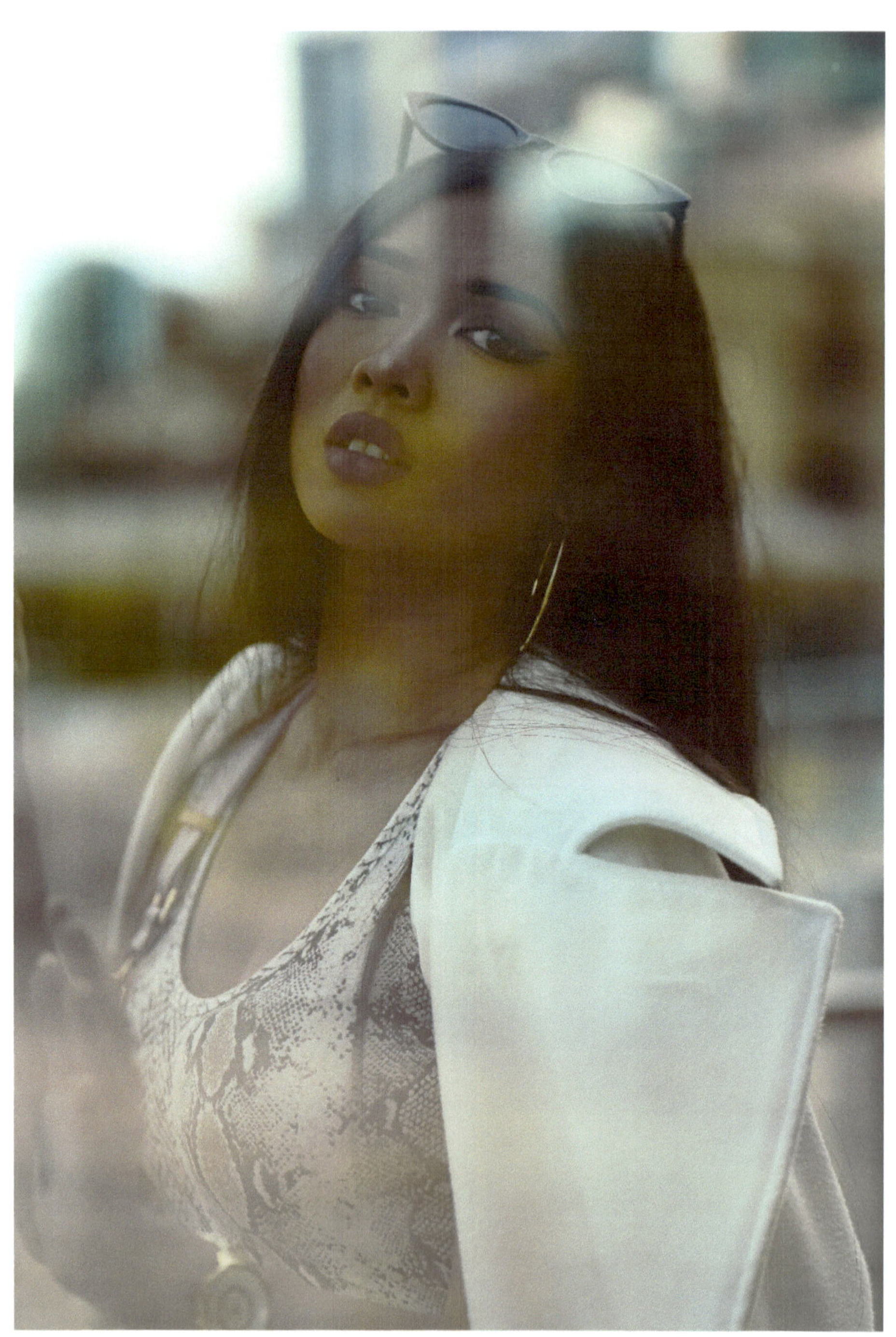

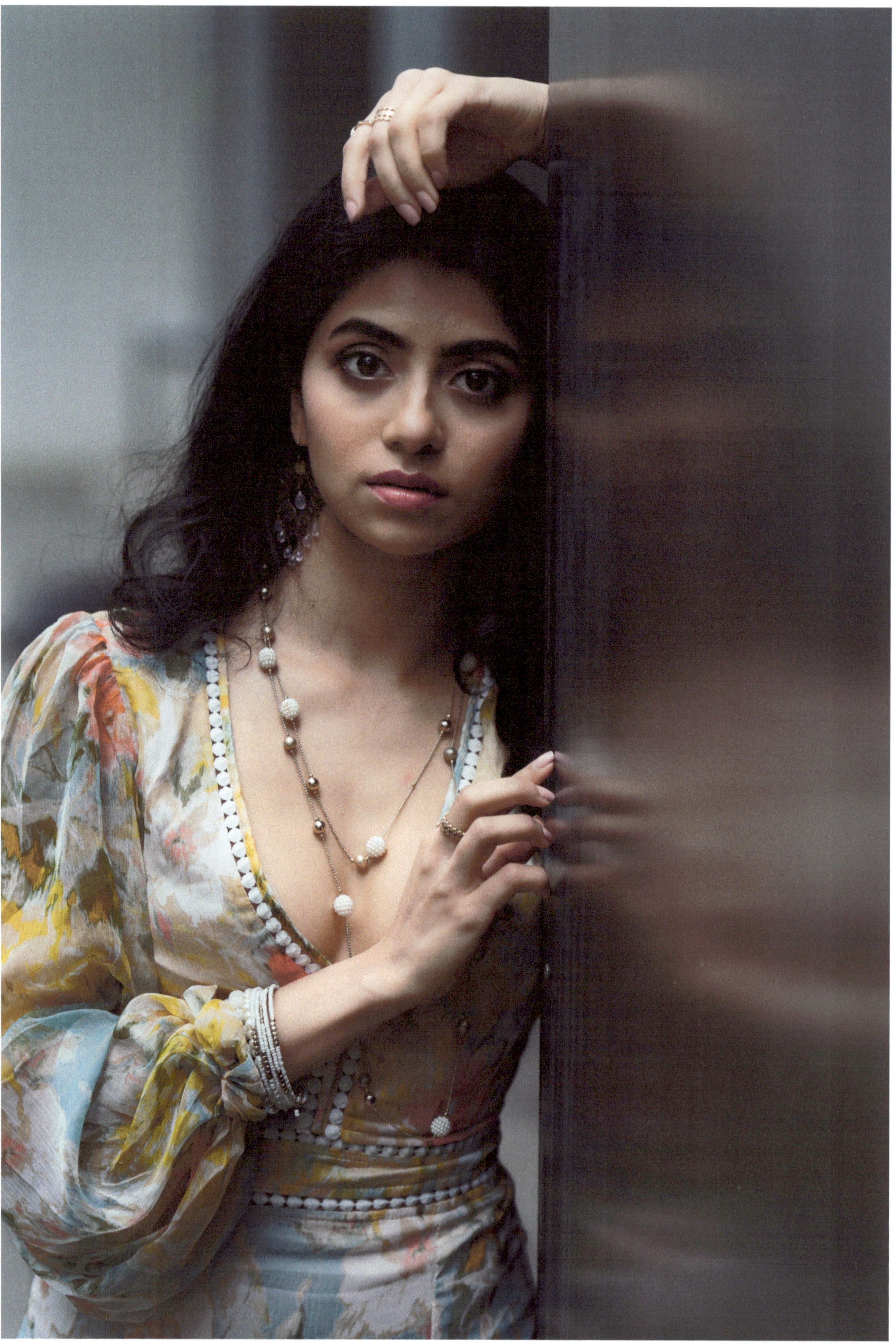

Chapter 6

Fantasy Meets Identity

"When fantasy and reality blend,
we discover parts of ourselves
we never knew existed."

Phoebe Riss

Fantasy Meets Identity

What happens when imagination meets reality? In these images, taken at Comic Con, the individuals photographed aren't just playing roles; they're bringing characters to life, merging their personal identity with the personas they portray. Each glance, each stance, tells a story, blurring the line between the person and the character they've chosen to embody. These moments, captured in natural light, reveal a deep connection between the person and the character.

The expressive power in these portraits comes from the ability to fully inhabit each character. From the fierce determination of a warrior to the quiet strength of a mysterious figure, there's a clear sense of ownership in how they present themselves, blending personal emotion with the story their character represents. The result is an intimate look at the passion and creativity that fuels each transformation.

While cosplay is often seen as an escape, these images reveal it as a powerful form of self-expression and identity exploration. Each costume becomes a vehicle to explore different facets of identity. The lines between reality and fantasy blur, allowing hidden strengths, vulnerabilities, and dreams to come forward. There's something uniquely liberating in stepping into a role that both reflects and contrasts with everyday life.

In this chapter, you're invited to see cosplay in a new light—not just as a celebration of characters, but as an exploration of identity, creativity, and self-expression. These images, taken in natural light, reveal how stepping into a character allows for boldness and transformation, offering inspiration to explore new dimensions of who we are. Whether you're drawn to the artistry of the costumes or the emotion behind the personas, there's a sense of connection here that resonates beyond the pages.

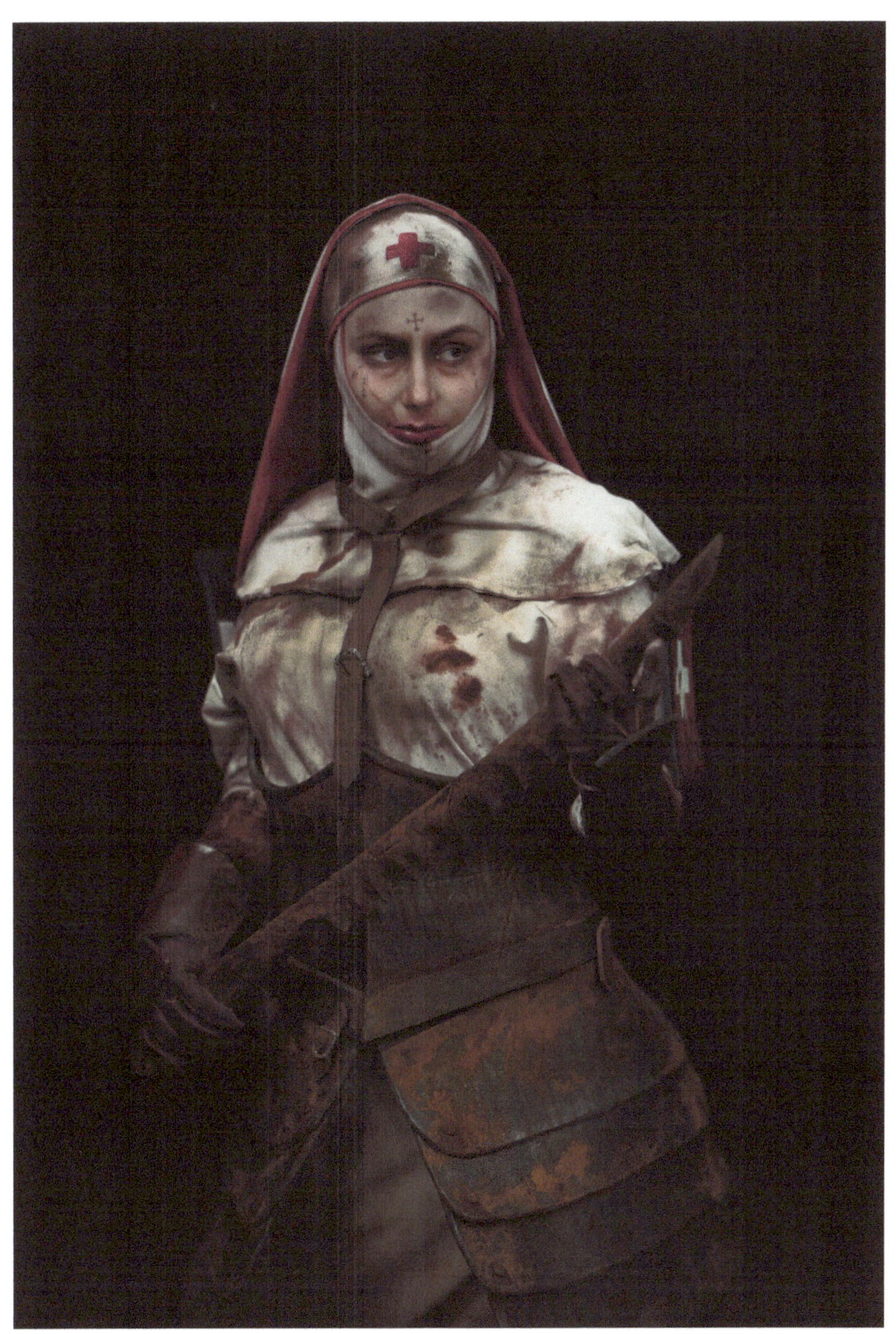

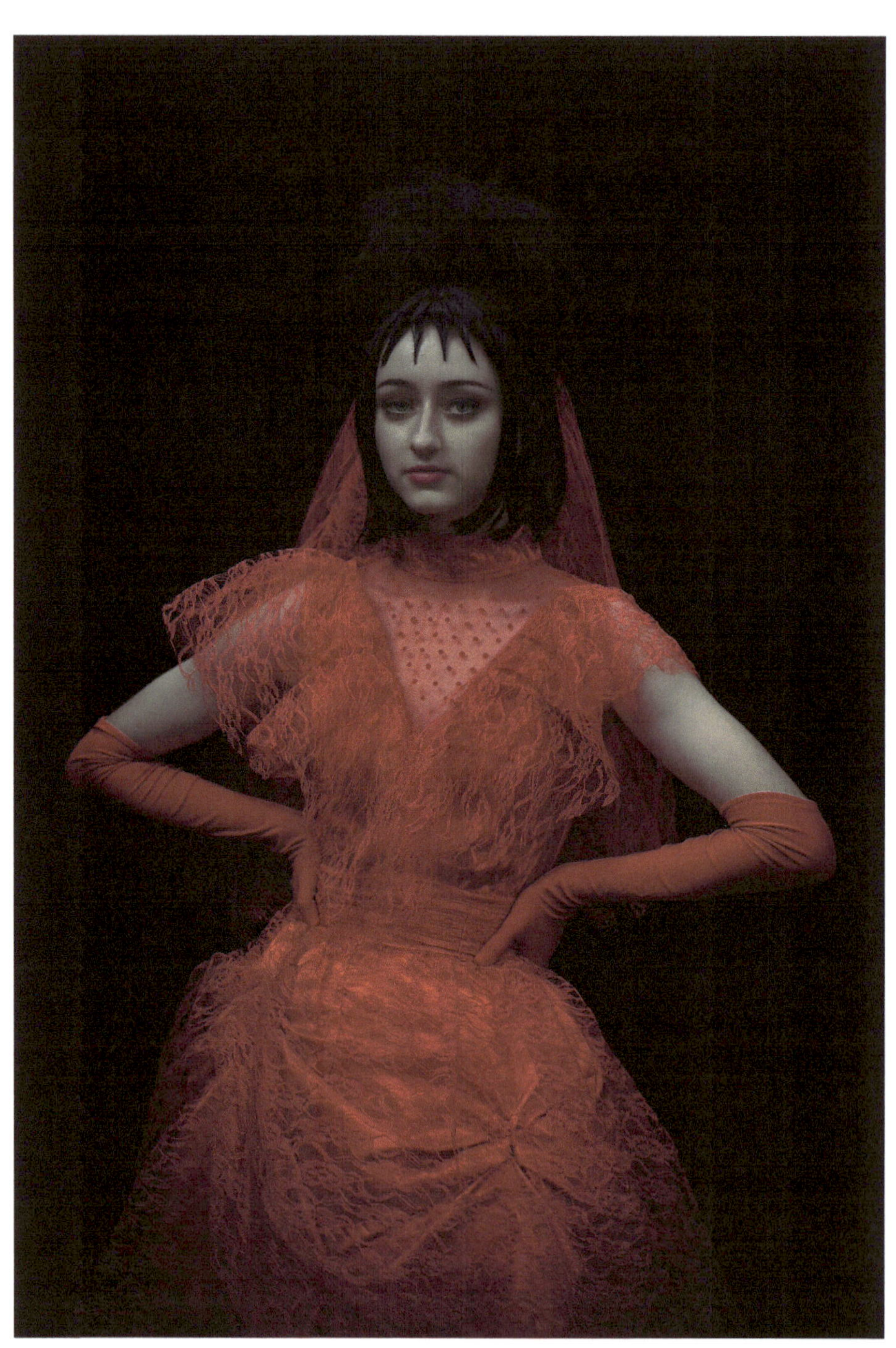

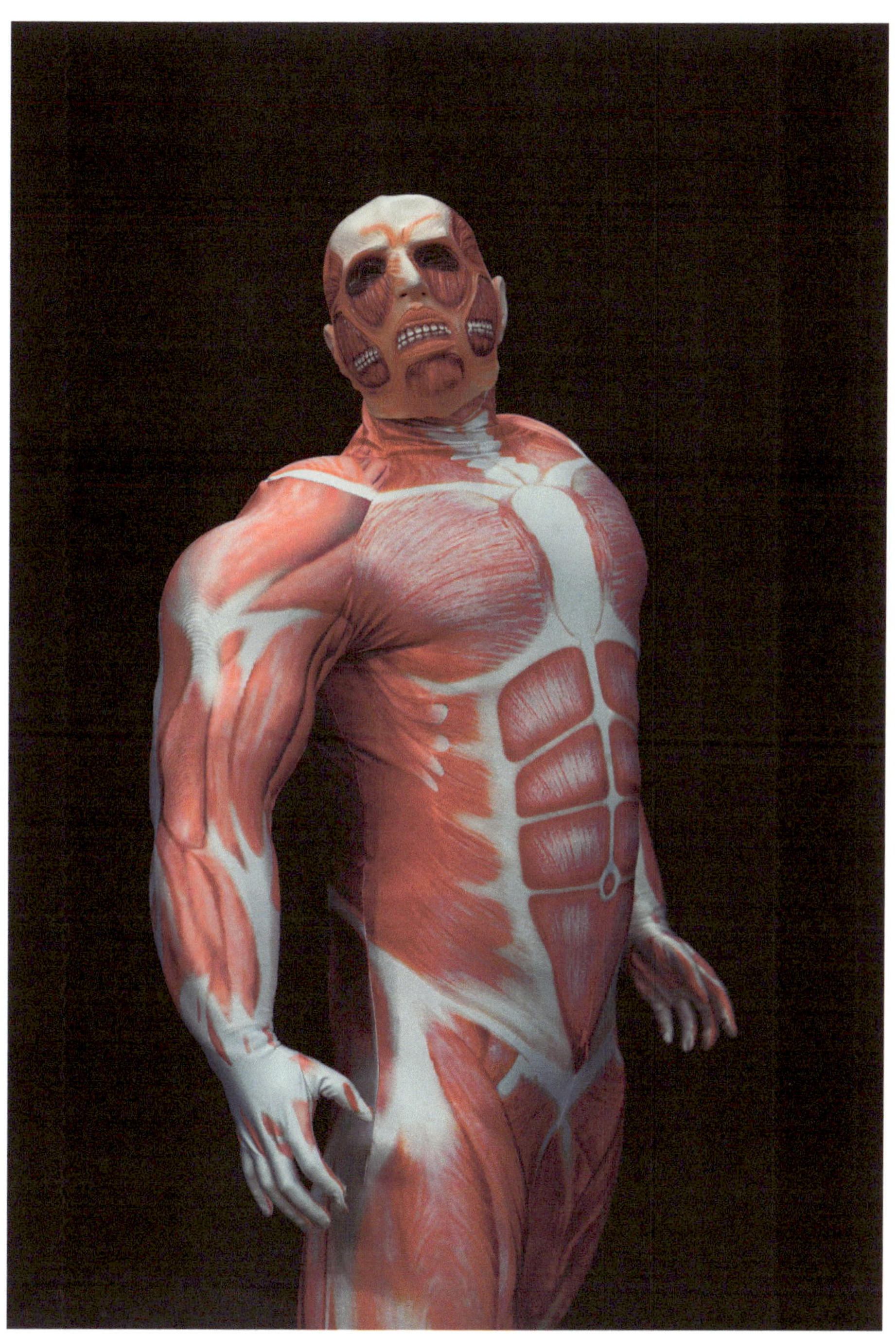

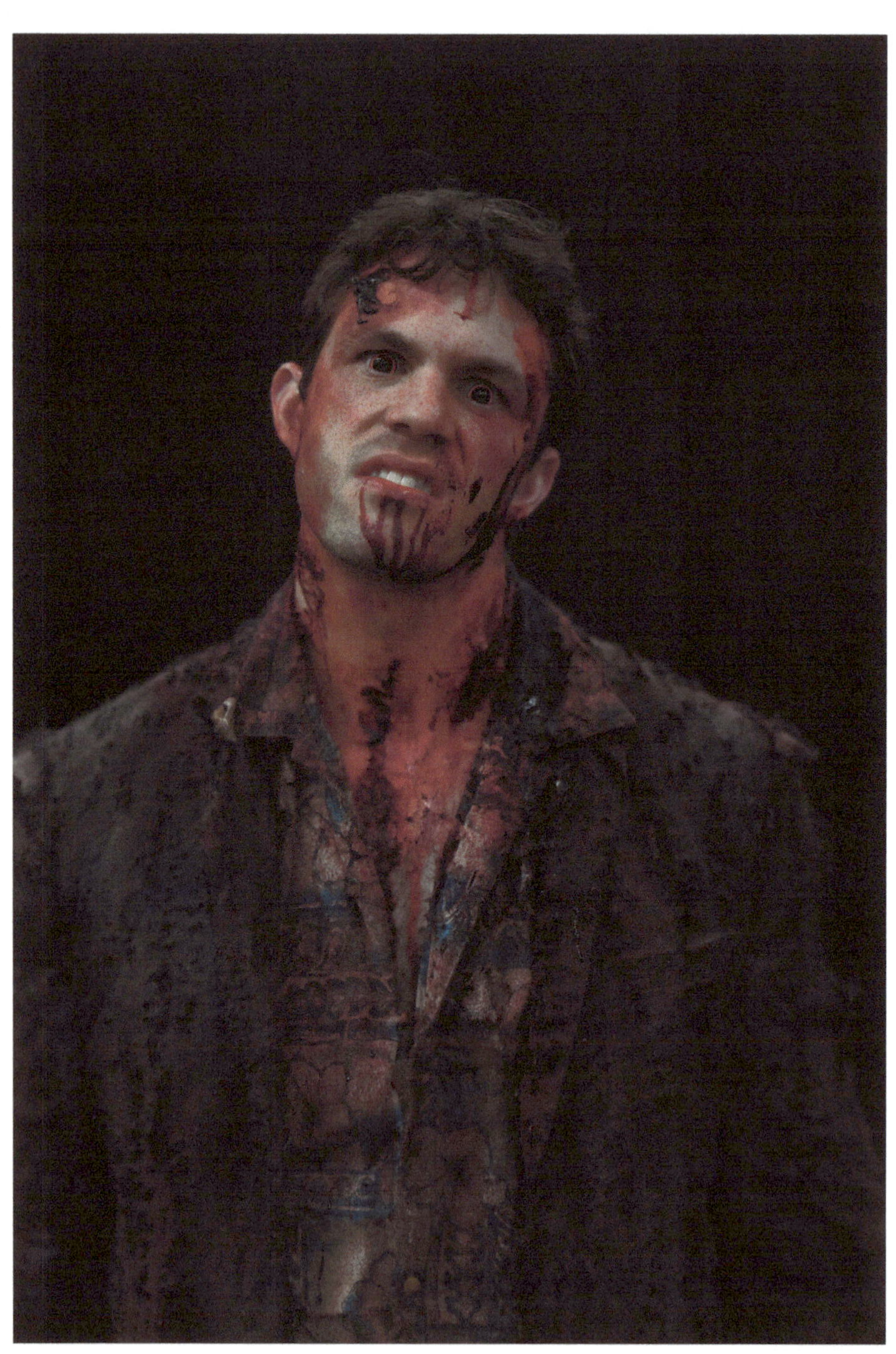

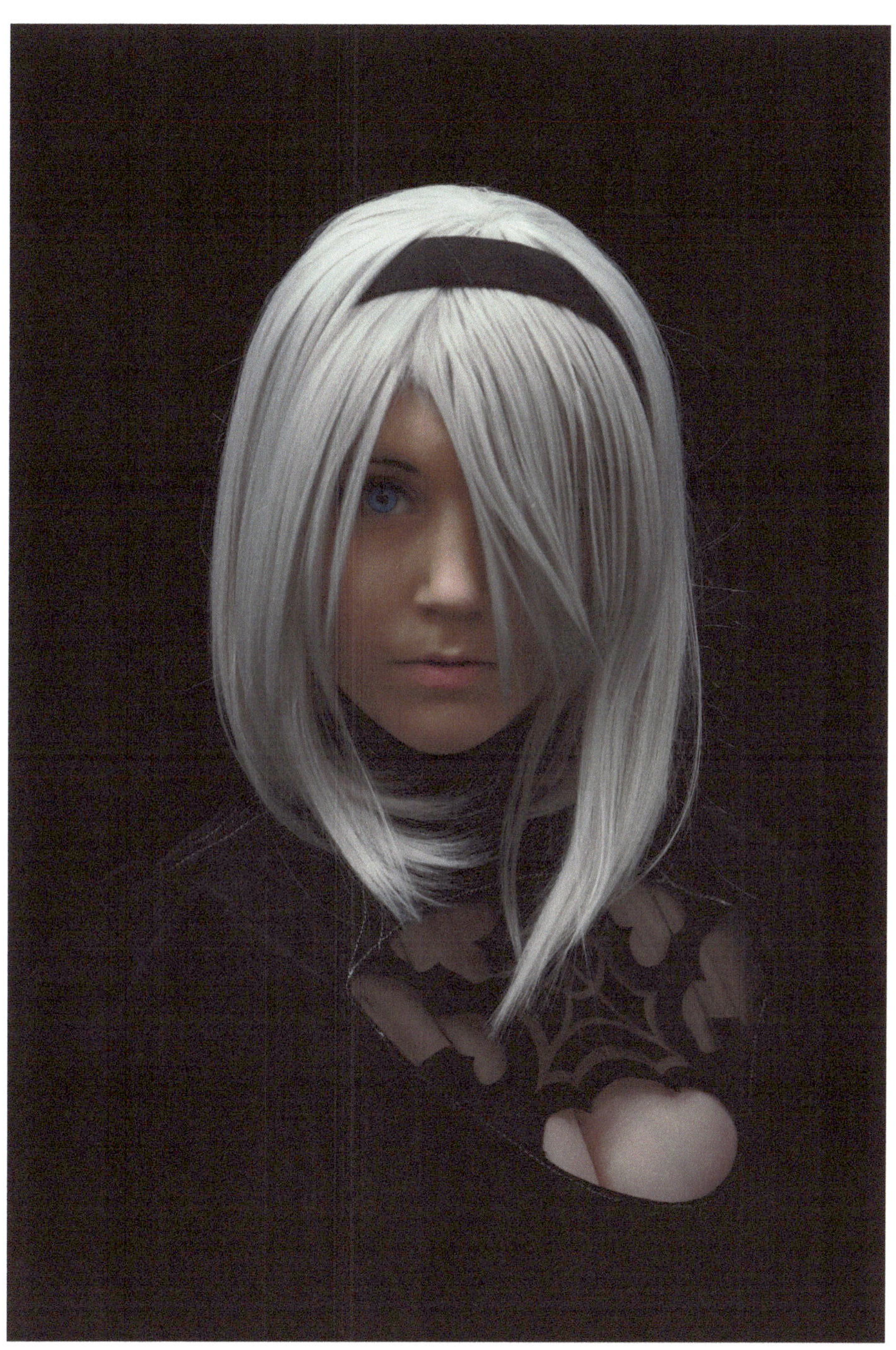

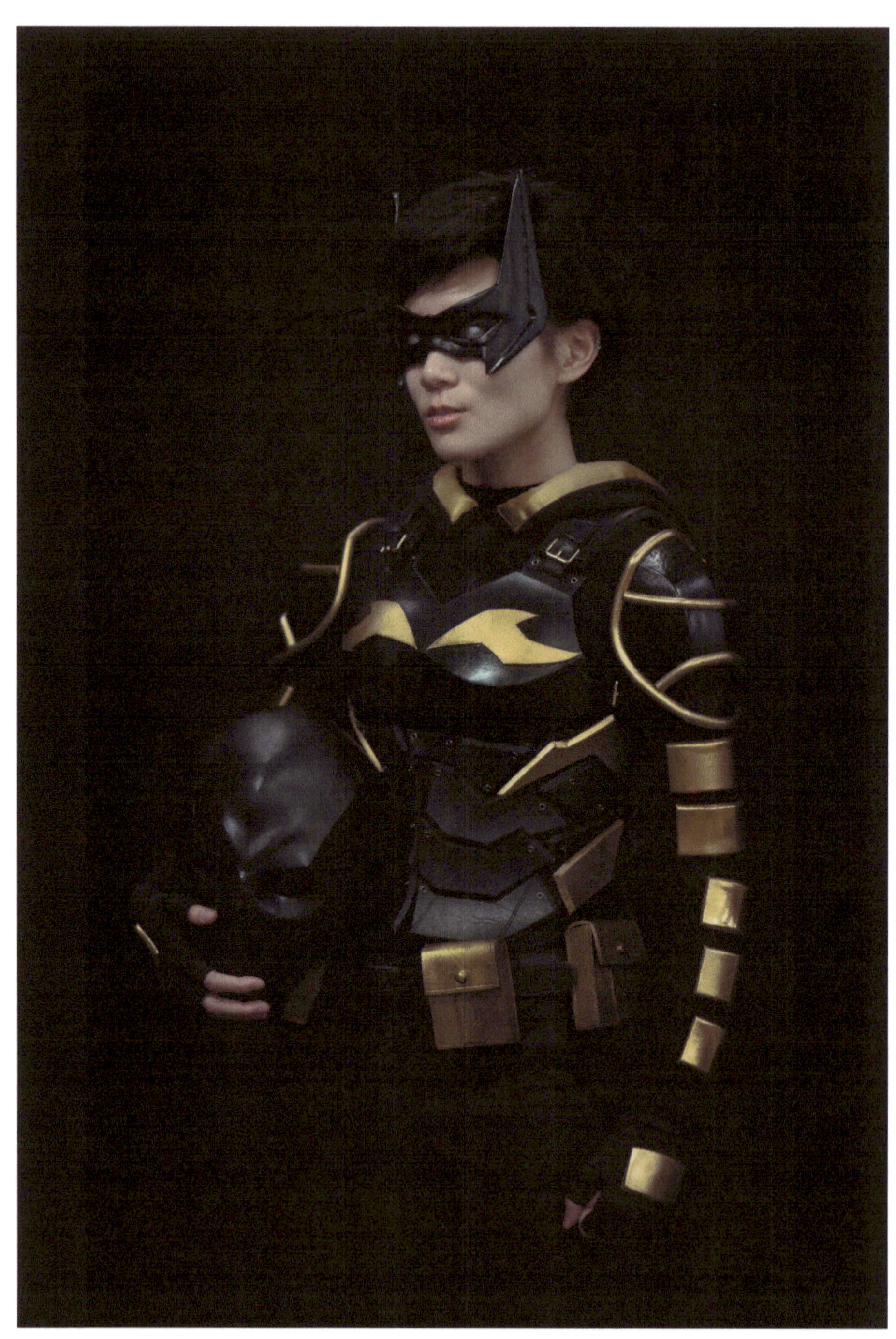

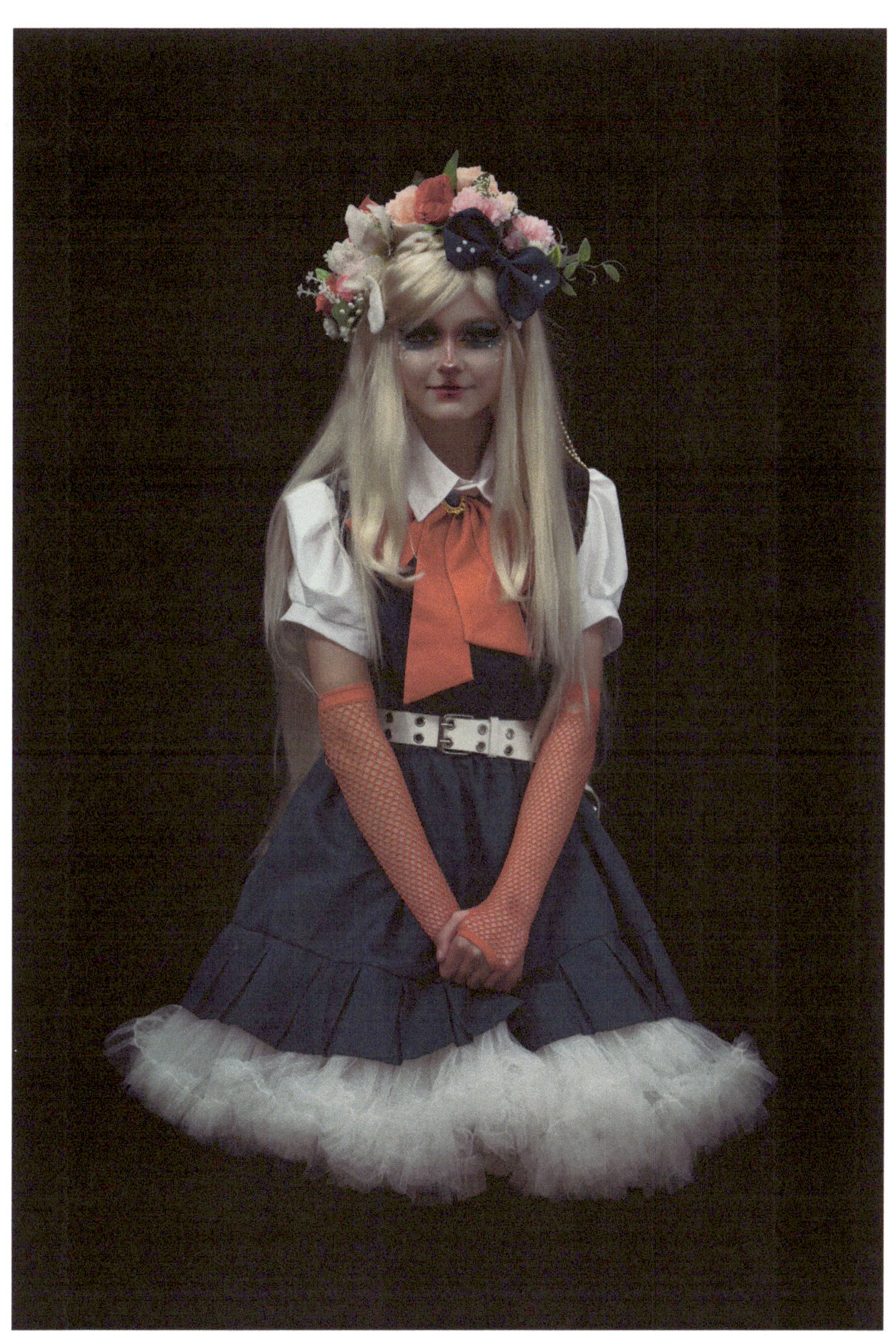

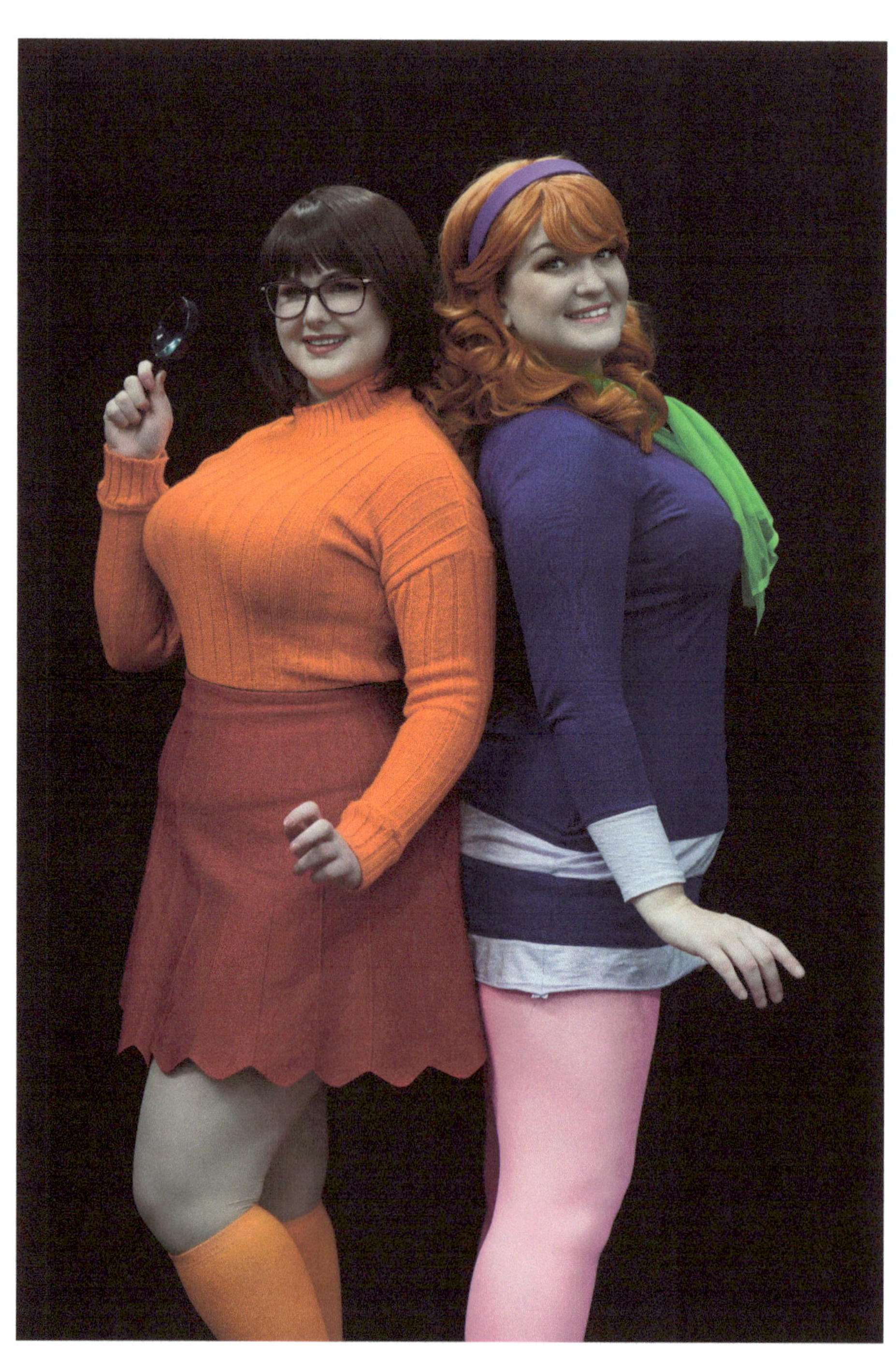

Chapter 7

Strike A Pose

"A pose is such a wonderful expression of emotion in how someone feels, it's like a painting that has artistic meaning yet not everyone can explain. It is a mysterious stance that someone might interpret differently, but yet seen beautiful and extraordinary. It can translate into anything from confidence, joy, sadness, and misery. It's like seeing through someone's soul and having a piece of their identity."

Pia Gould

Strike A Pose

Portraiture is not just about the person in the frame—it's about capturing the essence of a moment, movement, and emotion. This chapter brings that philosophy to life through a series of images that go beyond the traditional idea of posing. Each portrait reveals a unique energy, highlighting the way movement and expression create a connection with the environment. From dynamic movements to still moments of contemplation, the portraits create a visual narrative that speaks to authenticity and connection.

Through these photos, you're invited to explore how body language and subtle gestures can shift the entire mood of a portrait. There's an unspoken story in how one person stretches toward the light, or how another engages with their surroundings. By capturing these spontaneous moments, the chapter reveals the power of letting your subject express themselves naturally. This approach encourages you to see how spontaneity can lead to a deeper portrayal of identity.

The backgrounds and settings amplify the individuality of each portrait, whether it's a colorful street or a simple urban backdrop. Each image presents a harmony between the person and their environment, creating a sense of unity. It's in these little details—how expressions interact with the setting, or how a pose complements the scene—that the story unfolds. The subtle interactions between the individual and their surroundings emphasize the emotions conveyed through each portrait.

These portraits encourage you to embrace the fluidity of expression in your work. It's about letting go of the rigid idea of perfect composition and trusting in the energy of the moment. By focusing on how people move, interact, and reveal their true selves, you're empowered to create portraits that feel alive, full of movement, and deeply personal.

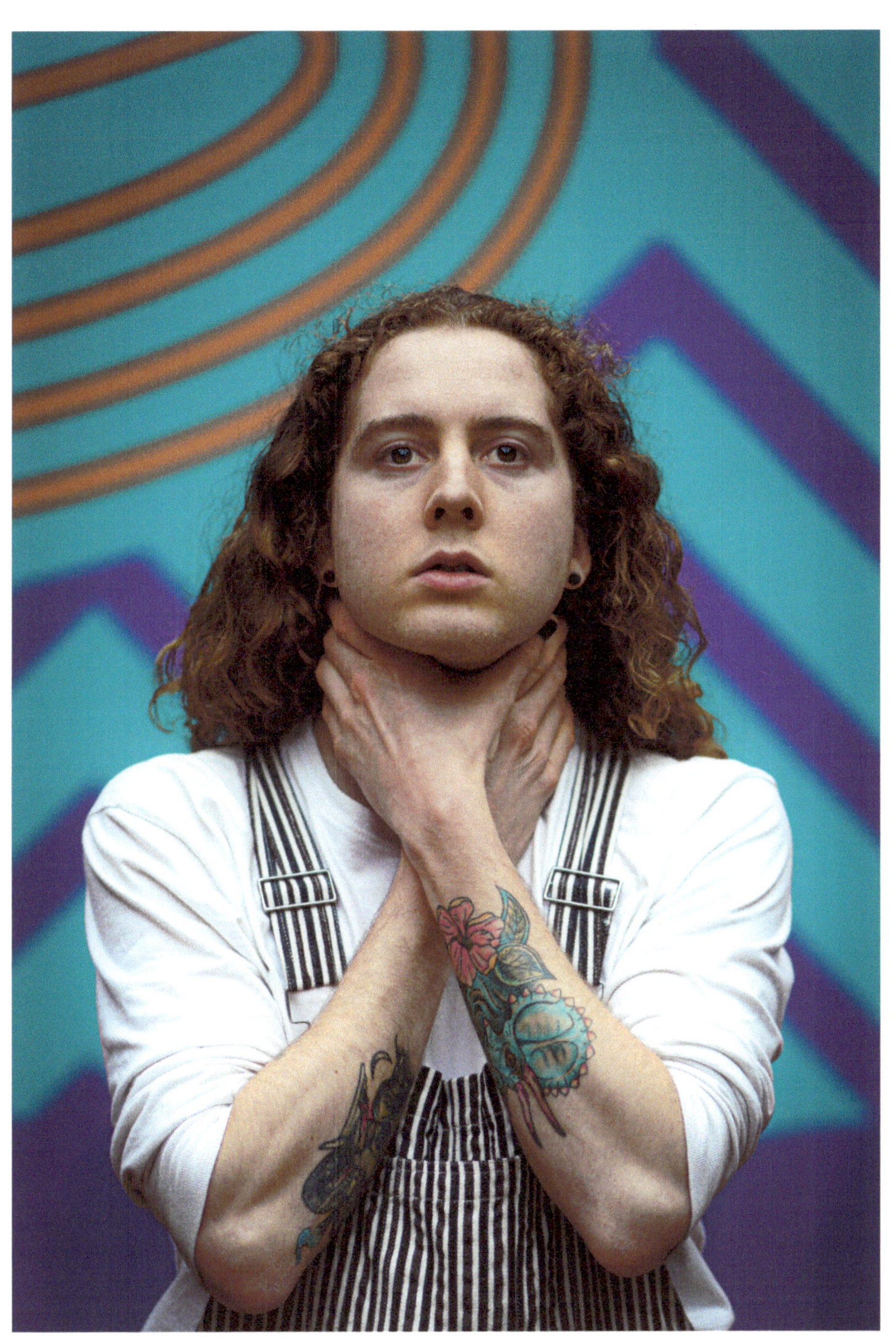

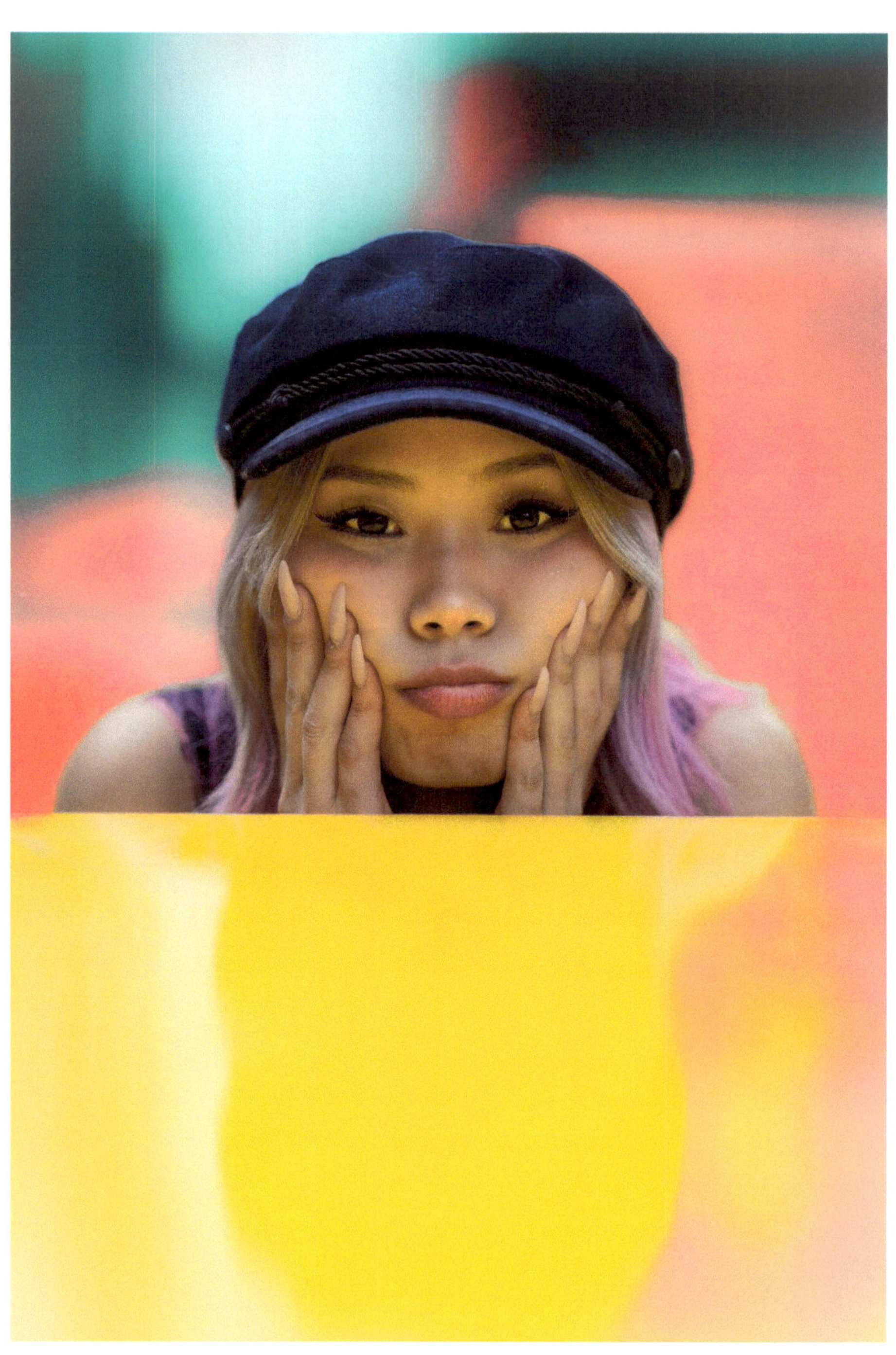

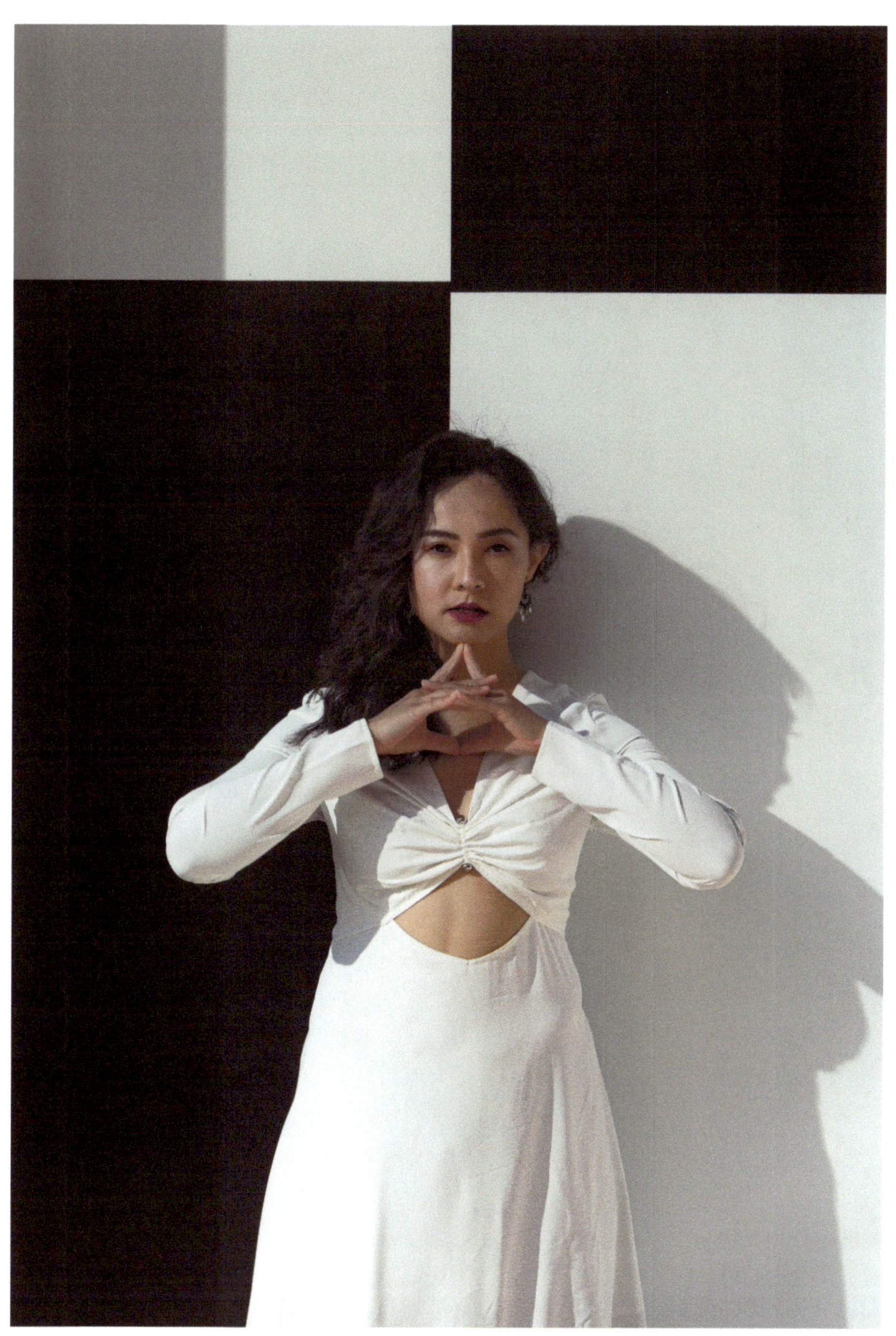

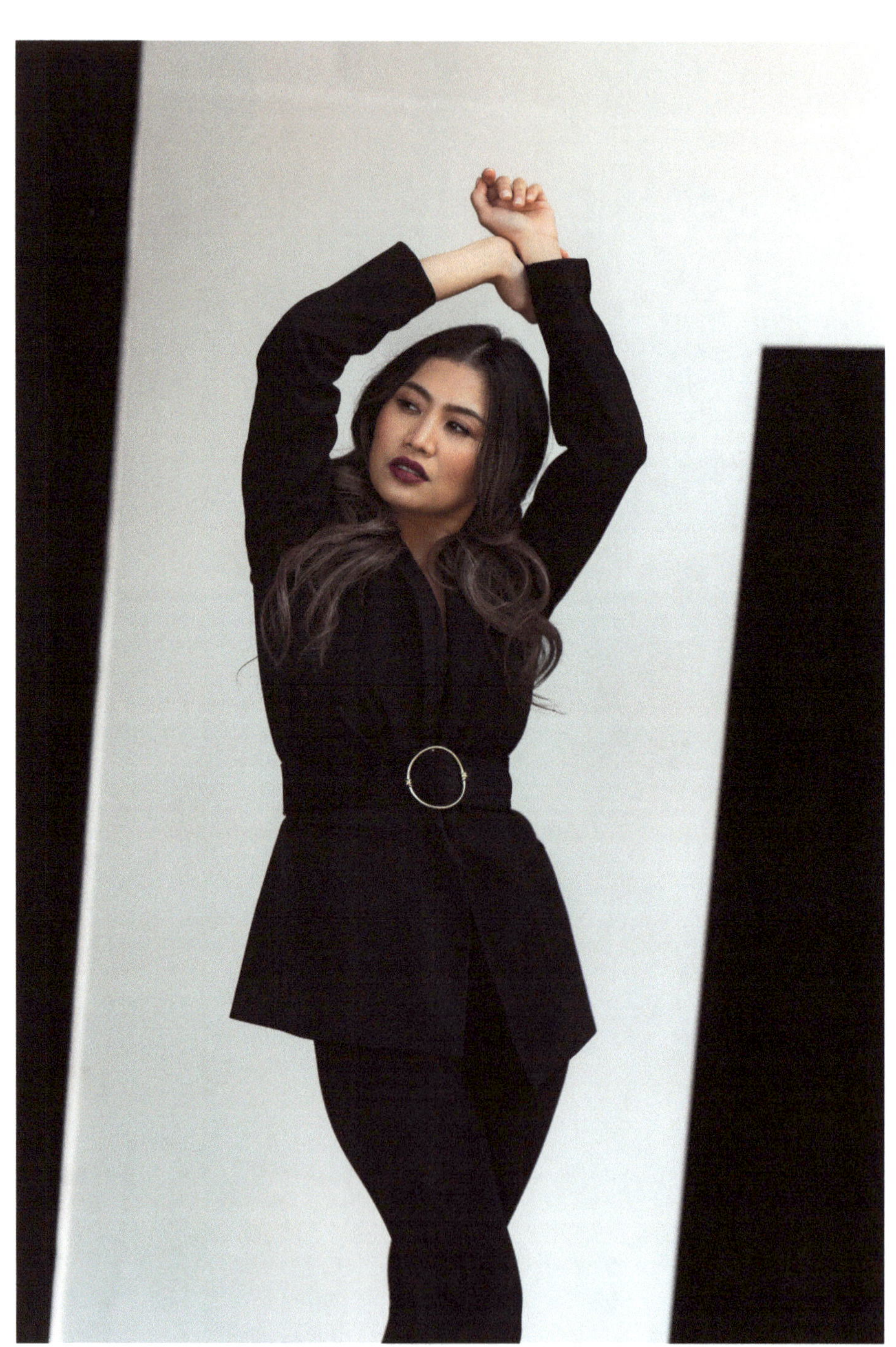

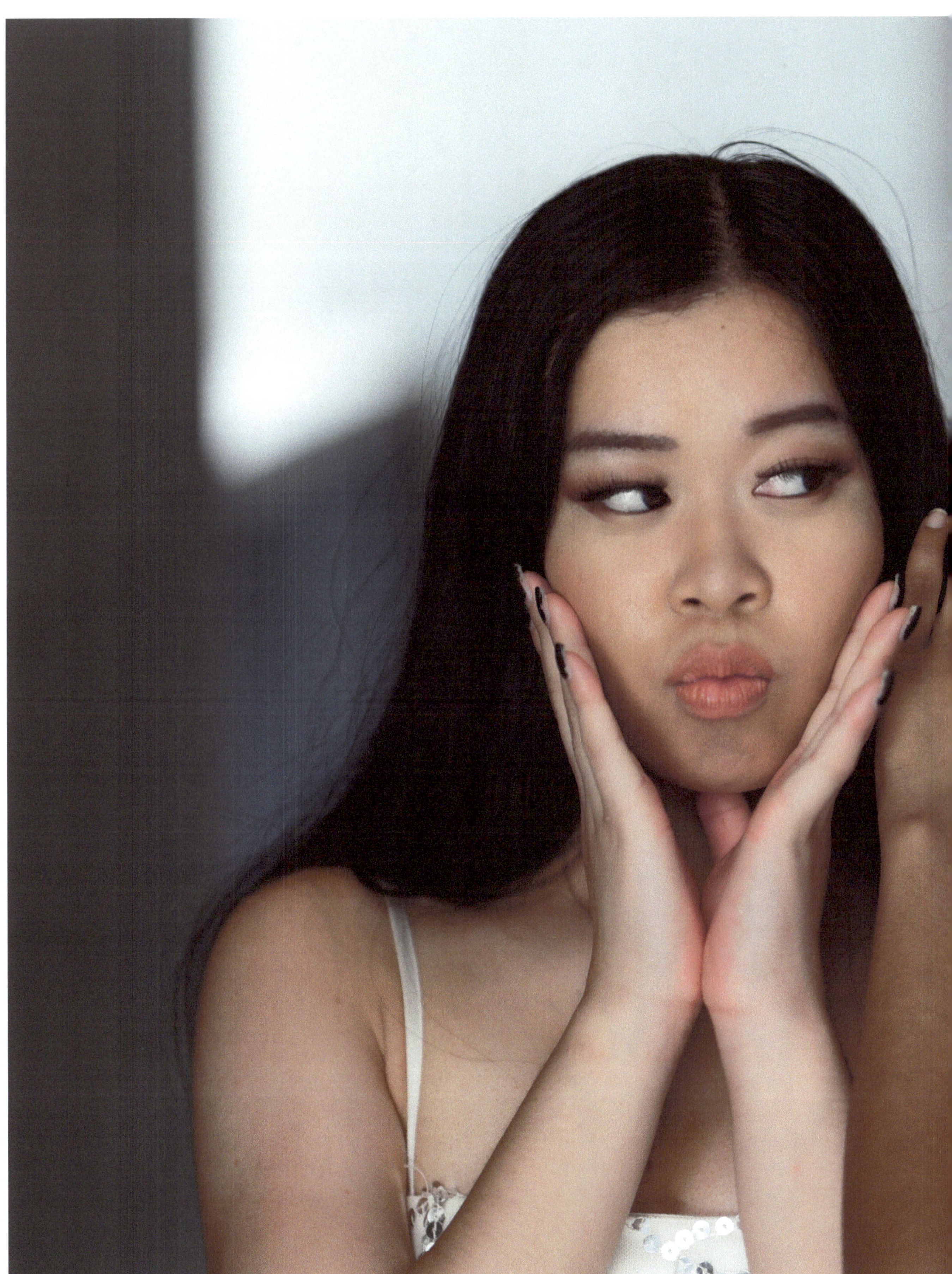

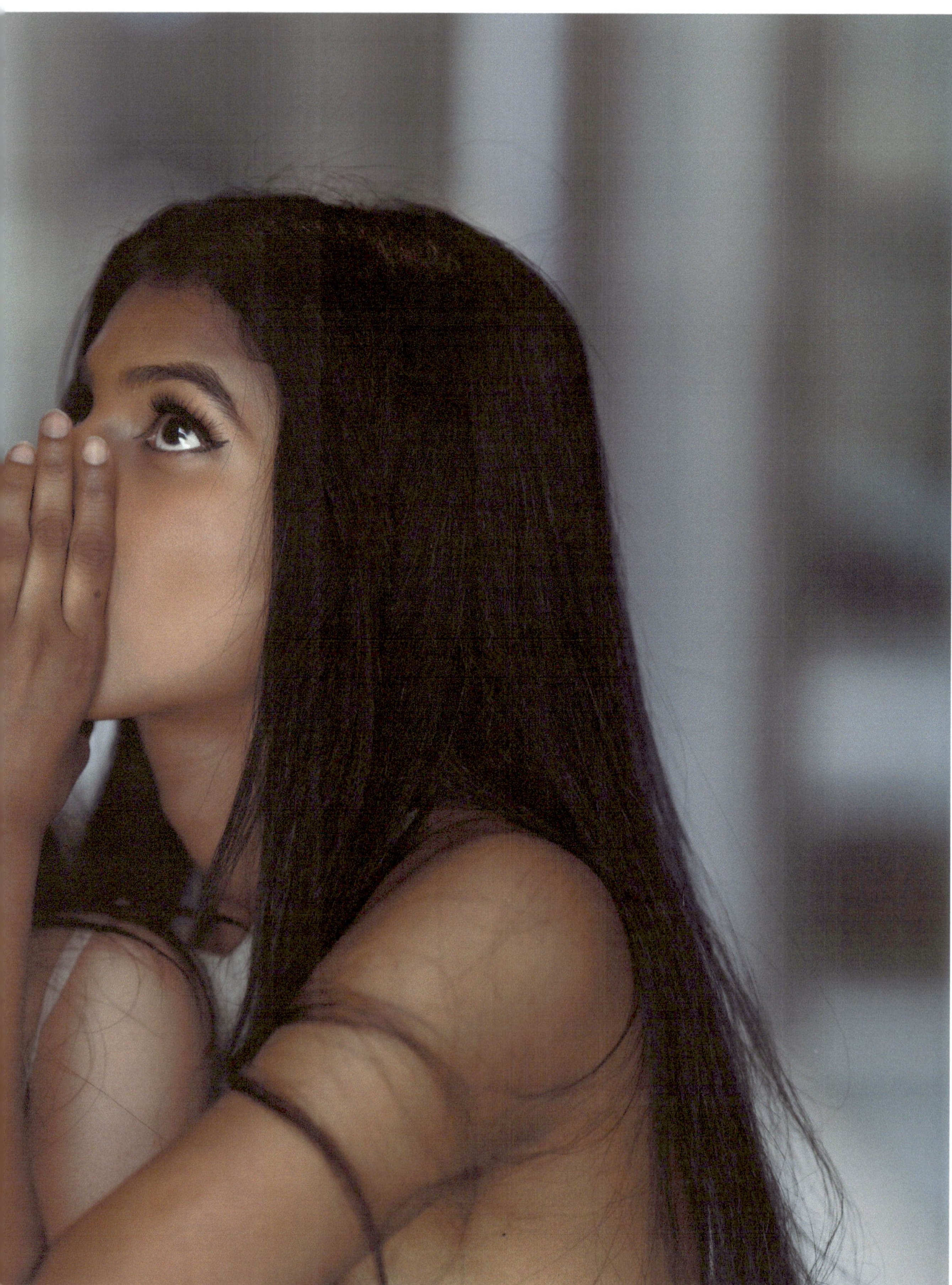

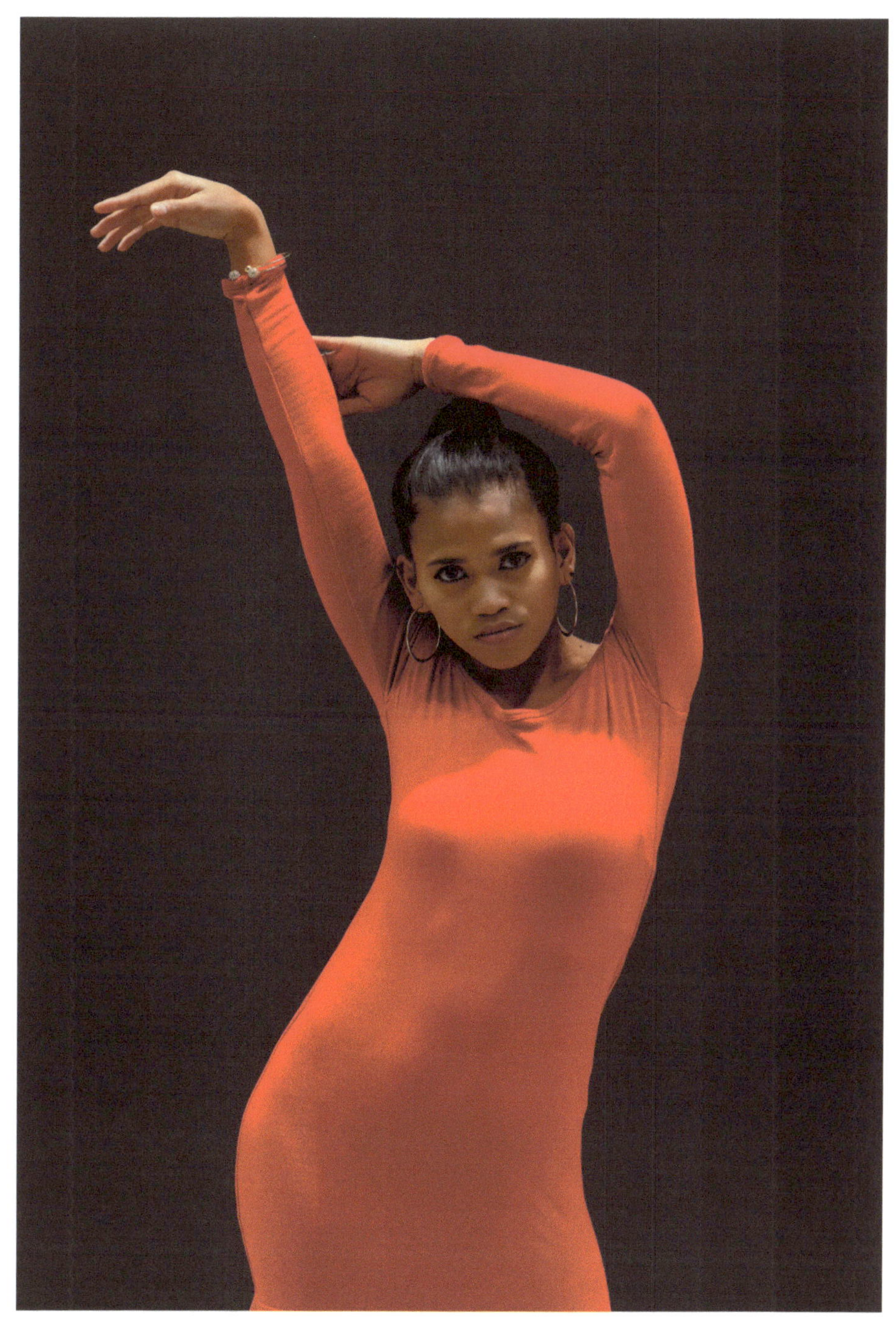

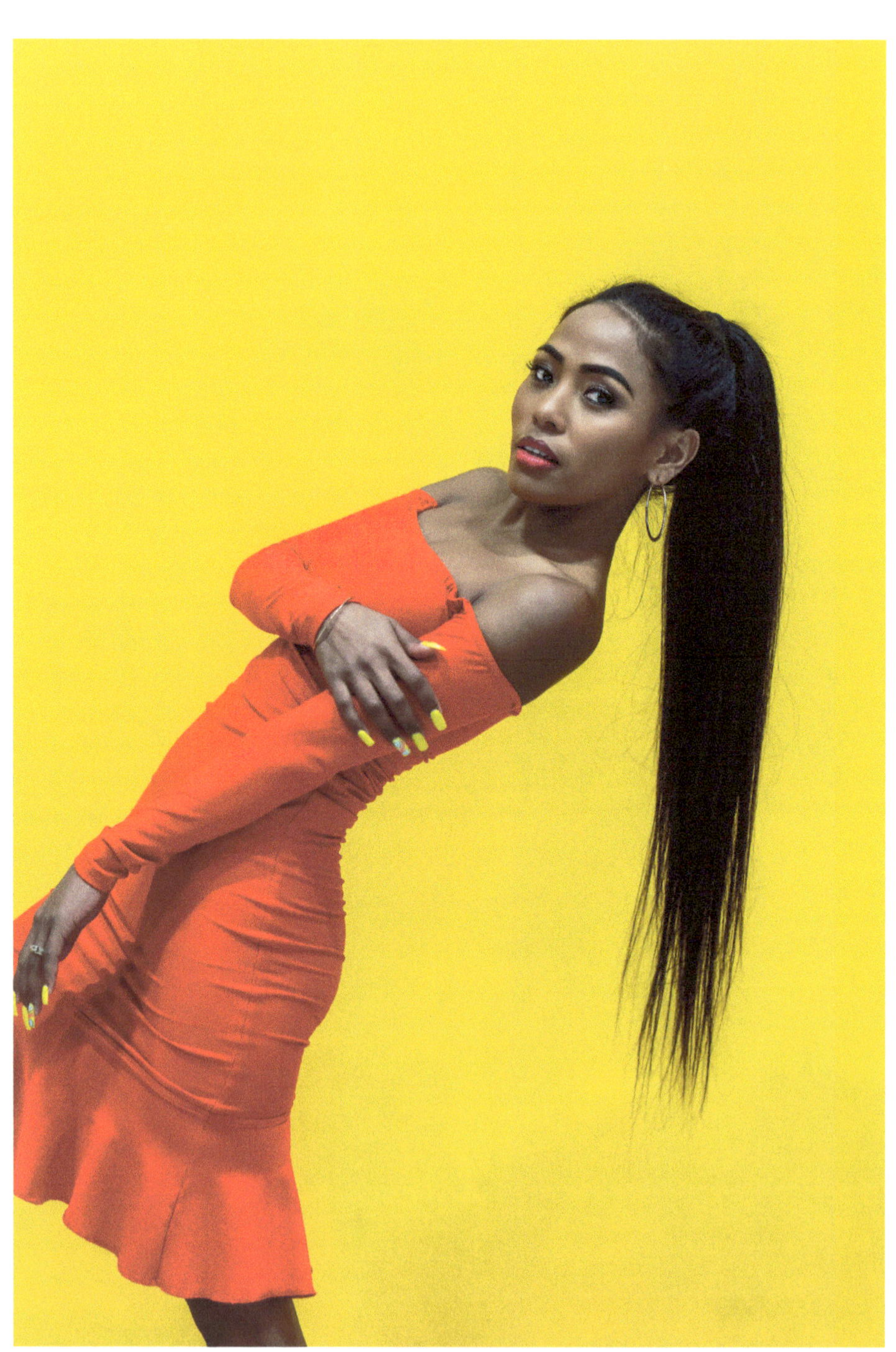

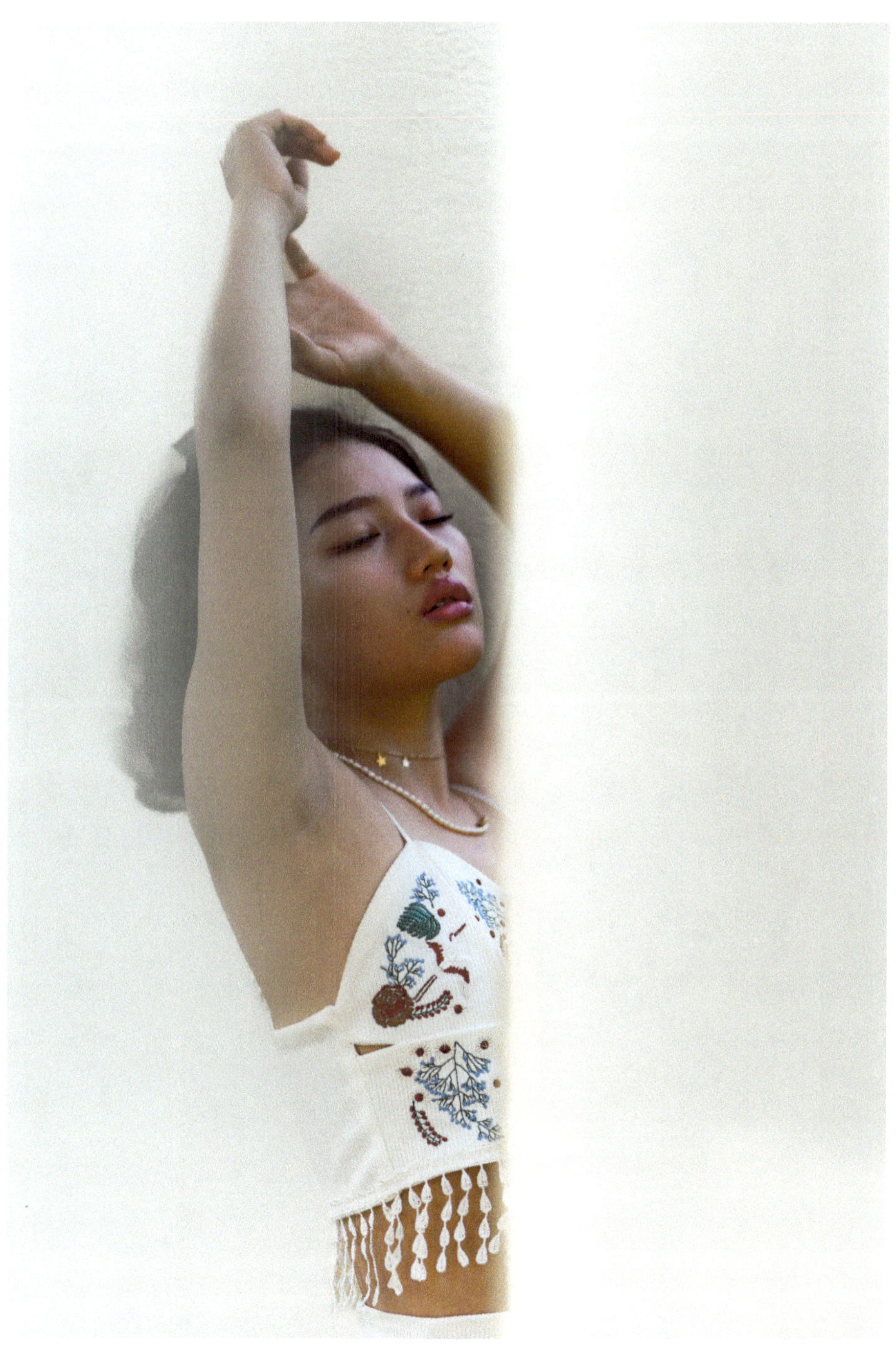

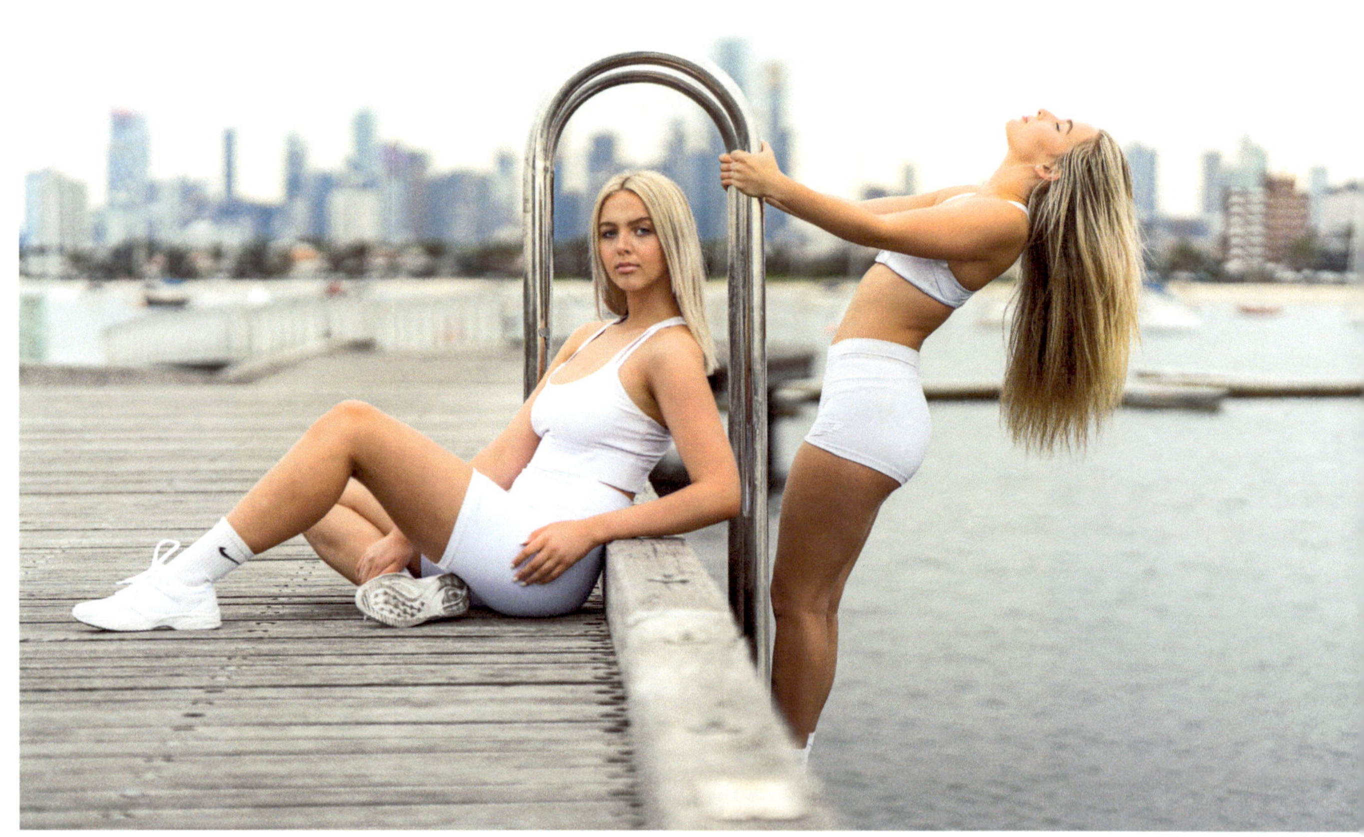

Chapter 8

The Dark Side

"Secrets, like shadows, bewilder in the dark. I am vaguely bewitched, and yet I am not. I live in the light but carry my shadow without it conquering me. Danger beneath the darkness isn't an illusion, but fear is a choice. I do not deny my shadows because I am in the light. I allowed my inner darkness and light to peacefully coexist as radiance, for I could not shake off the shadows. When I understood and accepted my shadow self, it gave me dimension and depth, just as stars cannot shine without darkness. I embraced my duality and became INVINCCIEBLE. Fear not, for shining through your brightest light is being who you truly are."

Vinccie Chow

The Dark Side

What happens when you step beyond the surface and explore what's behind the expression? This chapter delves into moments that embrace raw emotion and subtle intensity. Each photo invites you to look closer, to pause, and to wonder what story lies just beneath the exterior. The individuals in these images hold a certain quiet power, drawing the viewer in with expressions that suggest something deeper, something unsaid.

Even in stillness, there's a presence that fills the frame. Whether it's a piercing gaze or the play of shadows across a face, these portraits carry weight. The framing and composition work together to capture a balance between softness and strength, where vulnerability can be found within moments of confidence.

Each image tells its own unique story, yet together they weave a cohesive narrative. It's not just about what's seen at first glance, but about the layers underneath—whether it's a thoughtful stare, an exposed emotion, or an unexpected moment of reflection. The colors and tones, as well as the way light touches the skin, give life to these portraits, making them more than just images.

Through this series, there's an invitation to look deeper, to ask questions, and to experience the emotion that emanates from within. It's about the moments in between—the split second when a fleeting thought crosses the mind, captured for eternity.

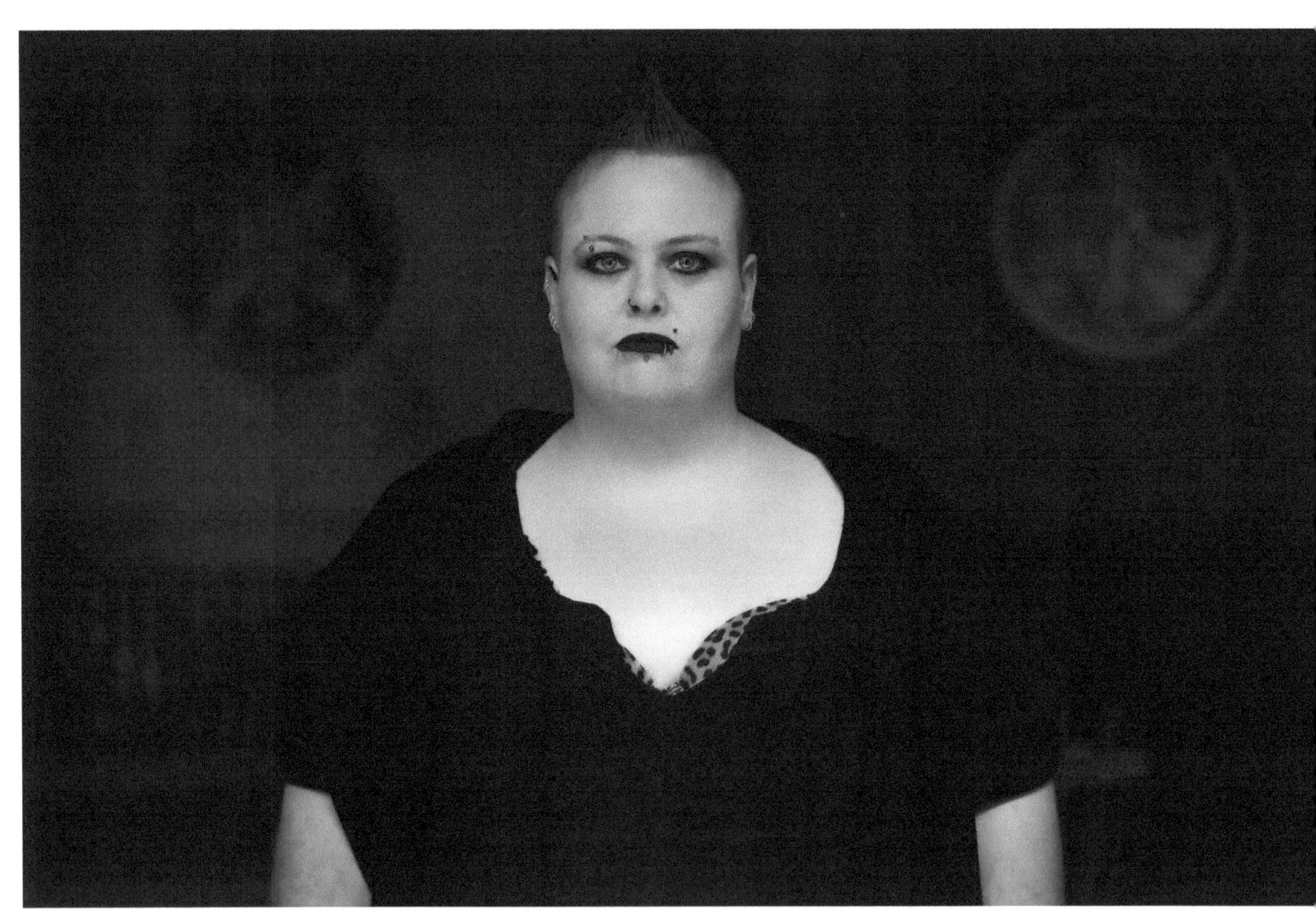

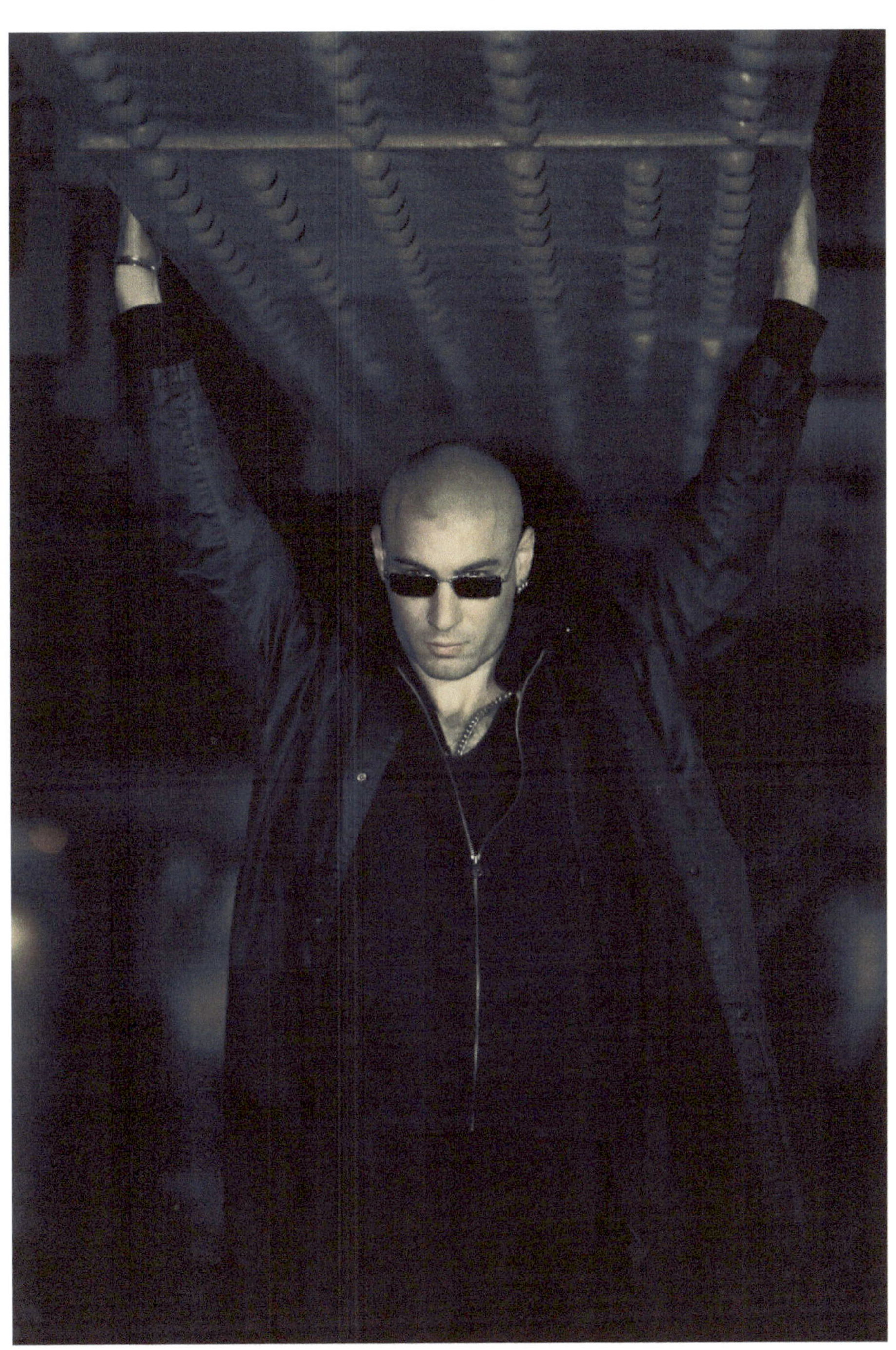

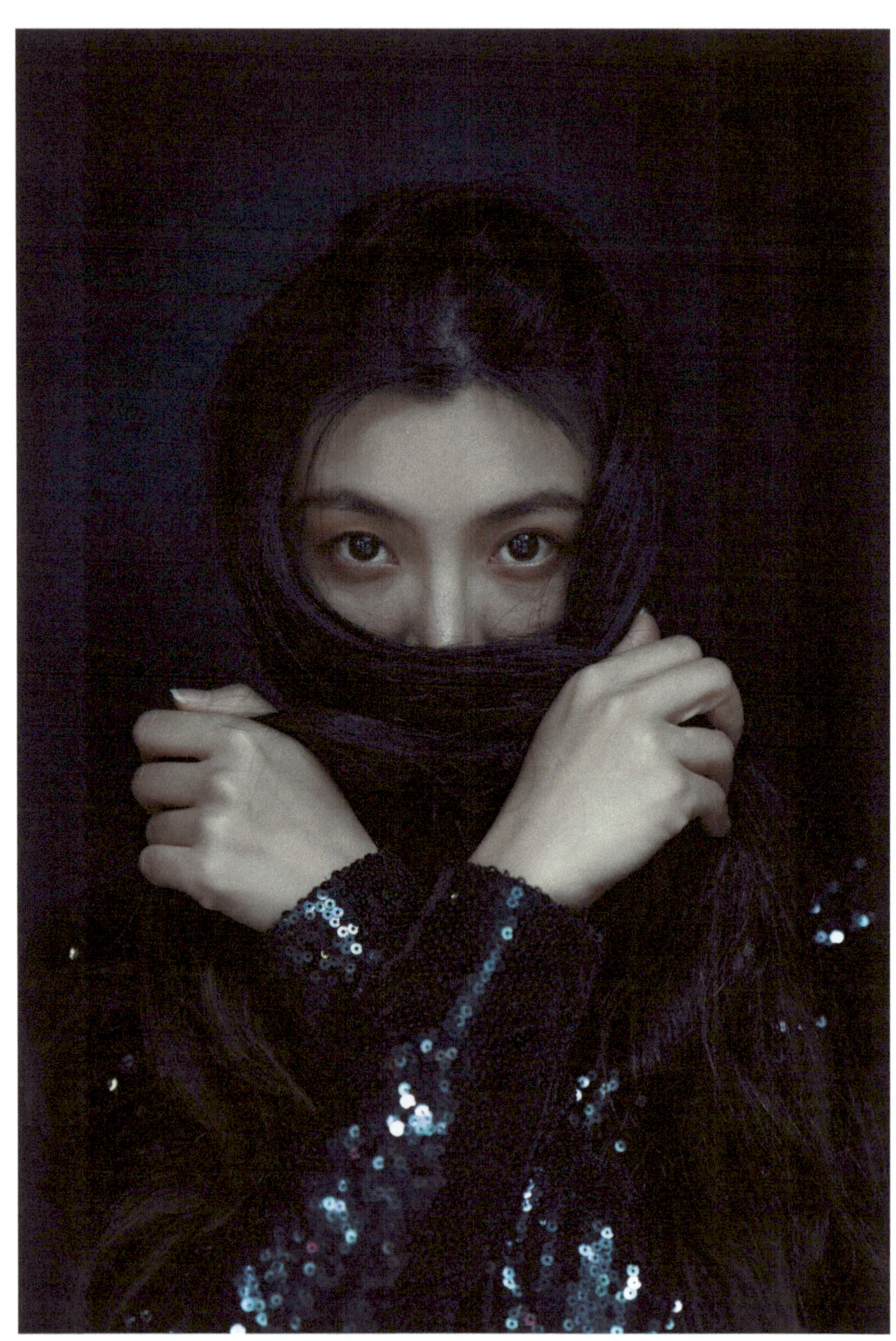

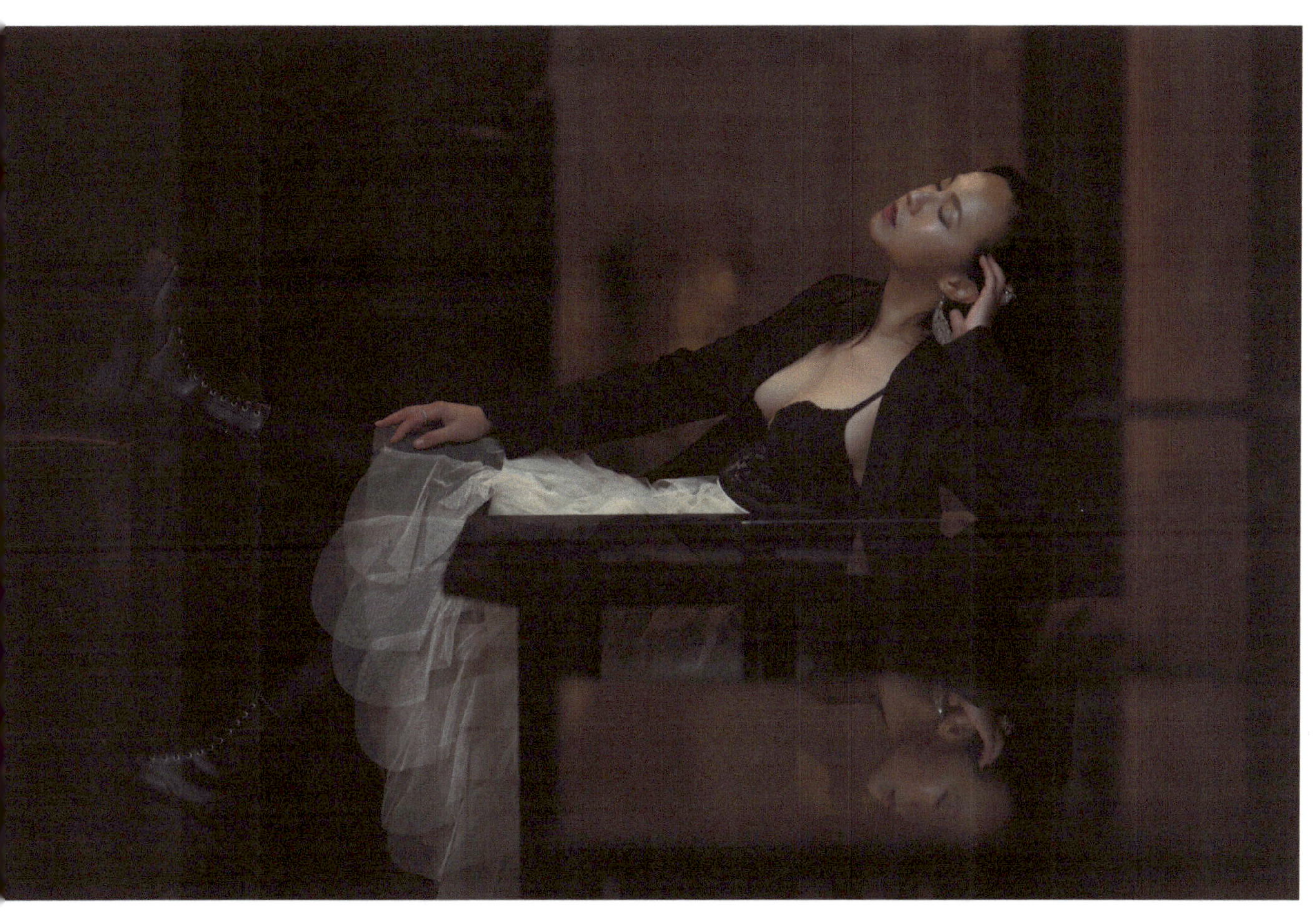

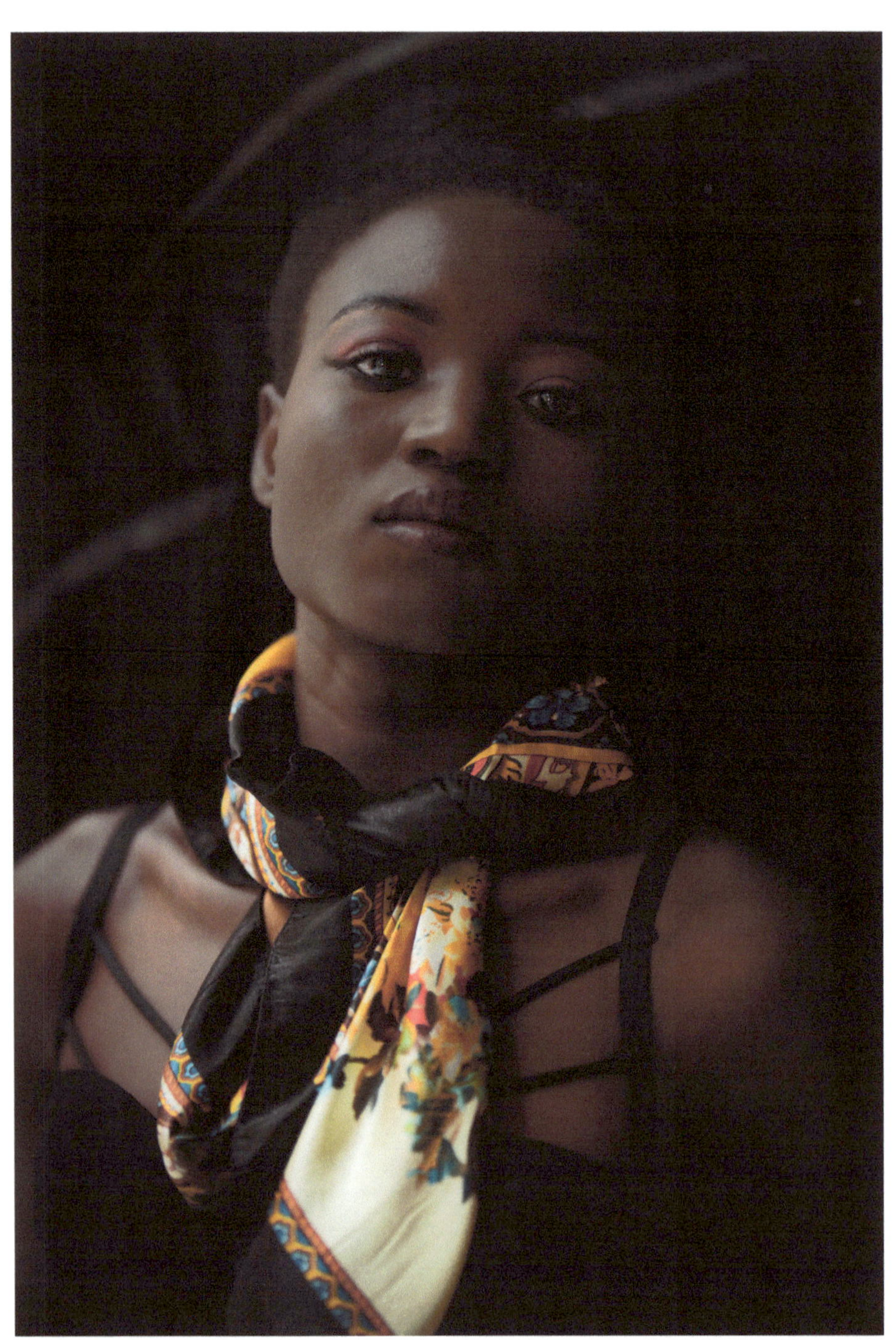

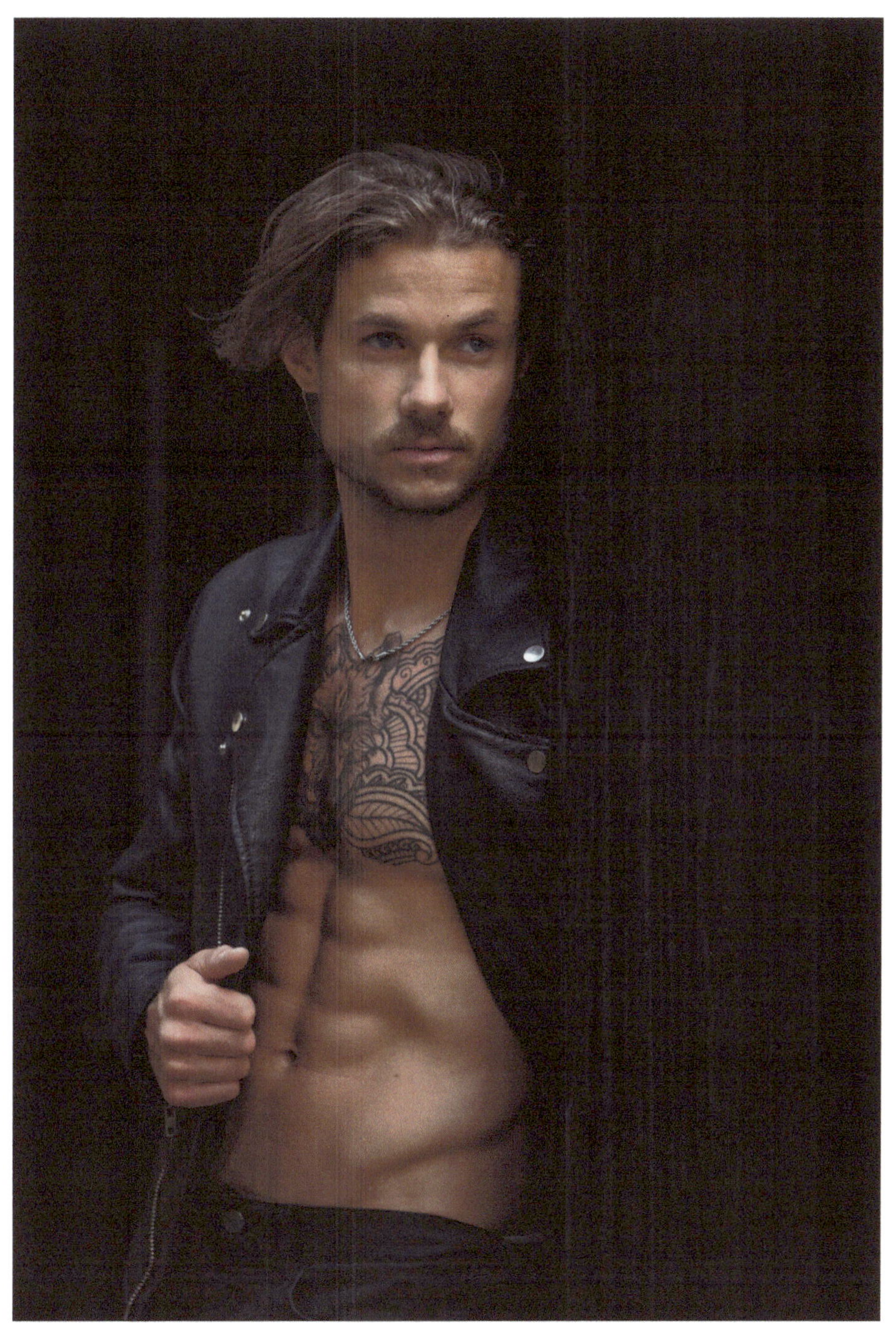

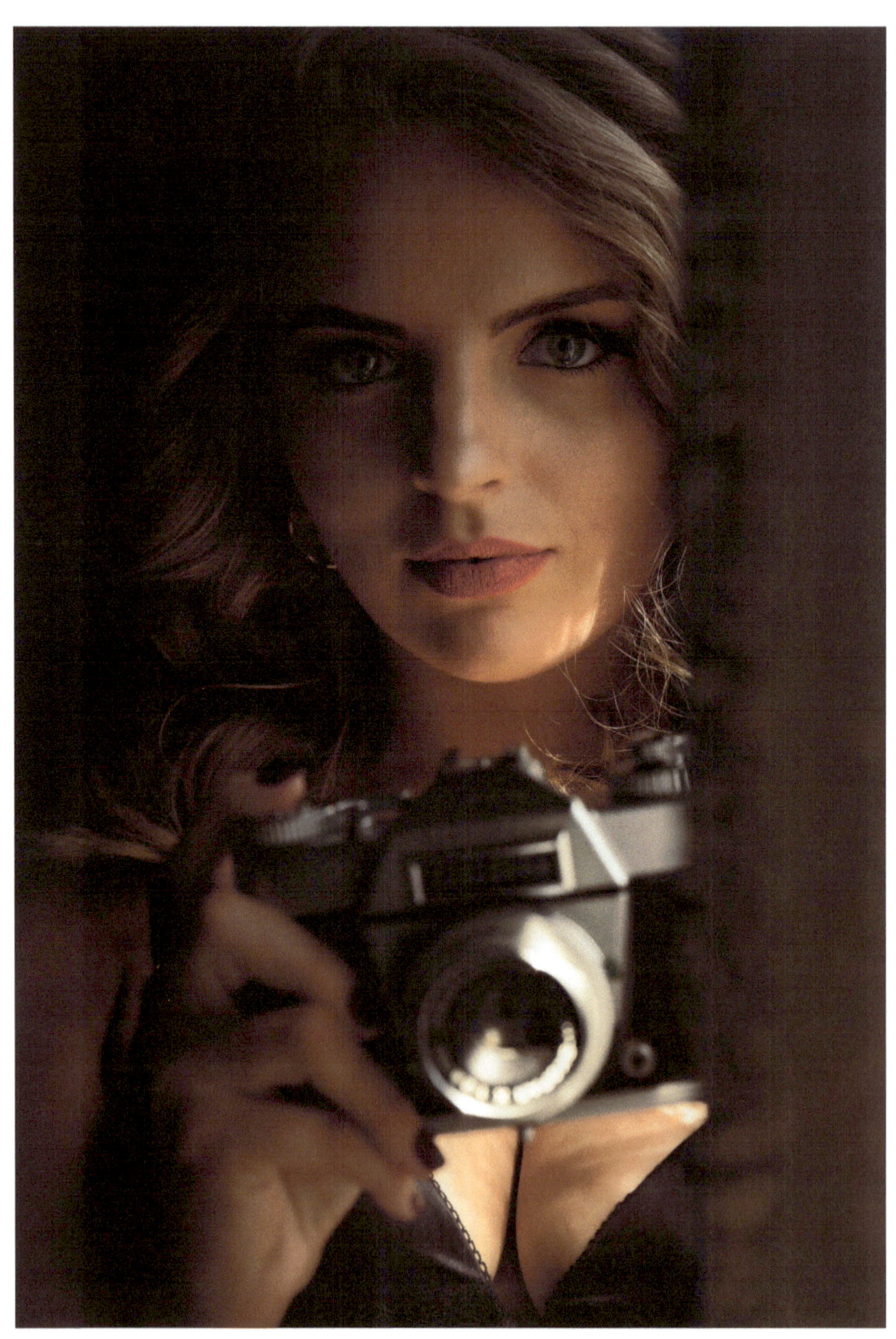

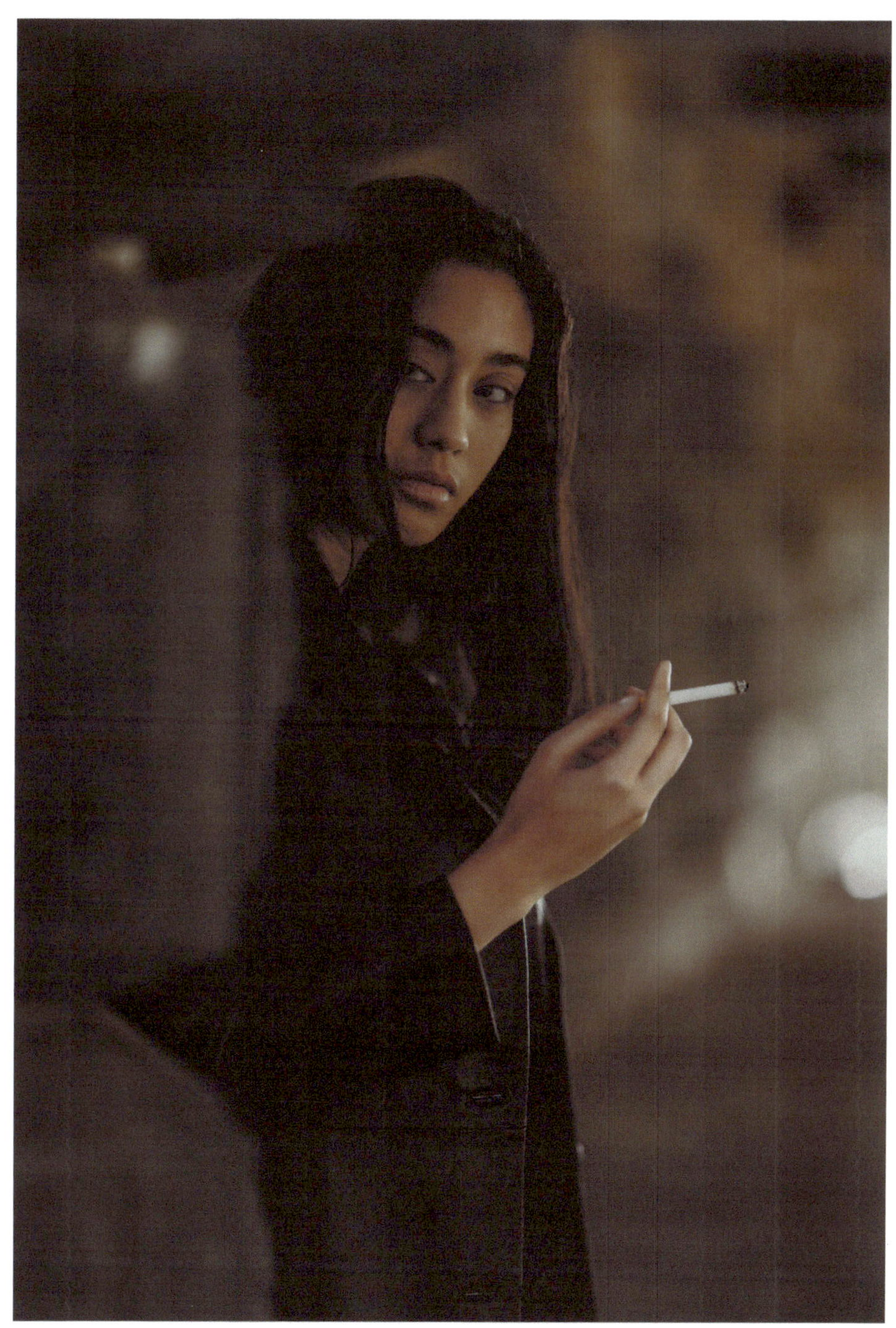

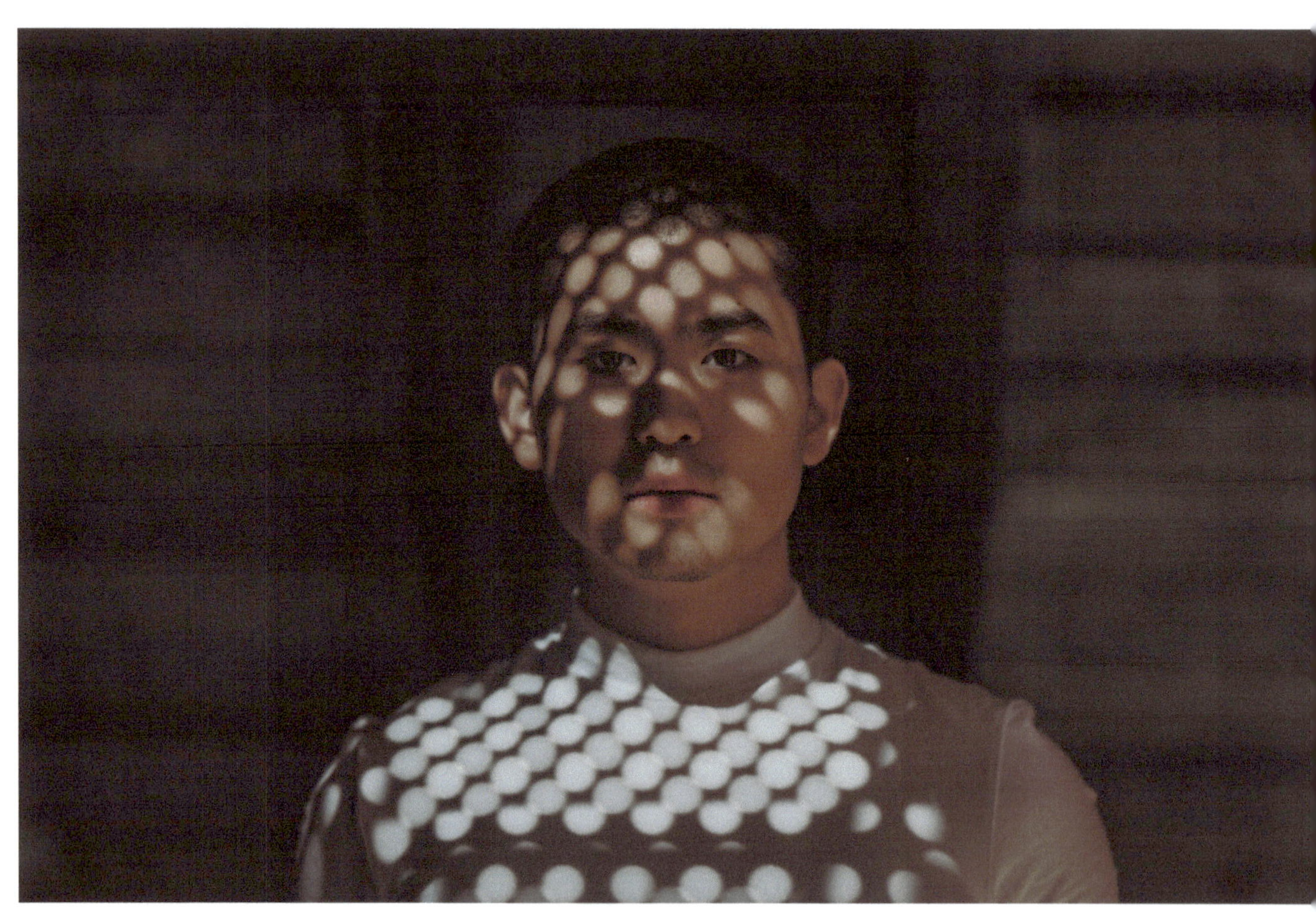

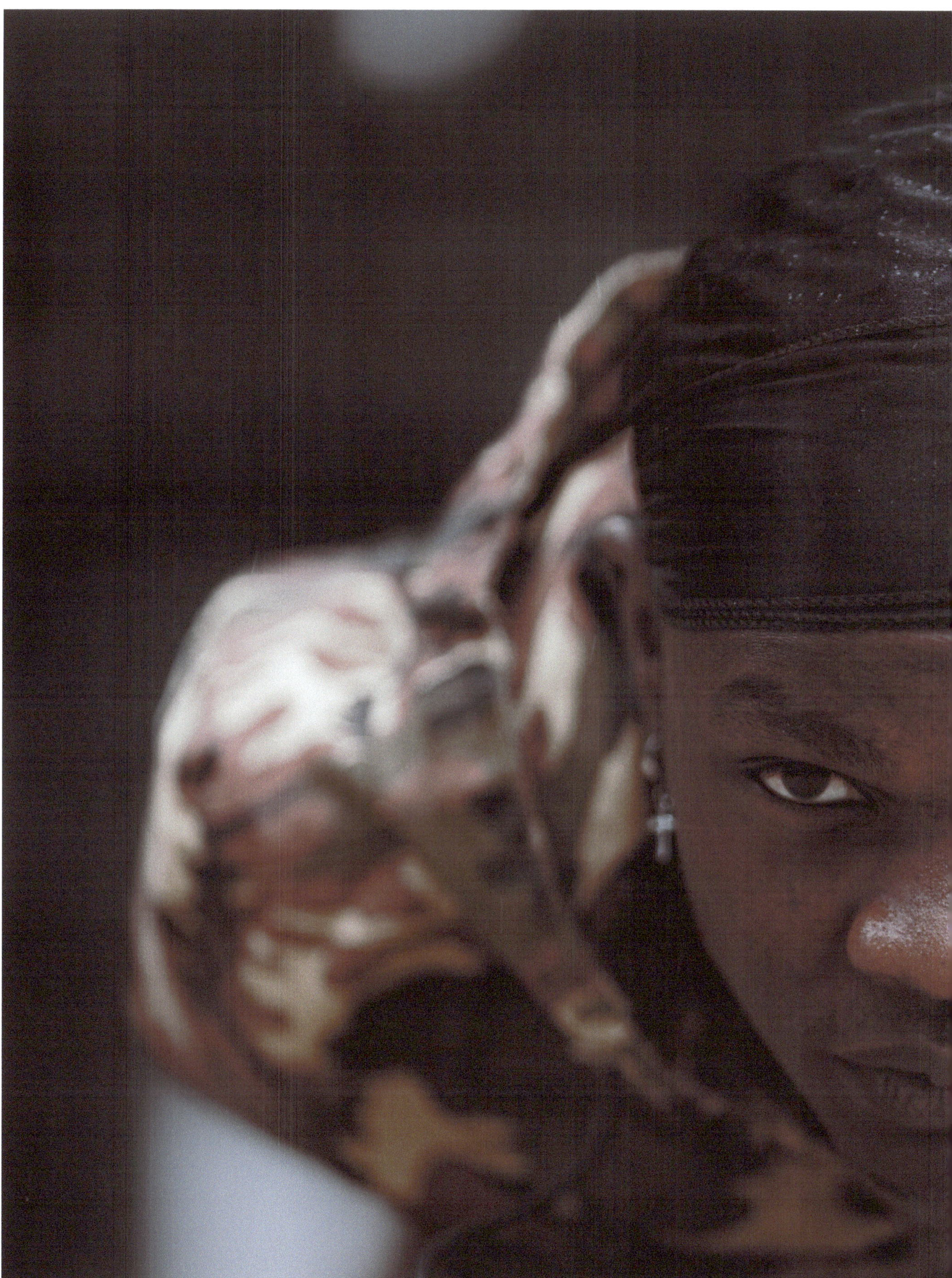

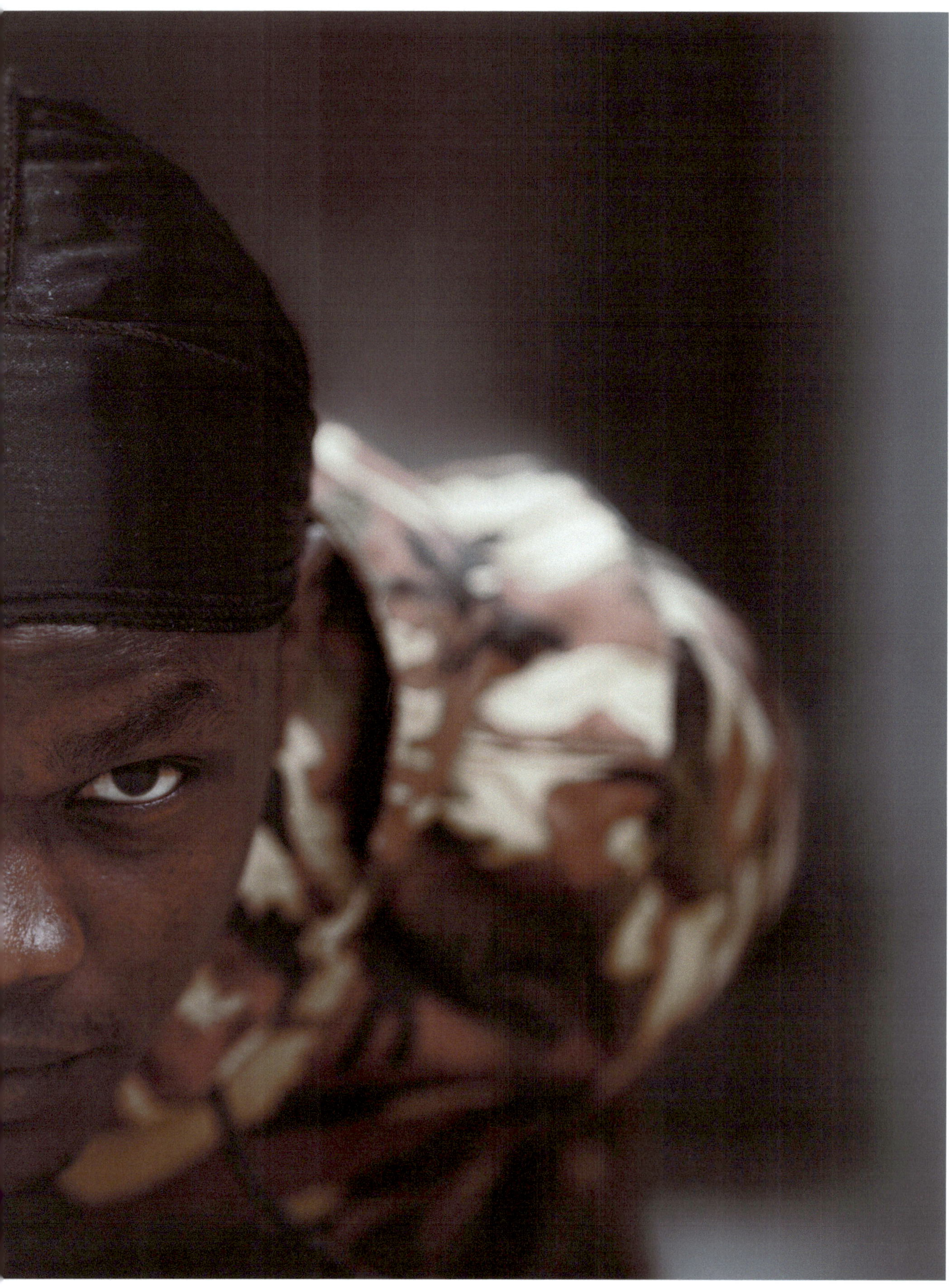

Chapter 9

Nature's Gentle Touch

"When I'm aligned with nature I recognize,

There is nothing to long for, and everything to hope for,

Joy and bliss are accessible to us in every moment,

Anxiety and worry are an unnatural state

because everything is in perfect flow."

Brielle Ying

Nature's Gentle Touch

This chapter embraces the natural world, showcasing the quiet connection between individuals and their environment. Each image highlights how being surrounded by nature enhances the creativity and expression of the person captured. It's about letting the natural elements inspire, leading to a sense of ease and spontaneity that brings the scene to life.

The setting goes beyond a mere backdrop—it plays an active role in shaping the mood. Whether it's soft light filtering through leaves or the textures of weathered wood and greenery, nature subtly enhances the energy of the portrait. The natural world isn't just framing the shot but blending with it, adding depth and richness to every image.

Creatively, the approach leans into the organic flow of working outdoors. Instead of rigid setups, these scenes thrive on the unpredictability of natural light and surroundings. It's about adapting to the environment, using what's available to bring out the best in the moment. This sense of adaptability and freedom allows for a more relaxed, genuine creative process.

At its heart, these images reflect how nature can inspire creativity. Being in natural settings encourages us to explore new ideas, step outside the usual routine, and embrace the beauty that surrounds us. Each portrait serves as a reminder that creativity flourishes when we're in tune with our environment.

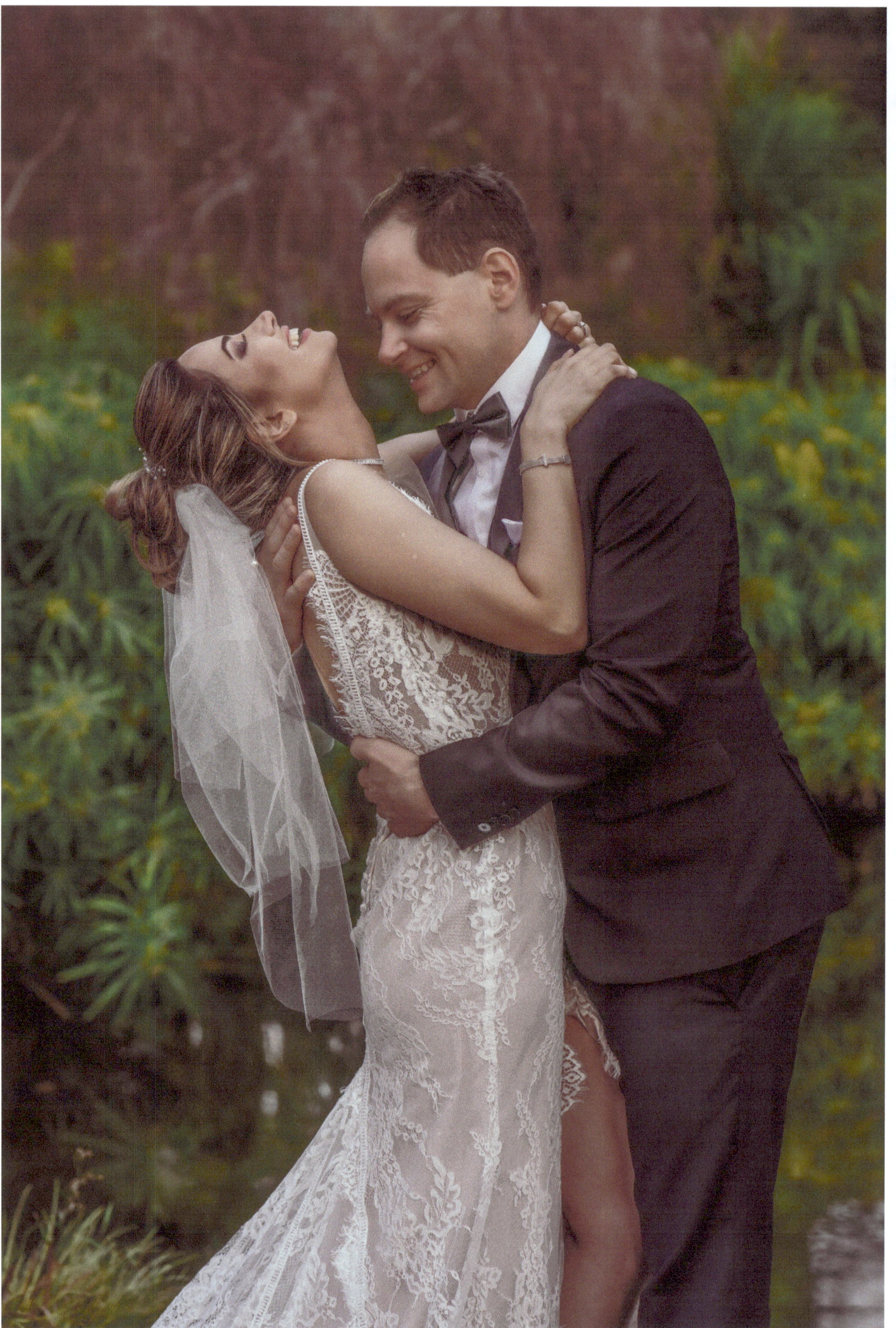

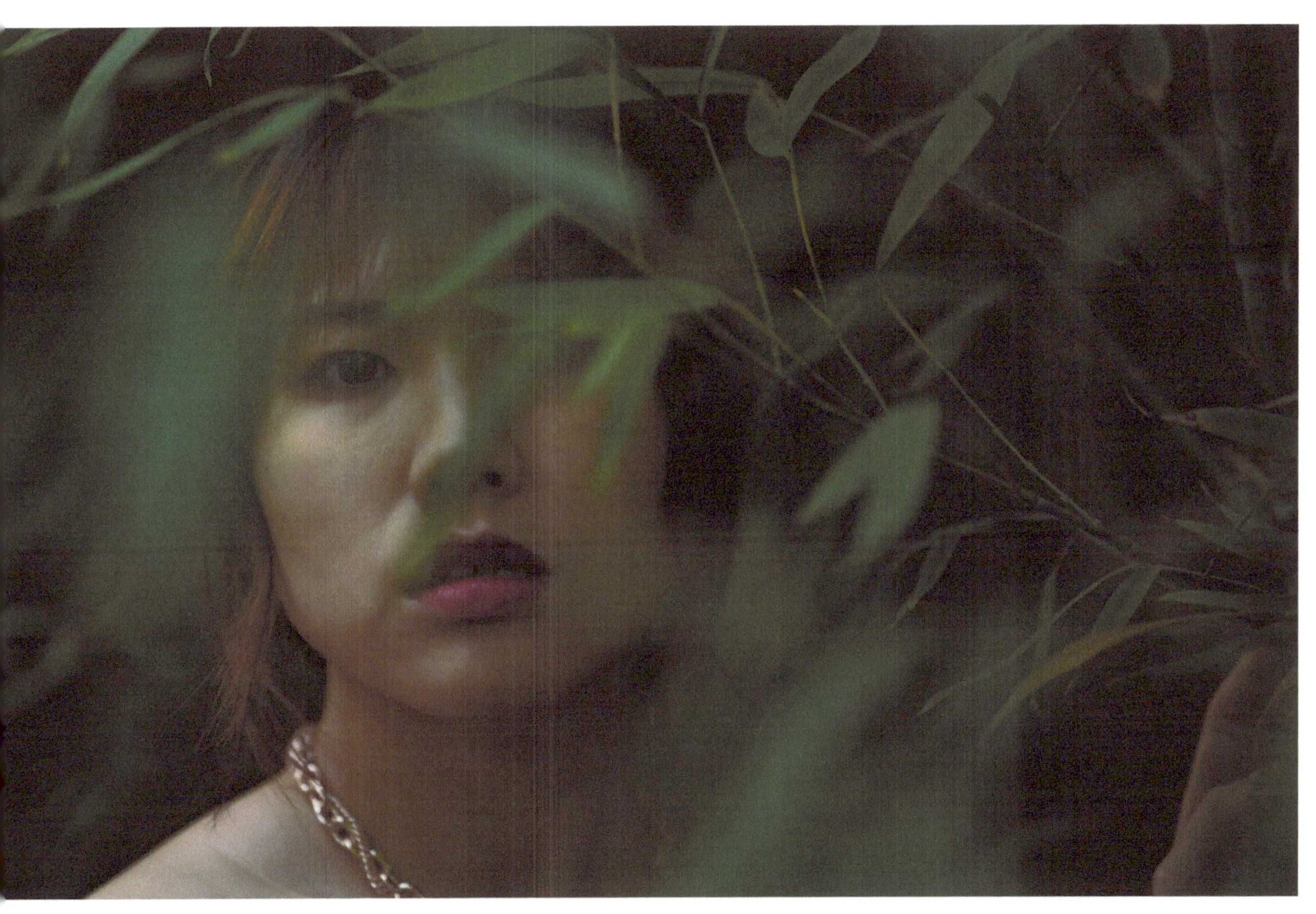

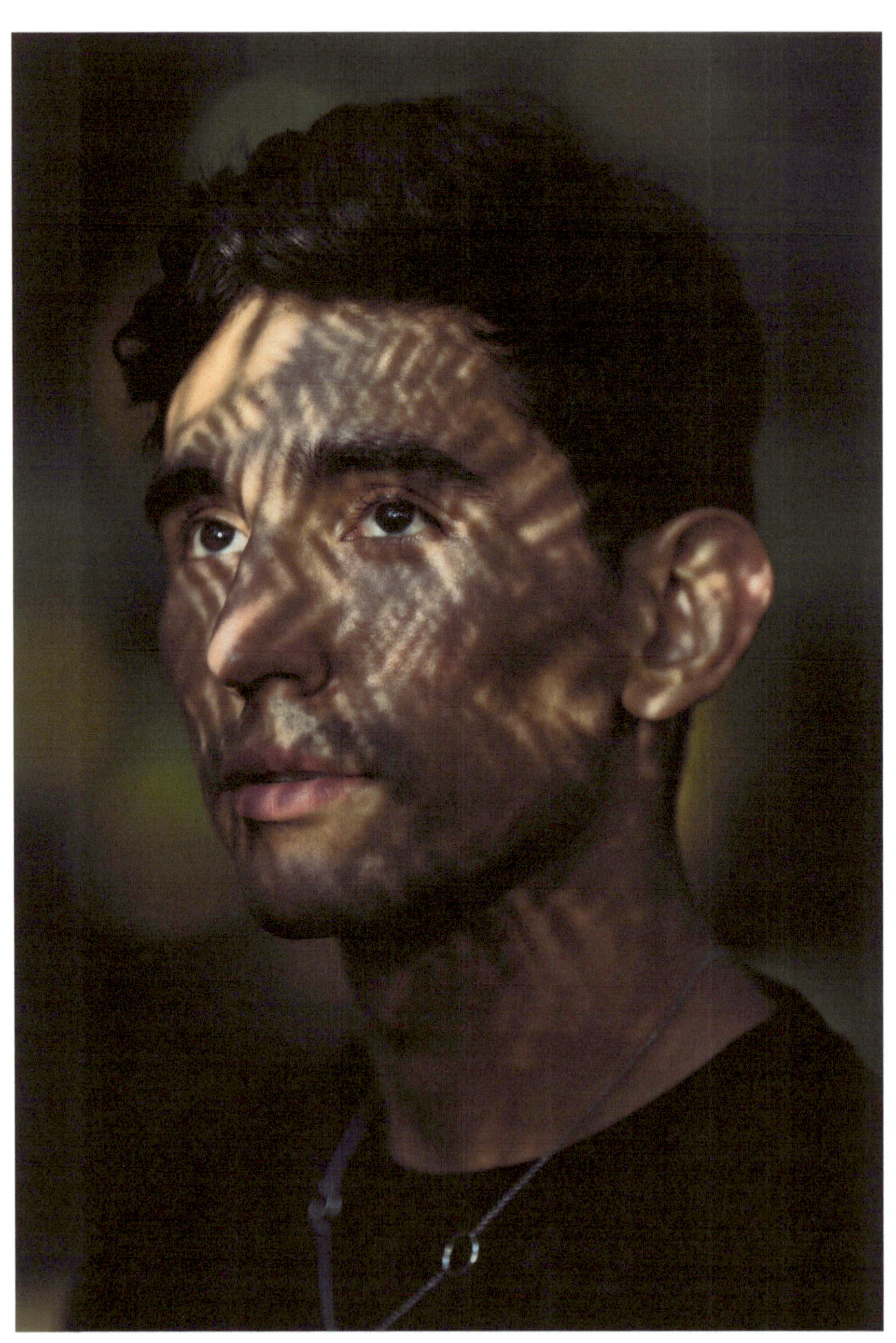

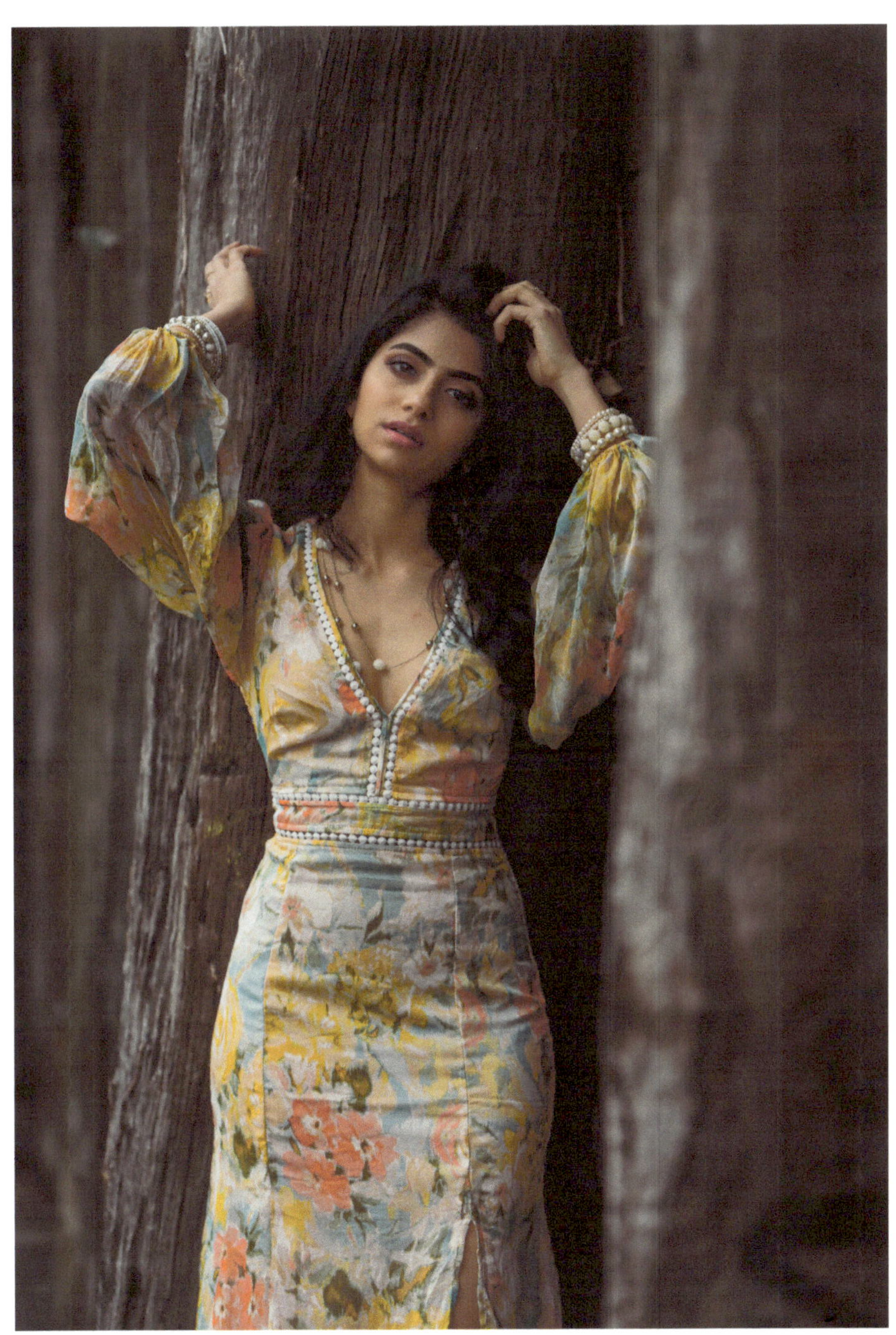

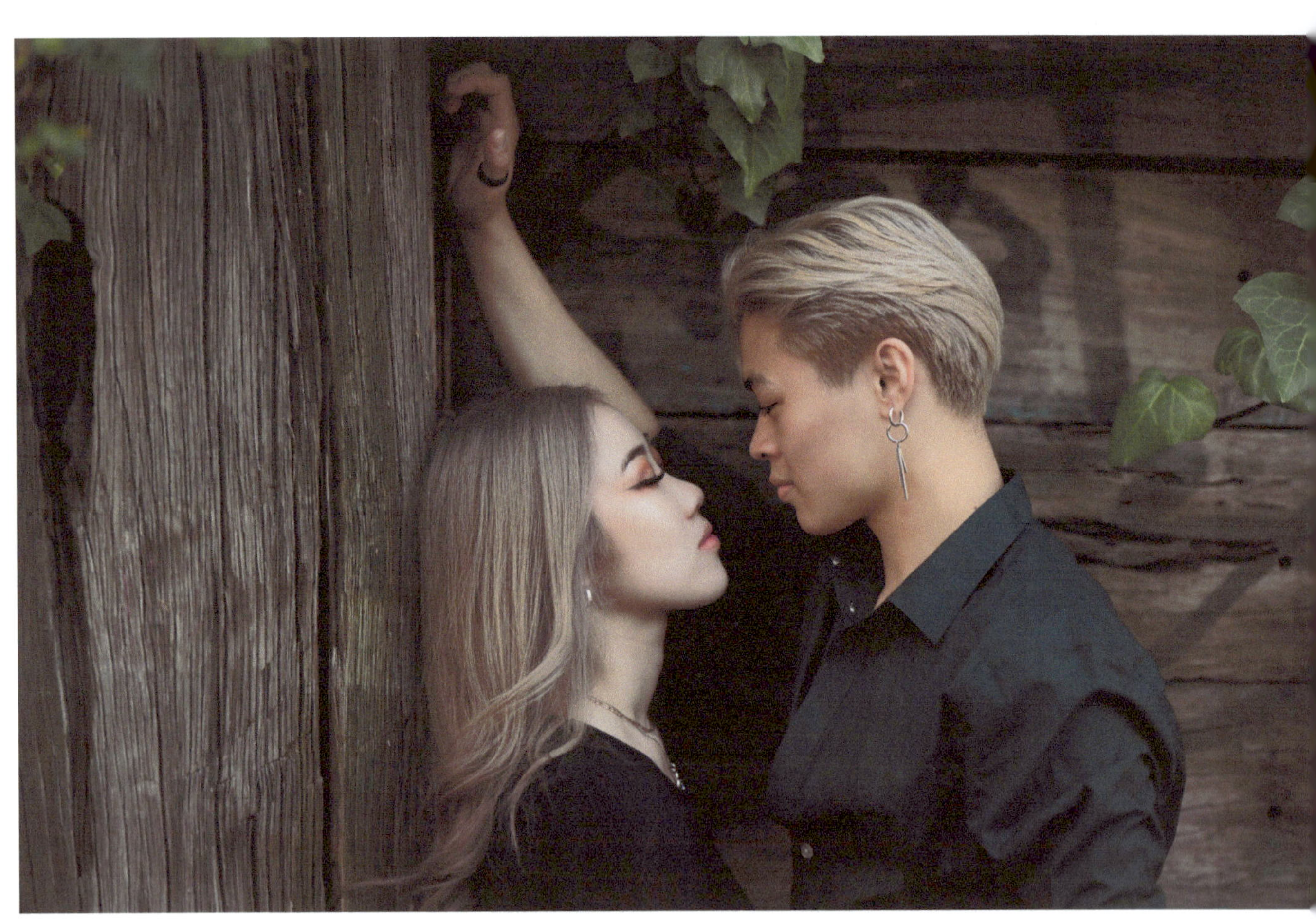

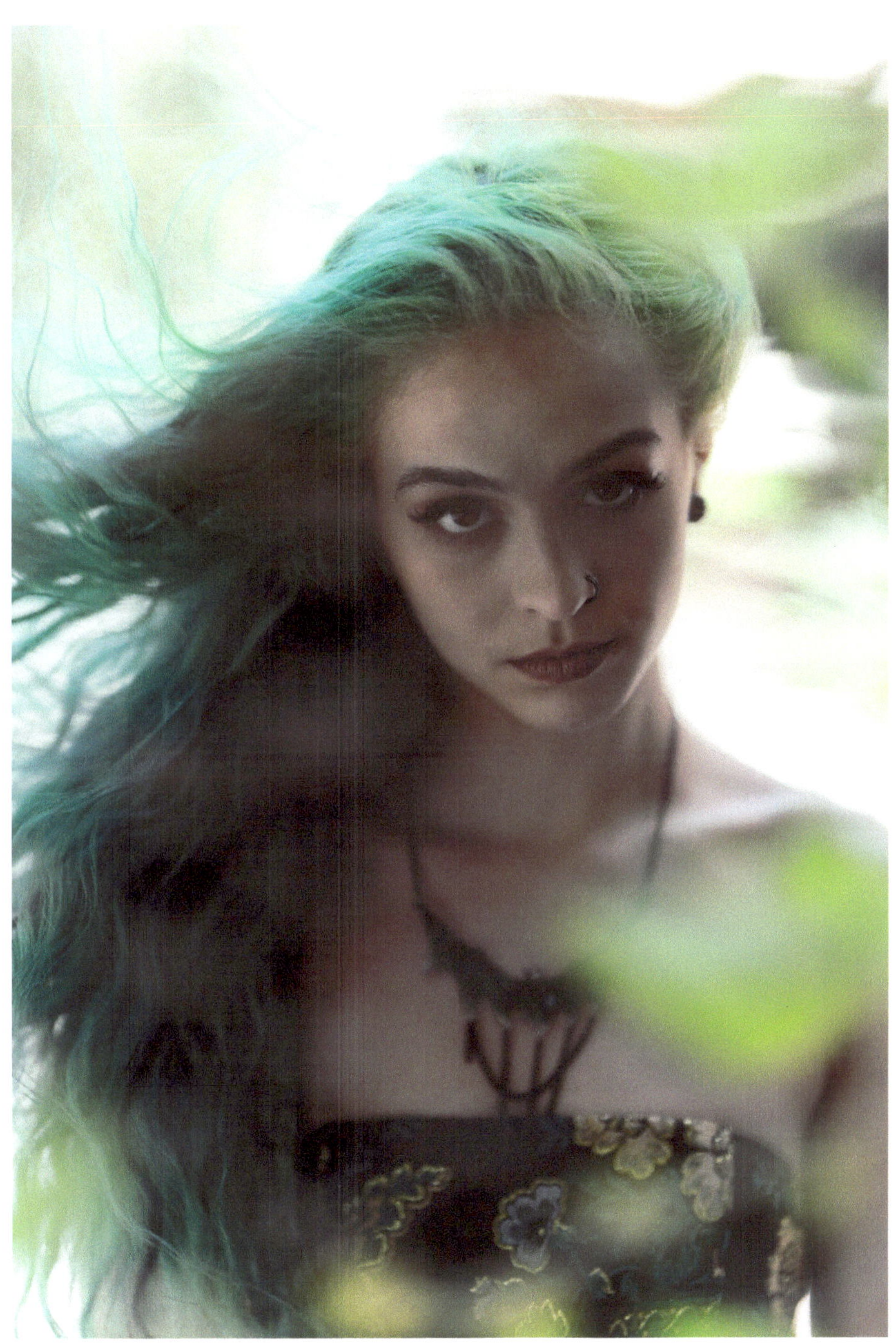

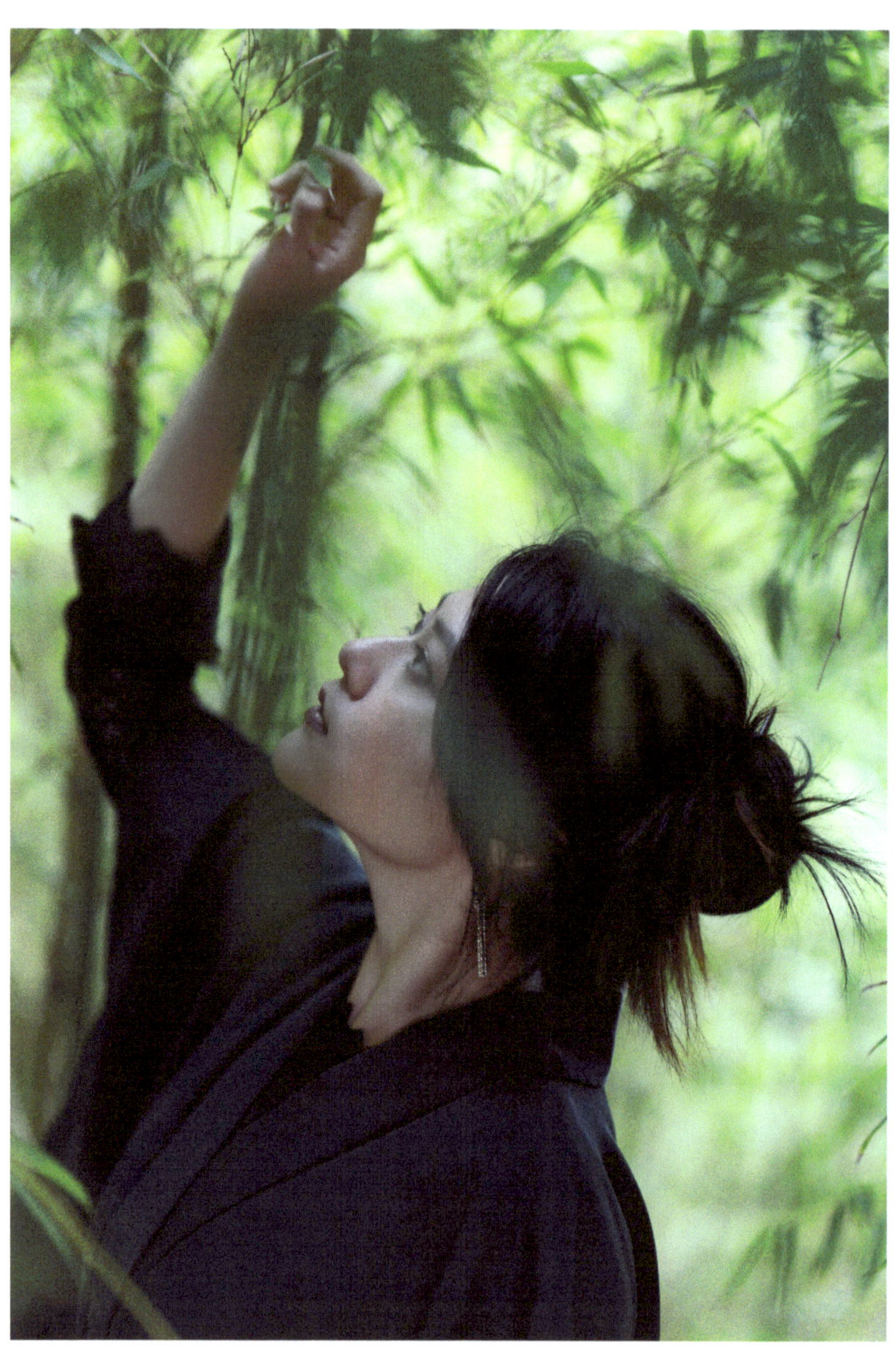

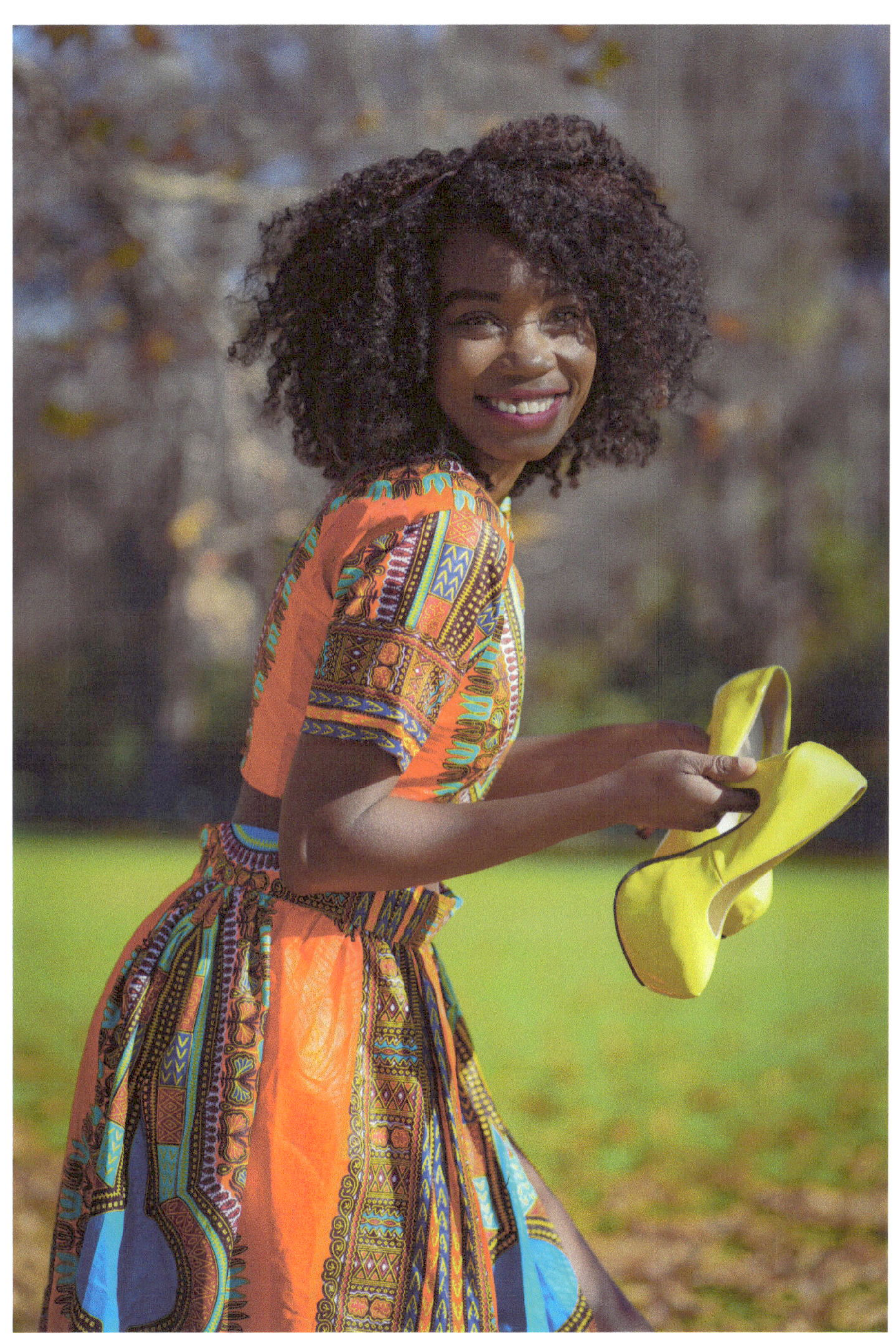

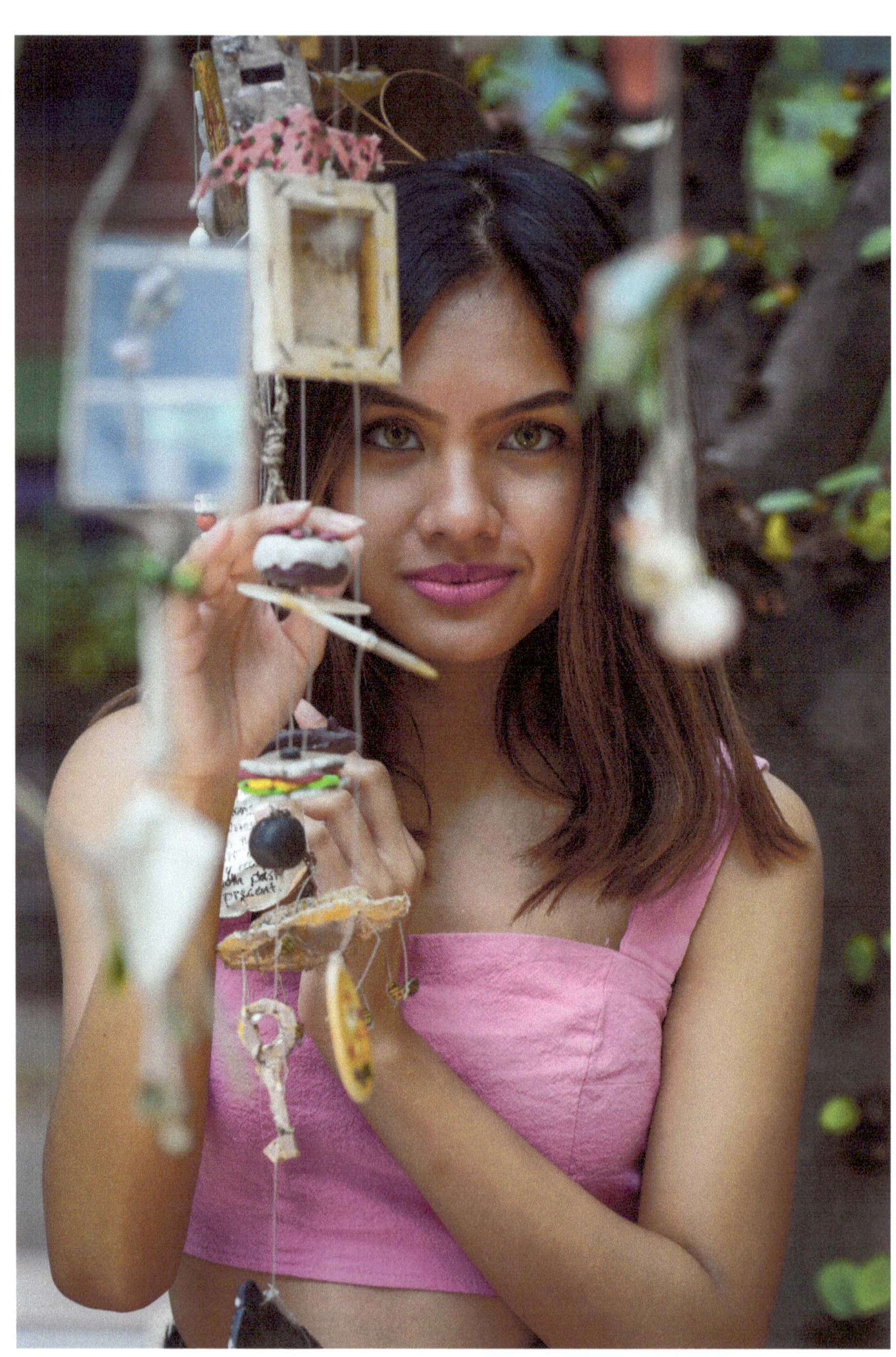

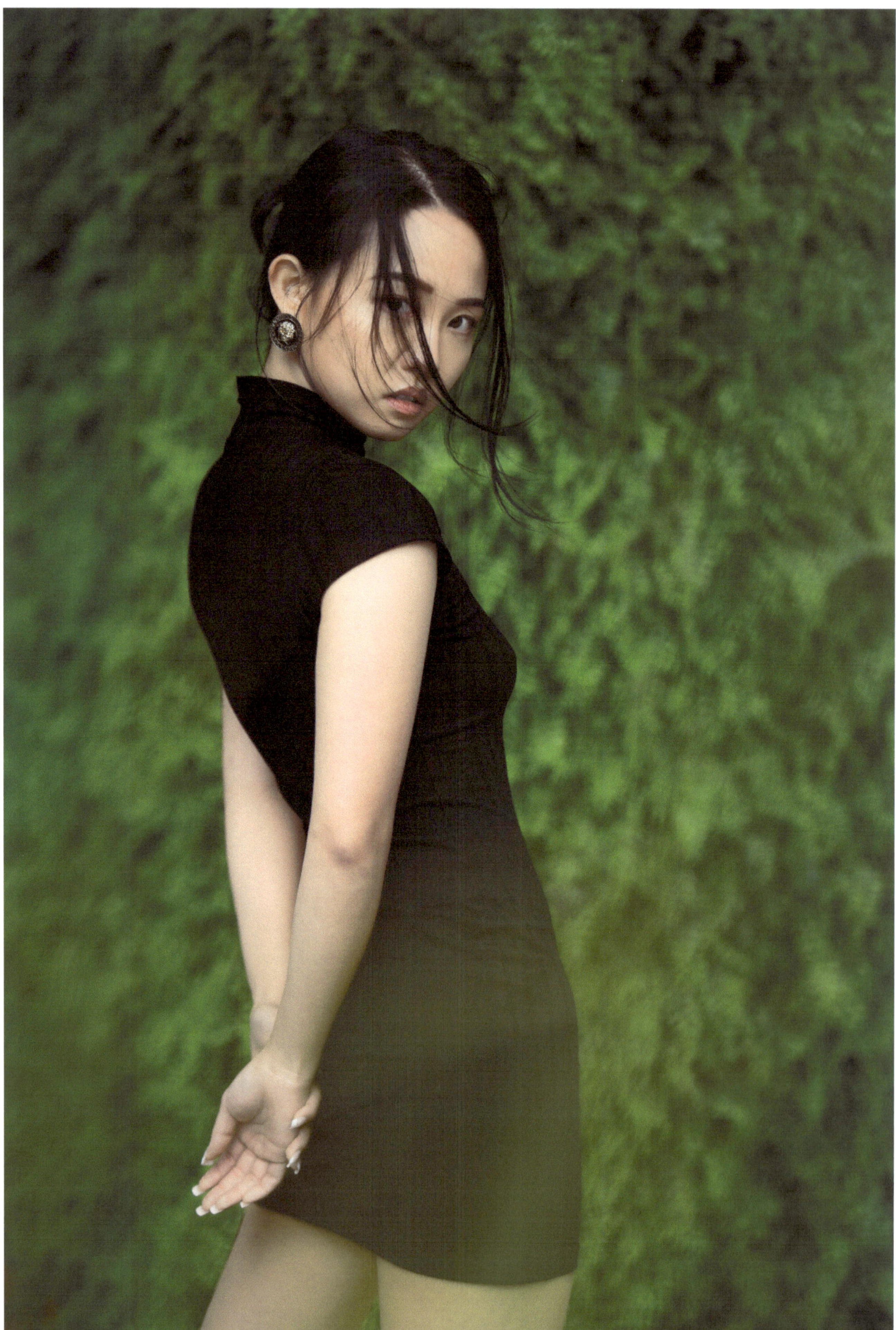

Chapter 10

City Lights

"In the glow of the city lights,
we find the courage
to explore who we truly are."

Yasmine Ke

City Lights

How do you feel when the city lights start to come alive? The night brings with it a certain magic, transforming not just the landscape, but also the energy within it. As the day fades, the familiar begins to shift, and the ordinary takes on new possibilities. It's as if the lights themselves invite us to step beyond the routine and explore who we might become when the world feels a little quieter, a little more hidden.

The city's glow intensifies, casting vibrant hues across every corner, encouraging a sense of freedom and play. The reflections from neon signs and shimmering windows ignite a boldness in every movement. As the night deepens, gestures feel more fluid, inspired by the glow that surrounds them. The atmosphere becomes alive, and everything—from colors to emotions—feels more daring under the changing light.

Amidst the illuminated streets, there's a sense of possibility that emerges, opening a path to embrace new versions of the self. Whether leaning into reflections or moving through the glow of city lights, each moment takes on a new significance. There's something liberating about being part of this landscape, where the night brings with it a sense of exploration and wonder, unrestrained by the usual rhythms of the day.

In these nighttime moments, the city transforms, offering a unique space for discovery. The glow of the lights becomes an invitation to be bolder and dream bigger, encouraging those who step into the night's embrace to reveal a side of themselves they might not have seen before—one that is vibrant, confident, and unafraid to explore what the night has to offer.

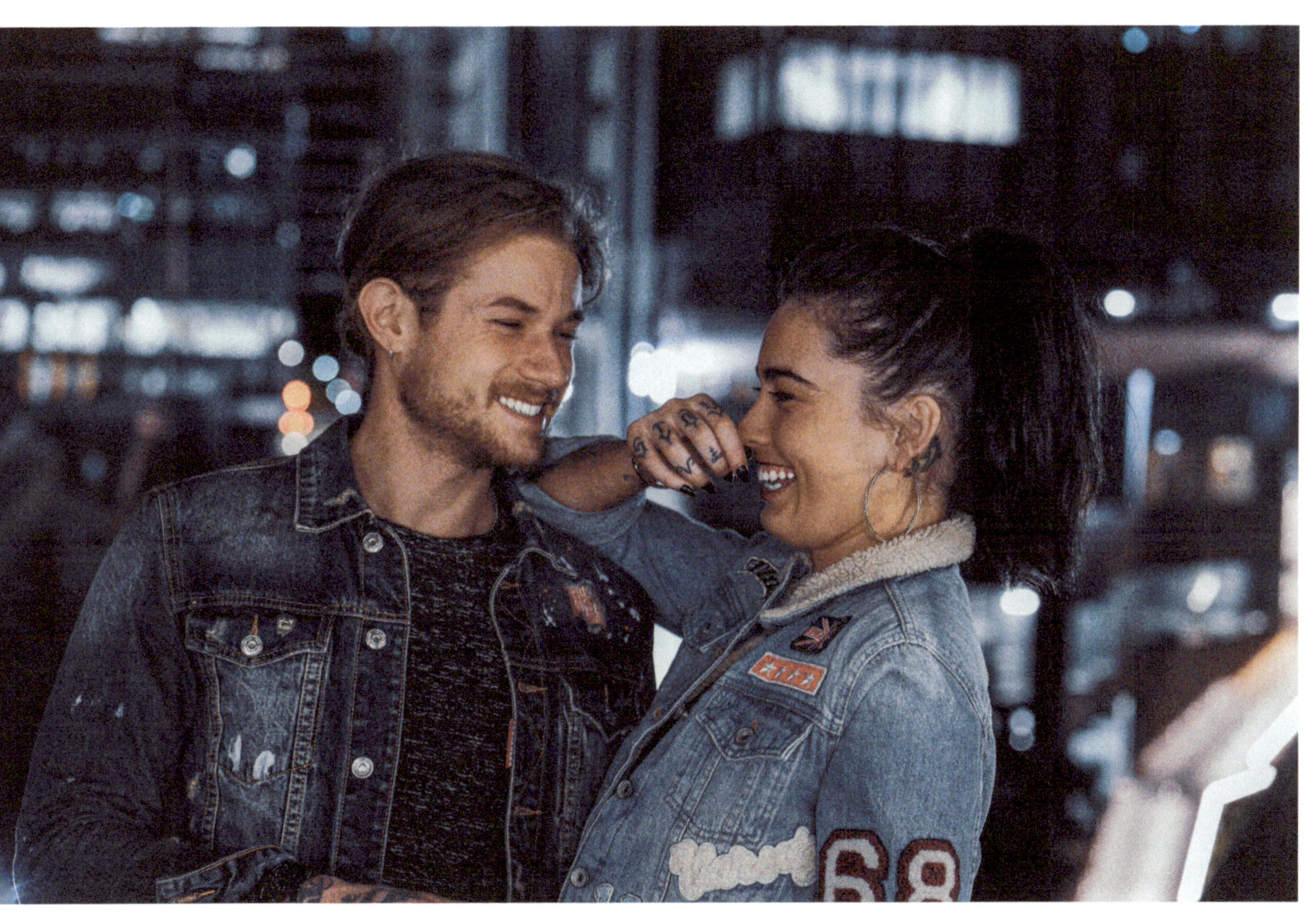

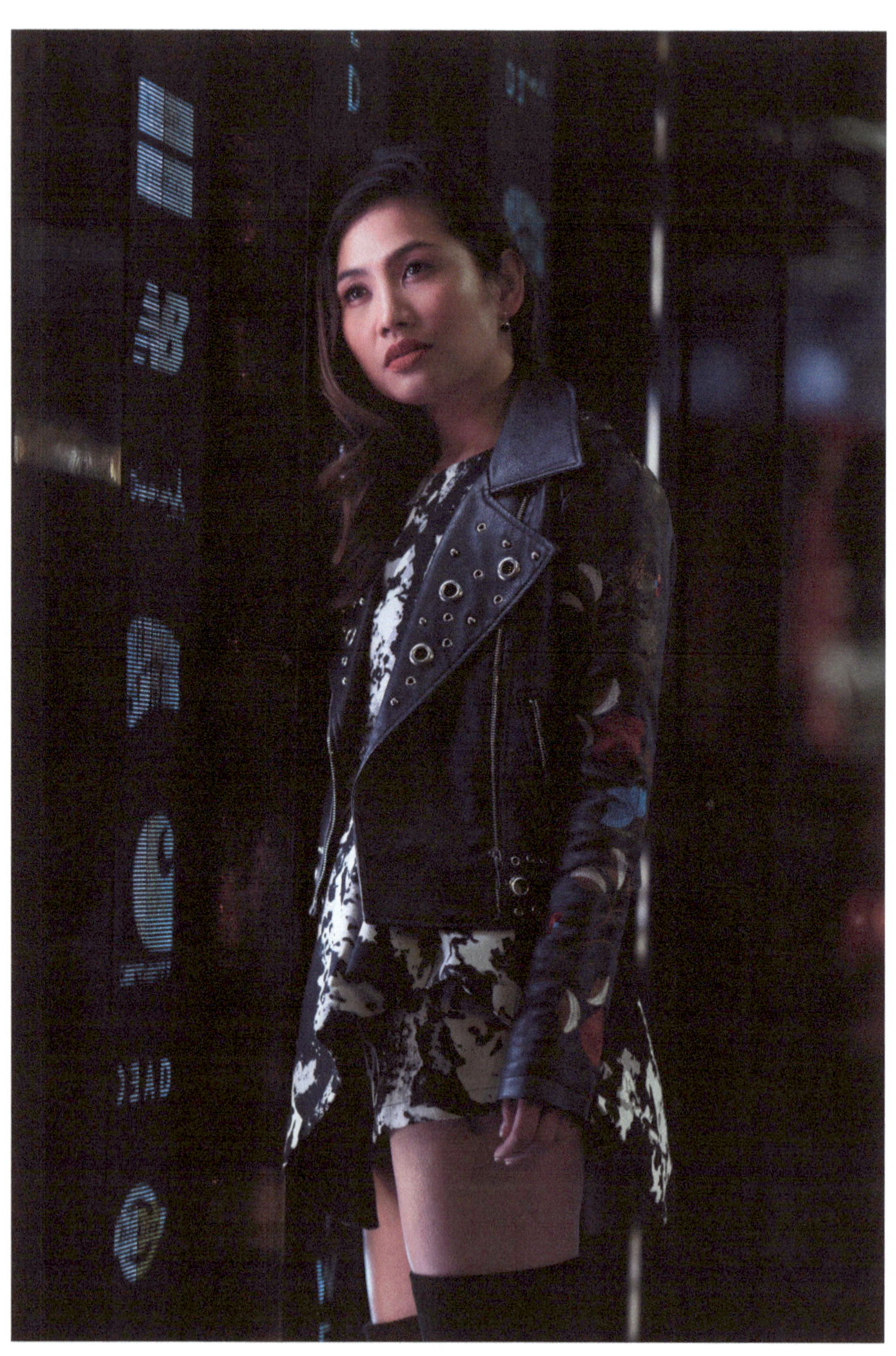

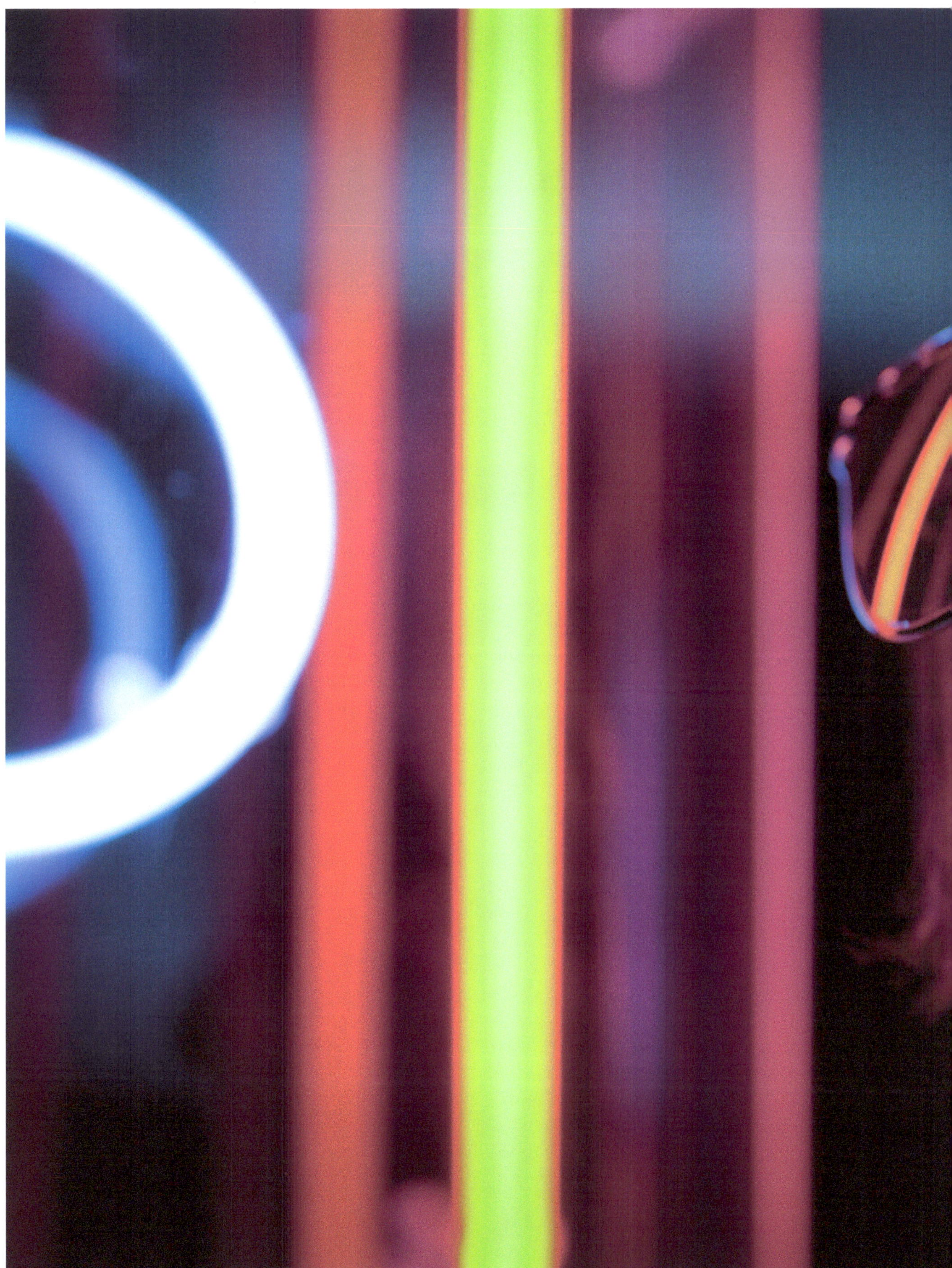

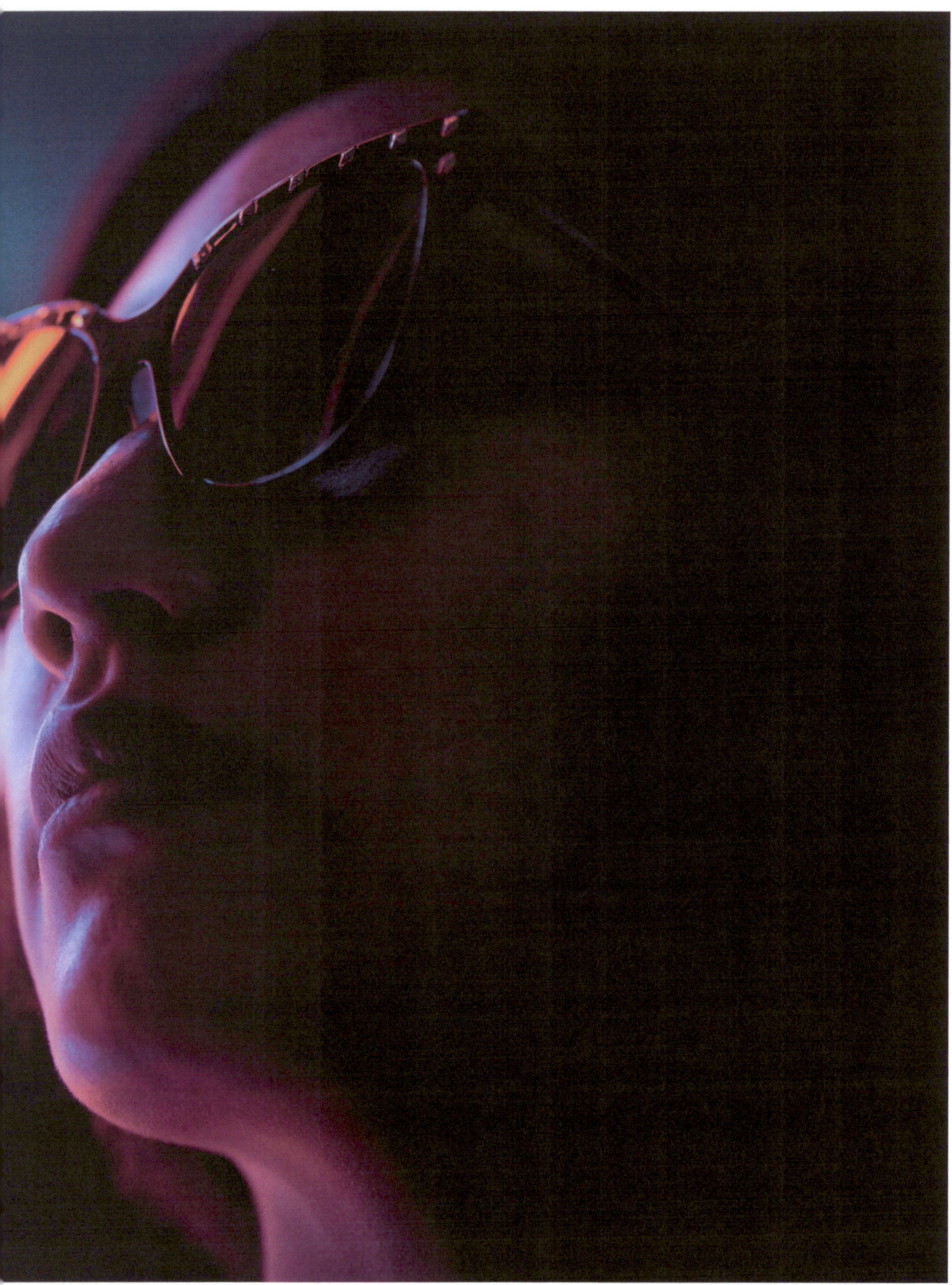

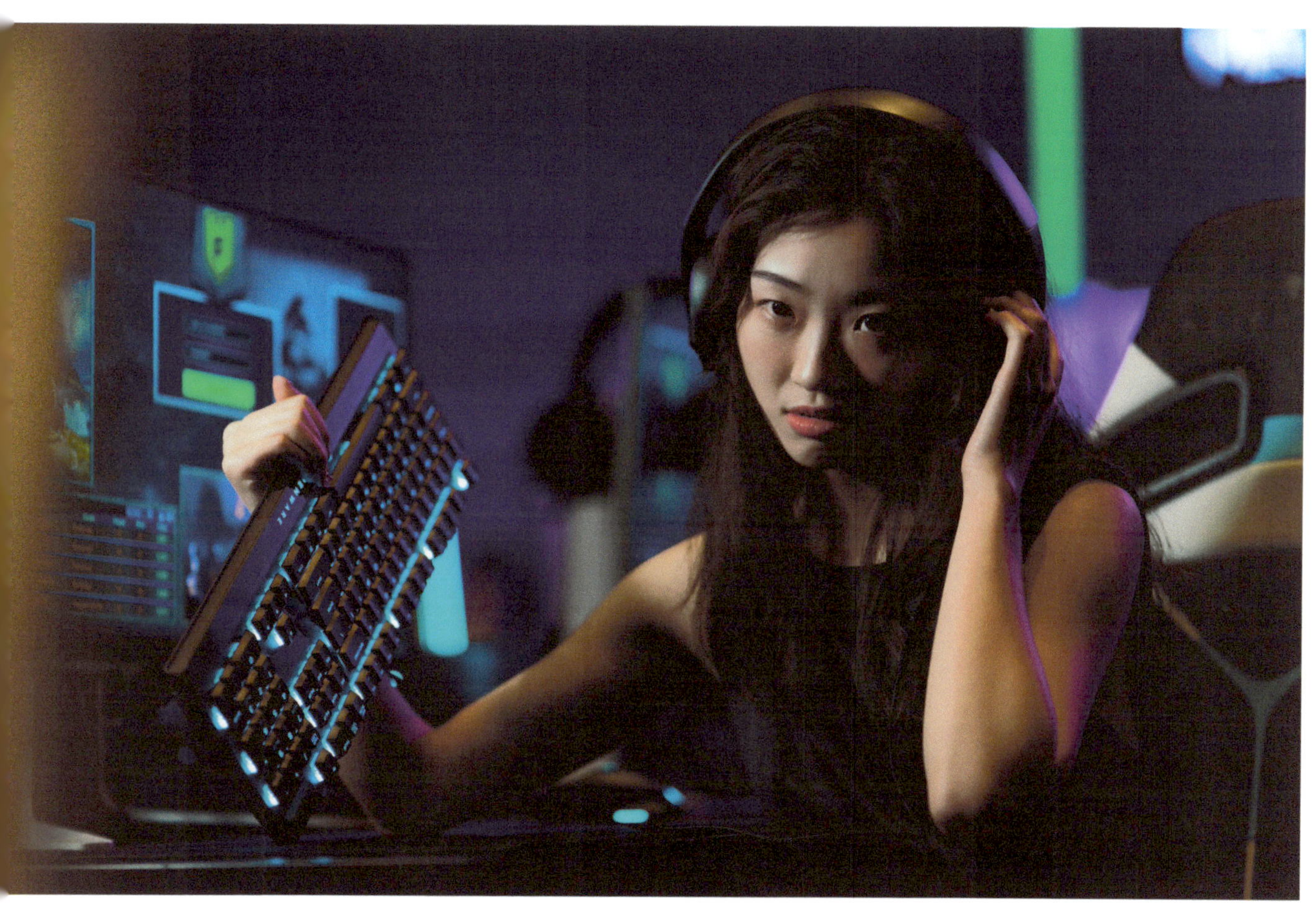

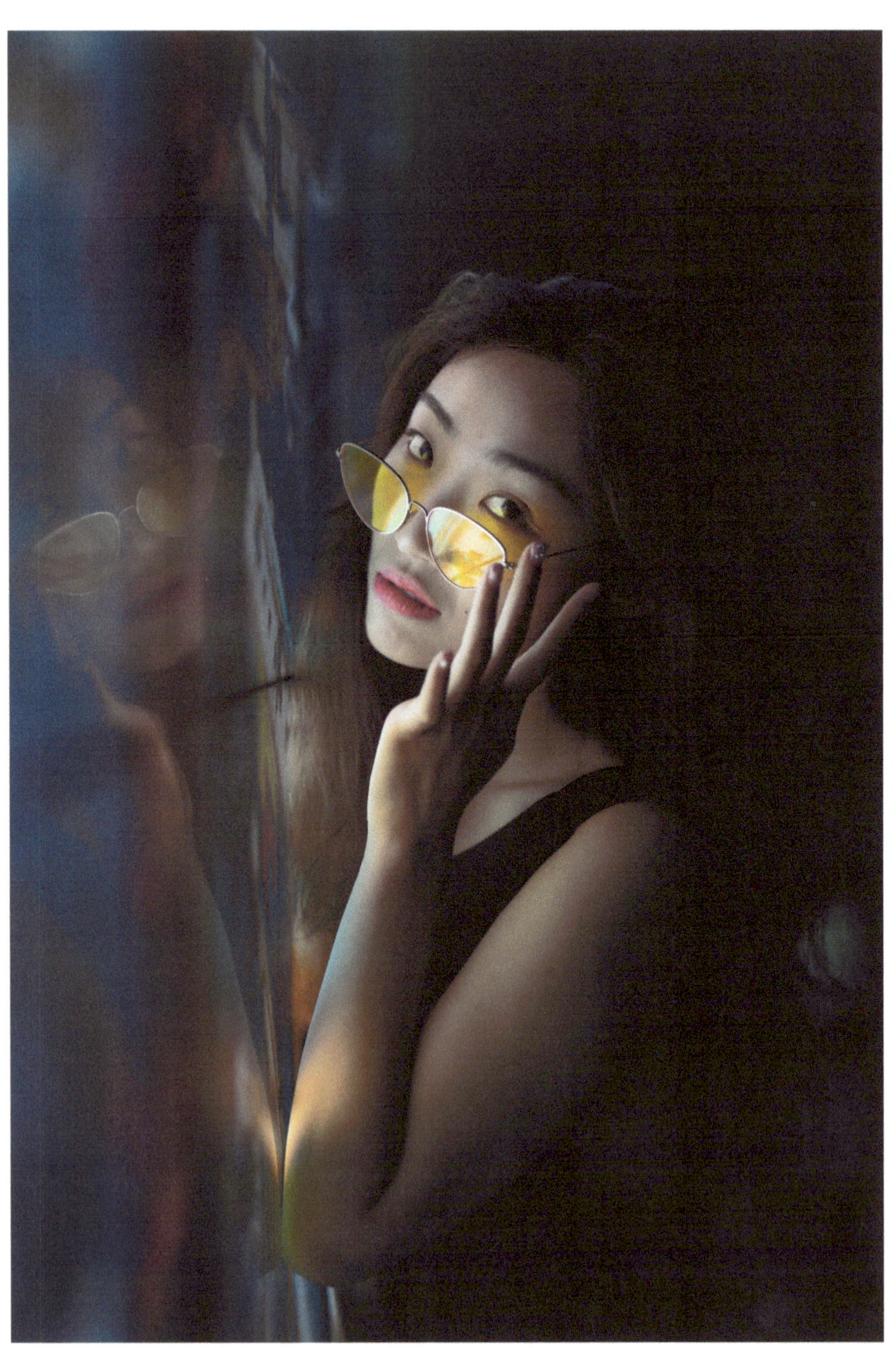

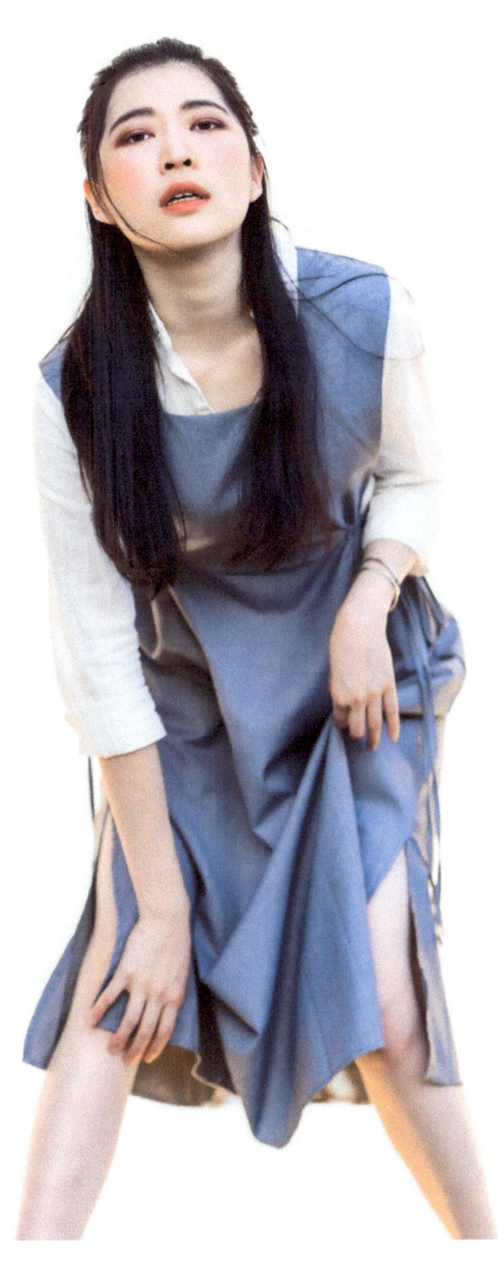

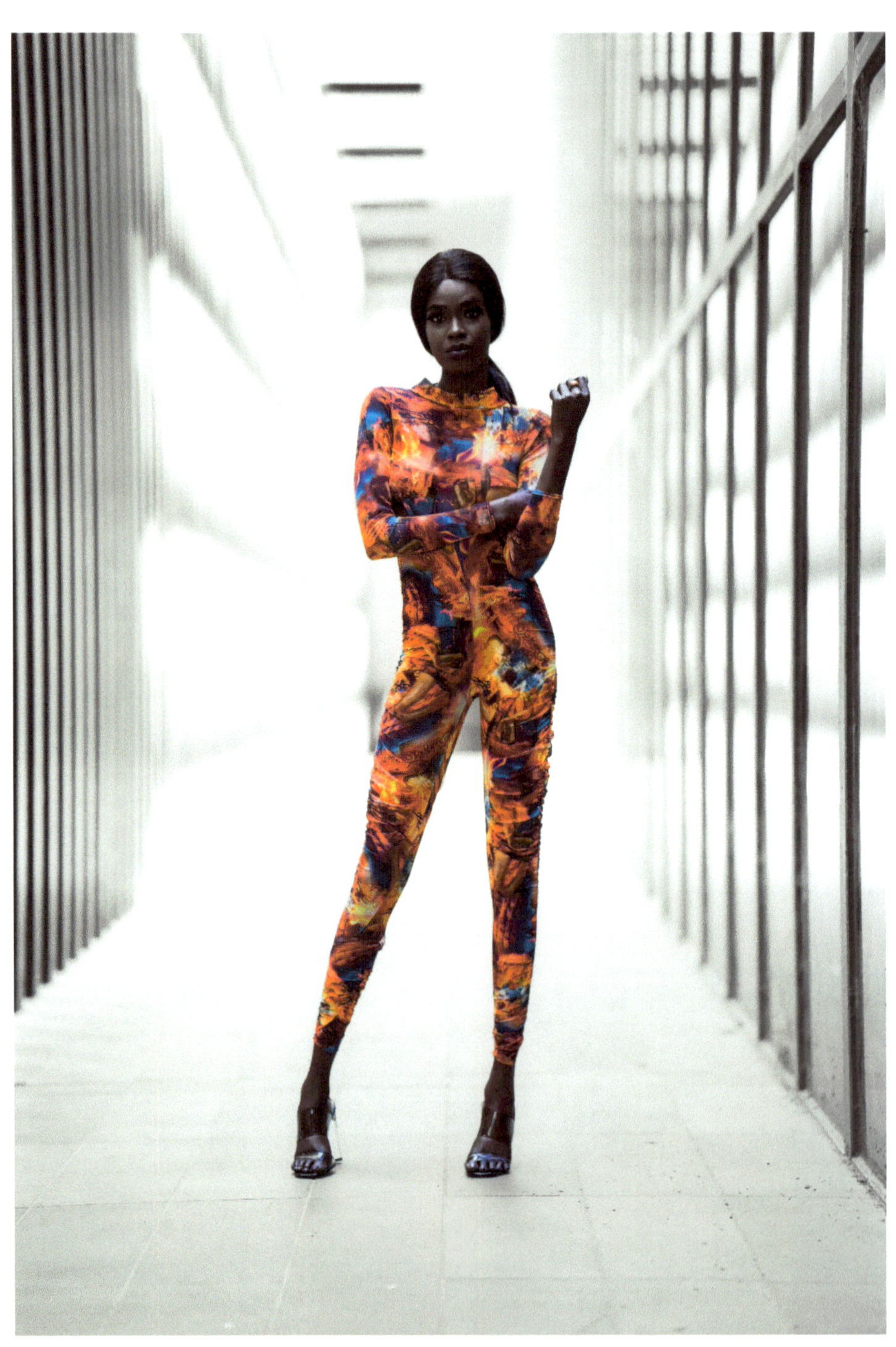

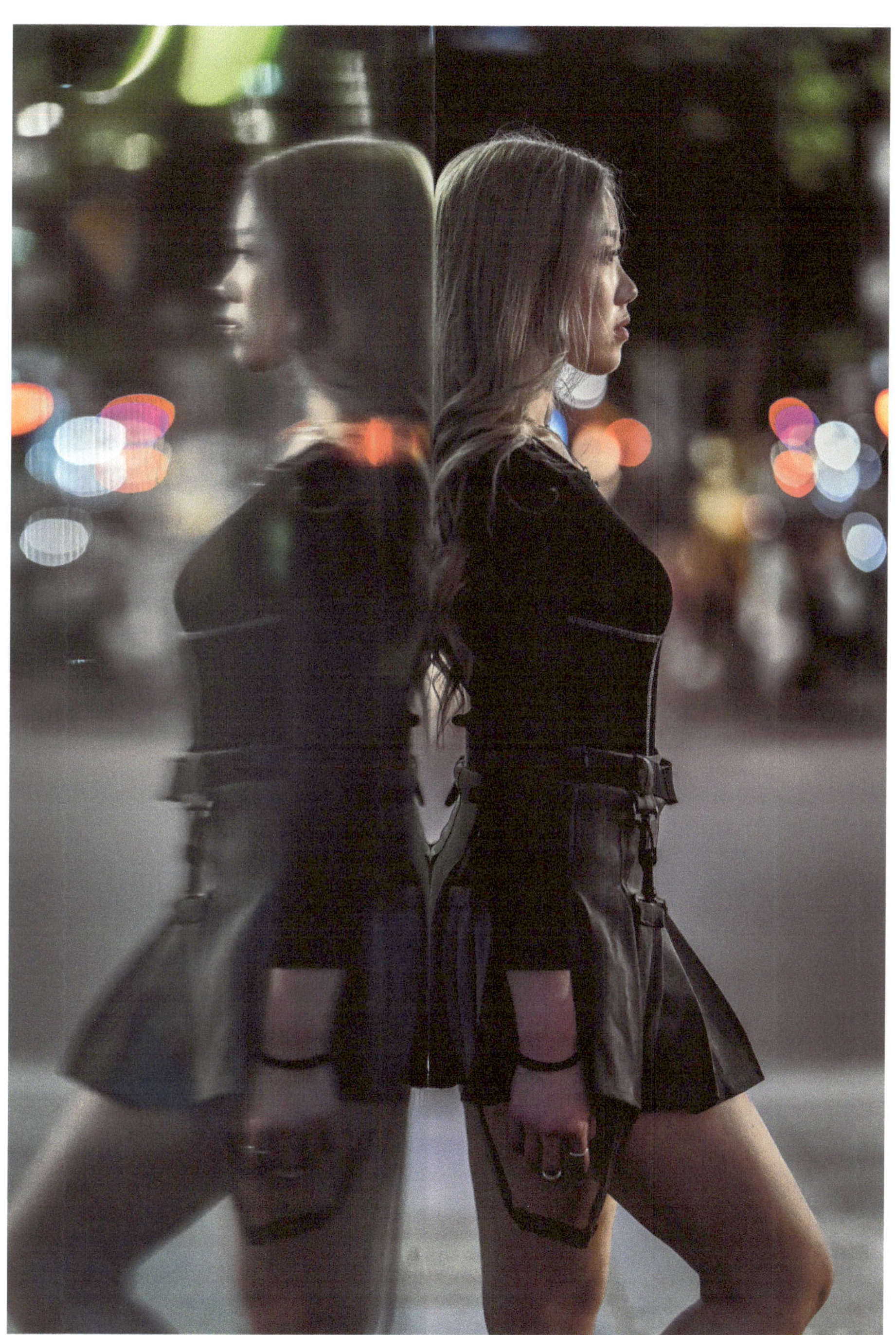

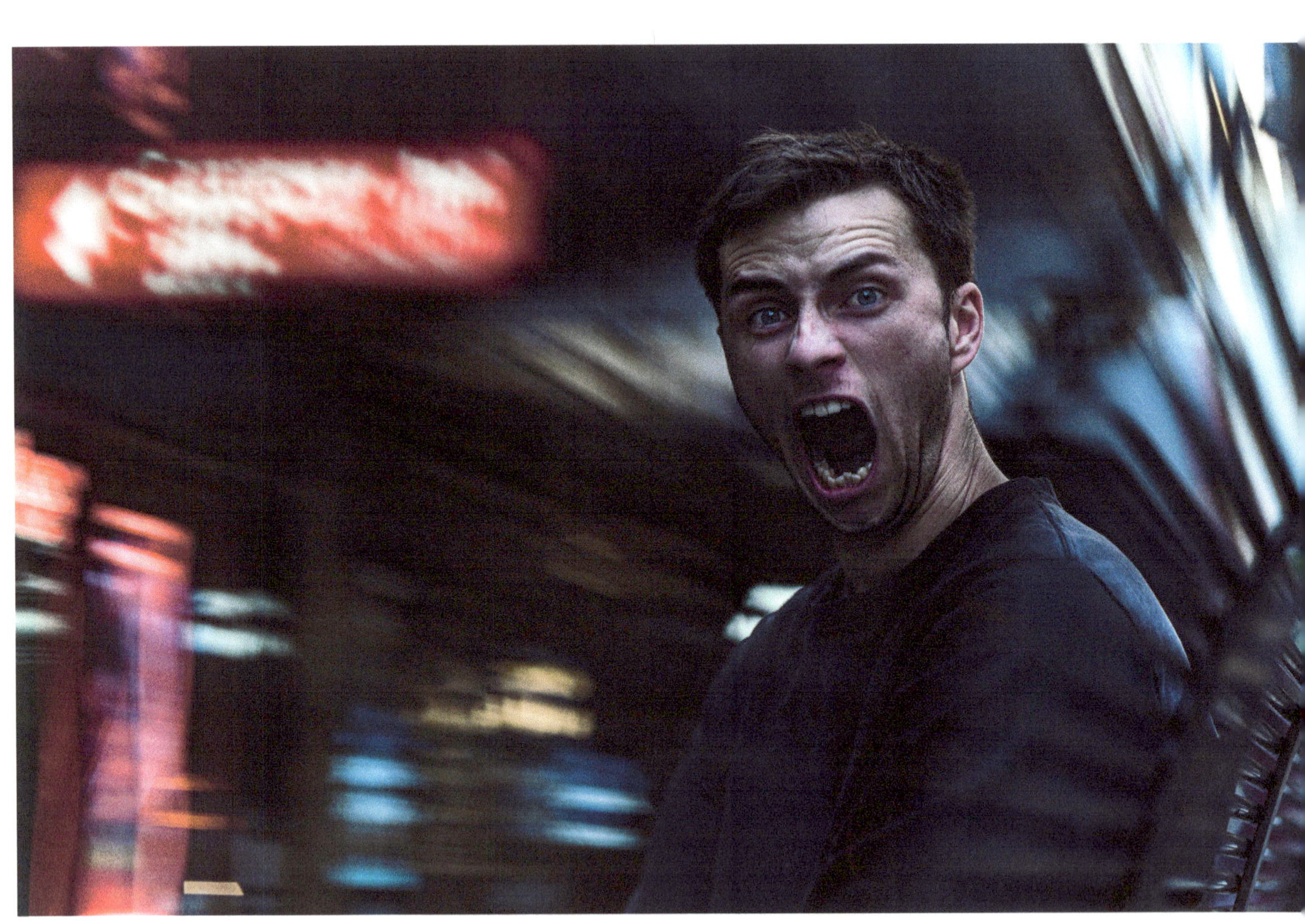

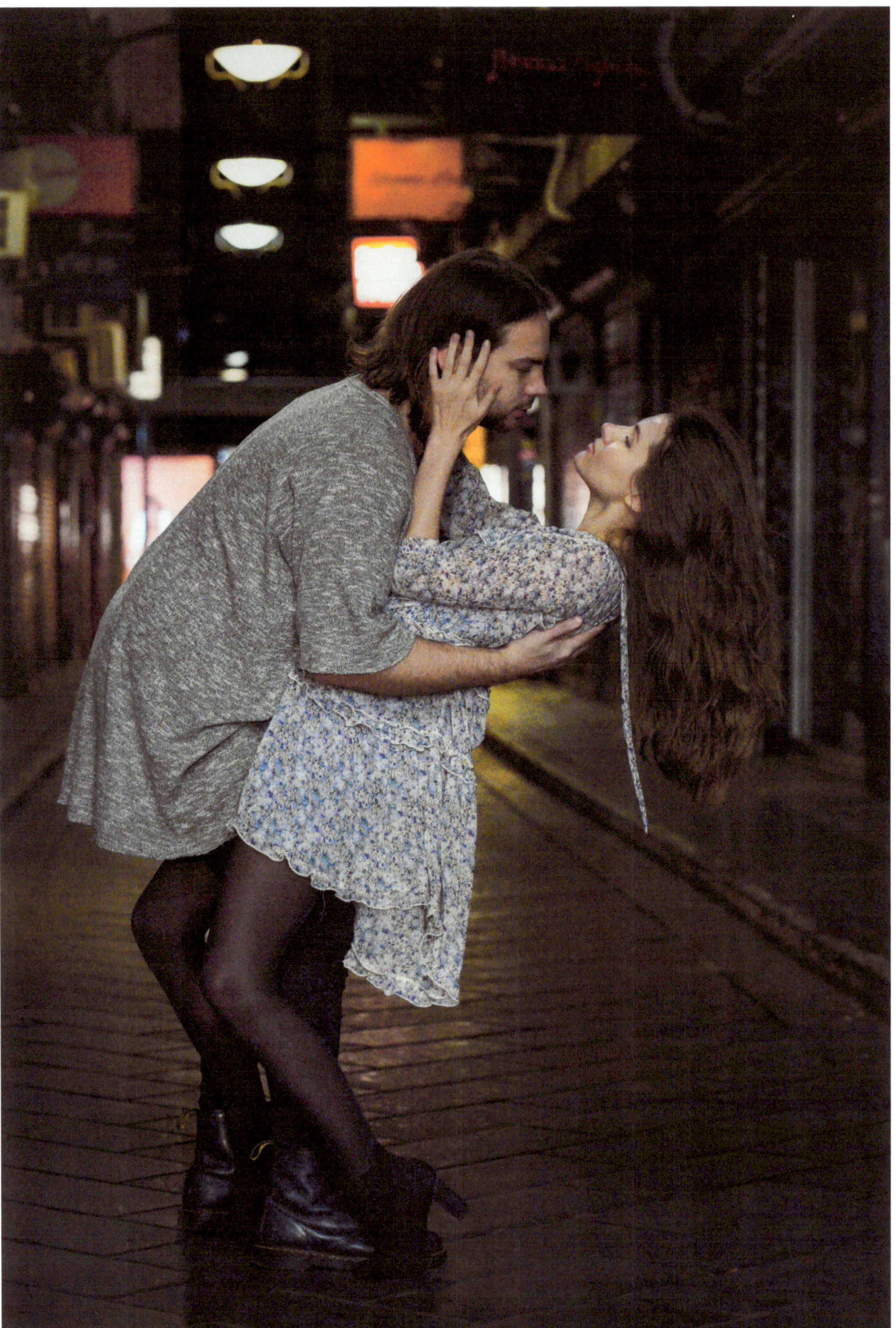

Chapter 11

Le Petit Palais

"It all comes together
when everyone shows up
with their own flair
and makes it stand out."

Elijah Dau

Le Petit Palais

At Le Petit Palais, the space came alive through the distinct interpretations brought by each participant. Wardrobe choices—from soft silks to sharp, tailored pieces—became an expression of creativity and confidence, reflecting the unique vision behind them. The elegance of the venue blended seamlessly with these bold choices, allowing freedom for every look to tell its own story.

While the charm of Le Petit Palais set the stage, it was the presence and artistry of those within it that captured attention. Whether through luxurious gowns, sleek suits, or avant-garde accessories, each look carried a sense of identity, elevating the atmosphere. The interplay between the surroundings and creative choices was powerful, making every detail feel intentional and full of purpose.

Adaptability became a key element as the day unfolded. Ideas shifted and evolved, allowing moments of elegance to meet unexpected bursts of boldness. What started as simple concepts turned into a collective expression of style and creativity, with the energy of the day driving experimentation and pushing beyond the ordinary.

All these moments, captured in a single day, felt timeless. The energy flowing through Le Petit Palais came from an unfiltered embrace of creativity, free from limitations. It wasn't just about collaboration; it was about pushing boundaries, exploring new ideas, and letting imagination take the lead. The experience reminded everyone that boldness and authenticity can combine to create something truly extraordinary, inspiring a deeper sense of creativity and a drive to keep dreaming bigger.

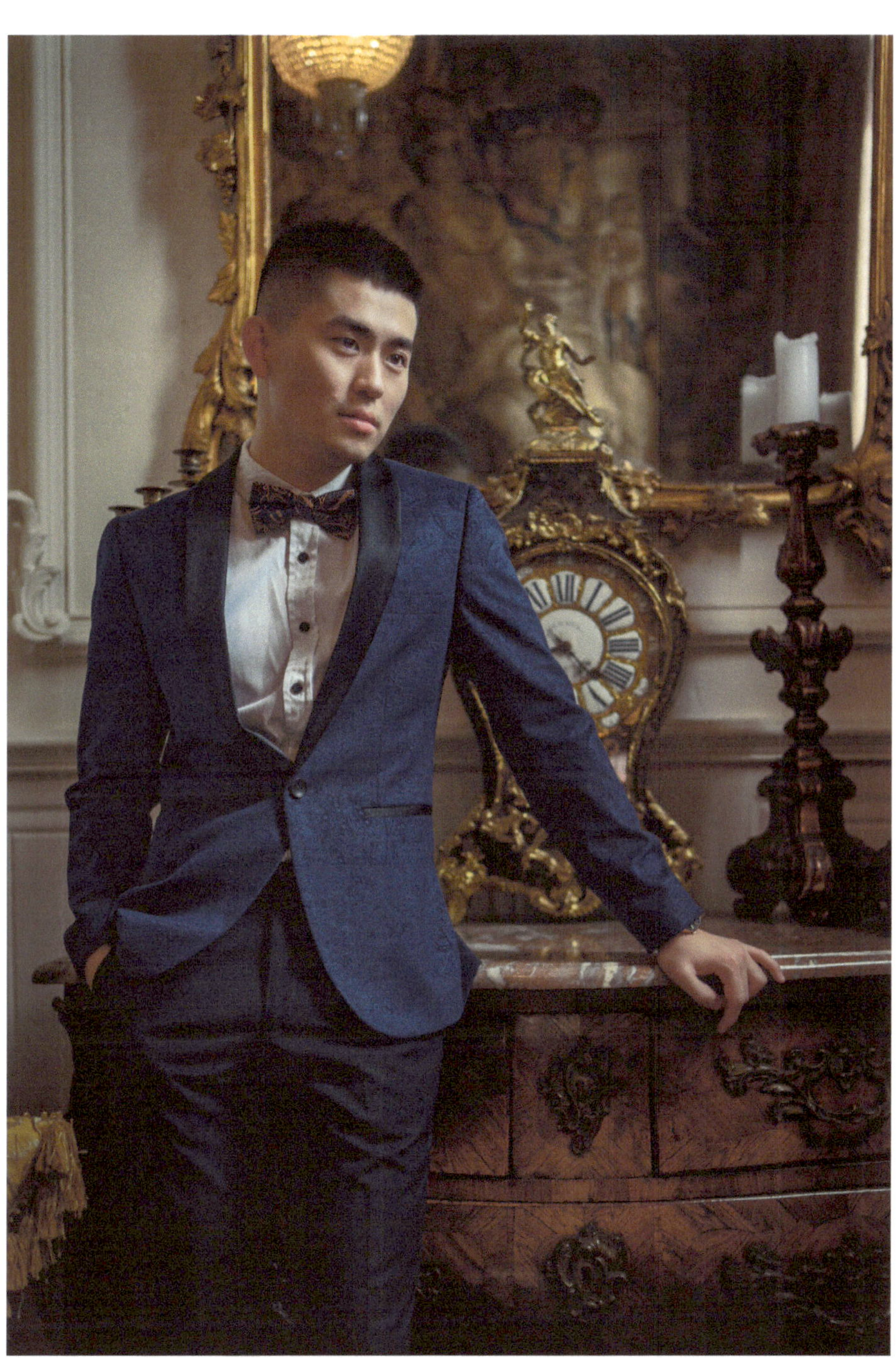

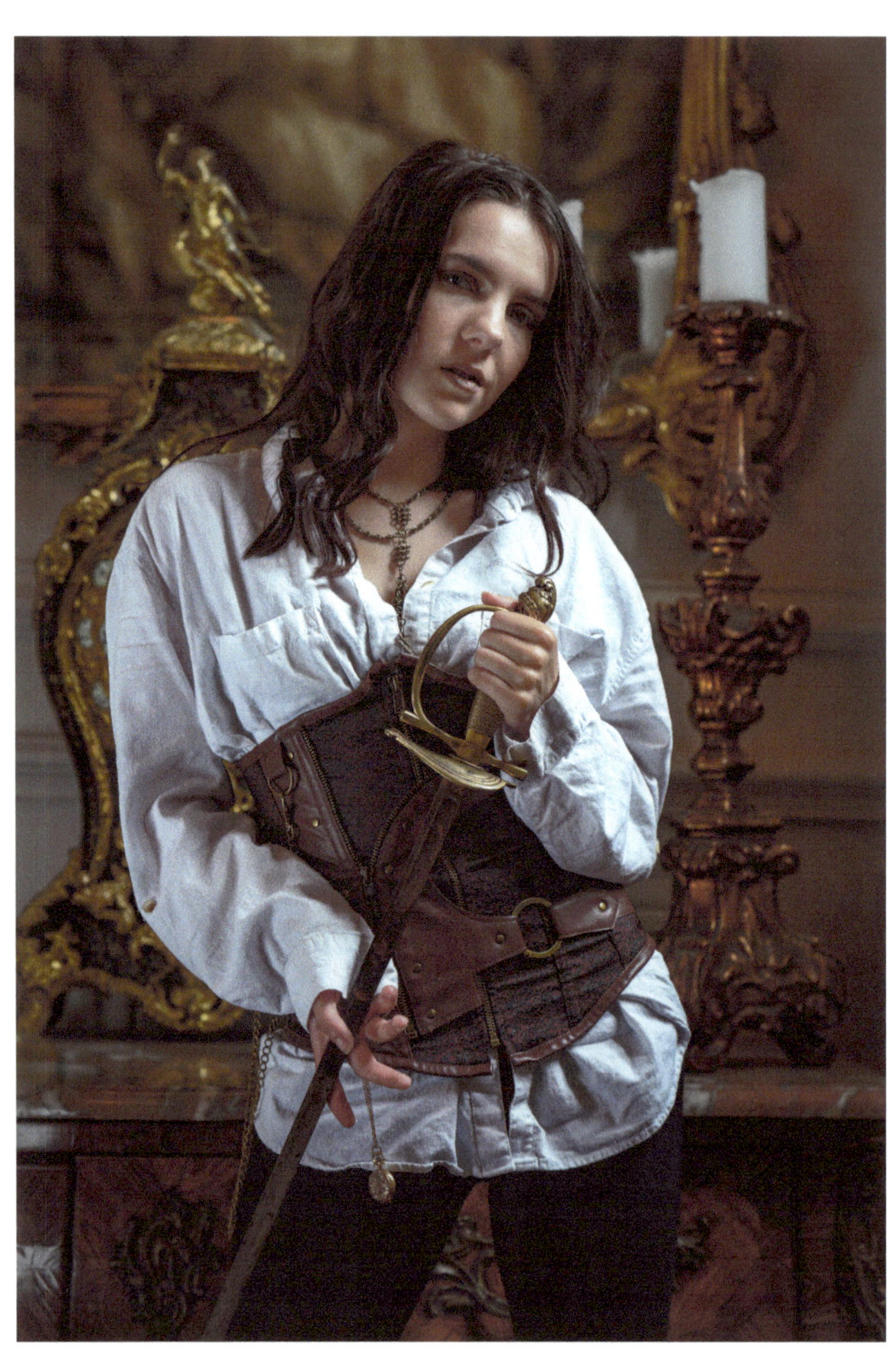

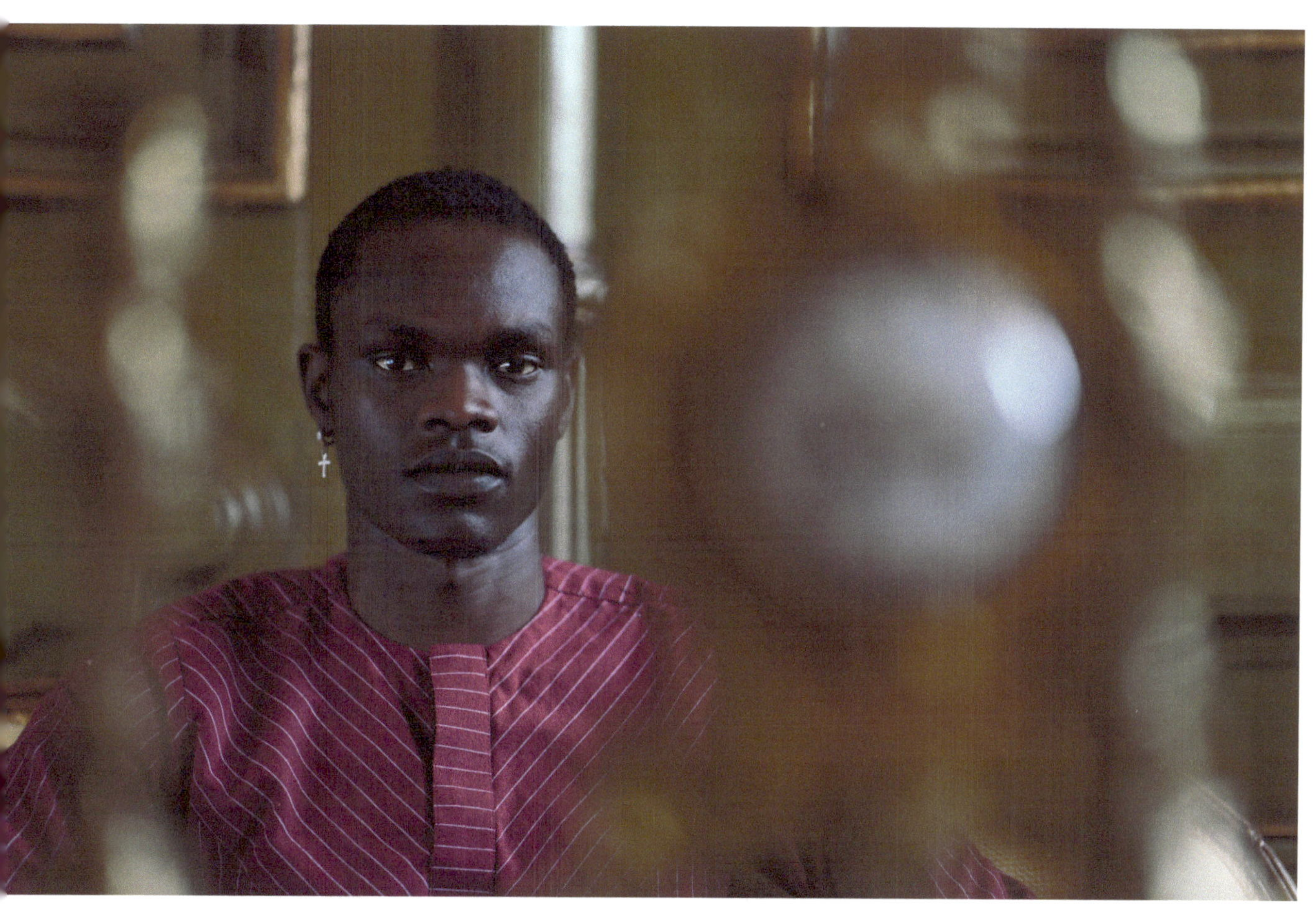

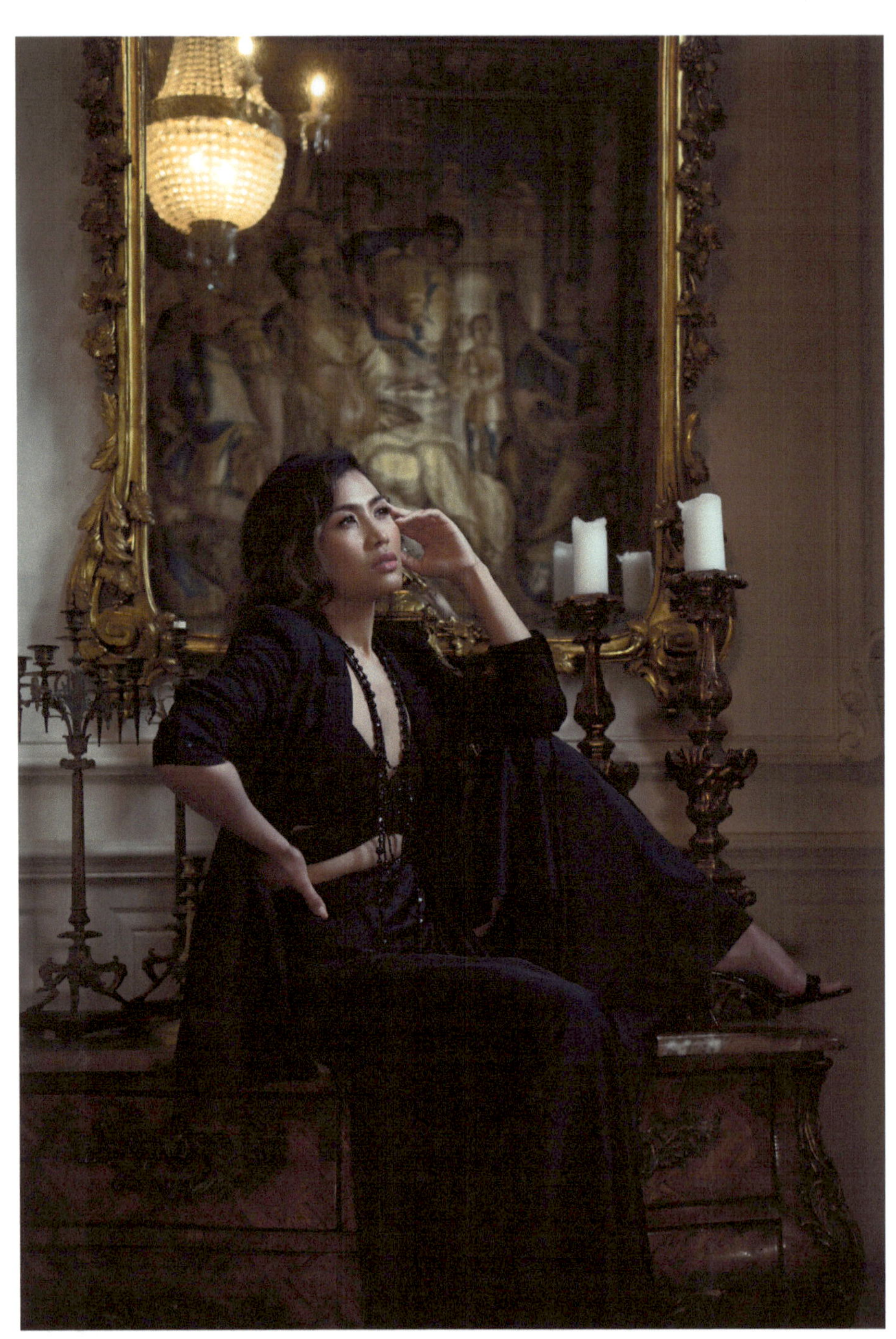

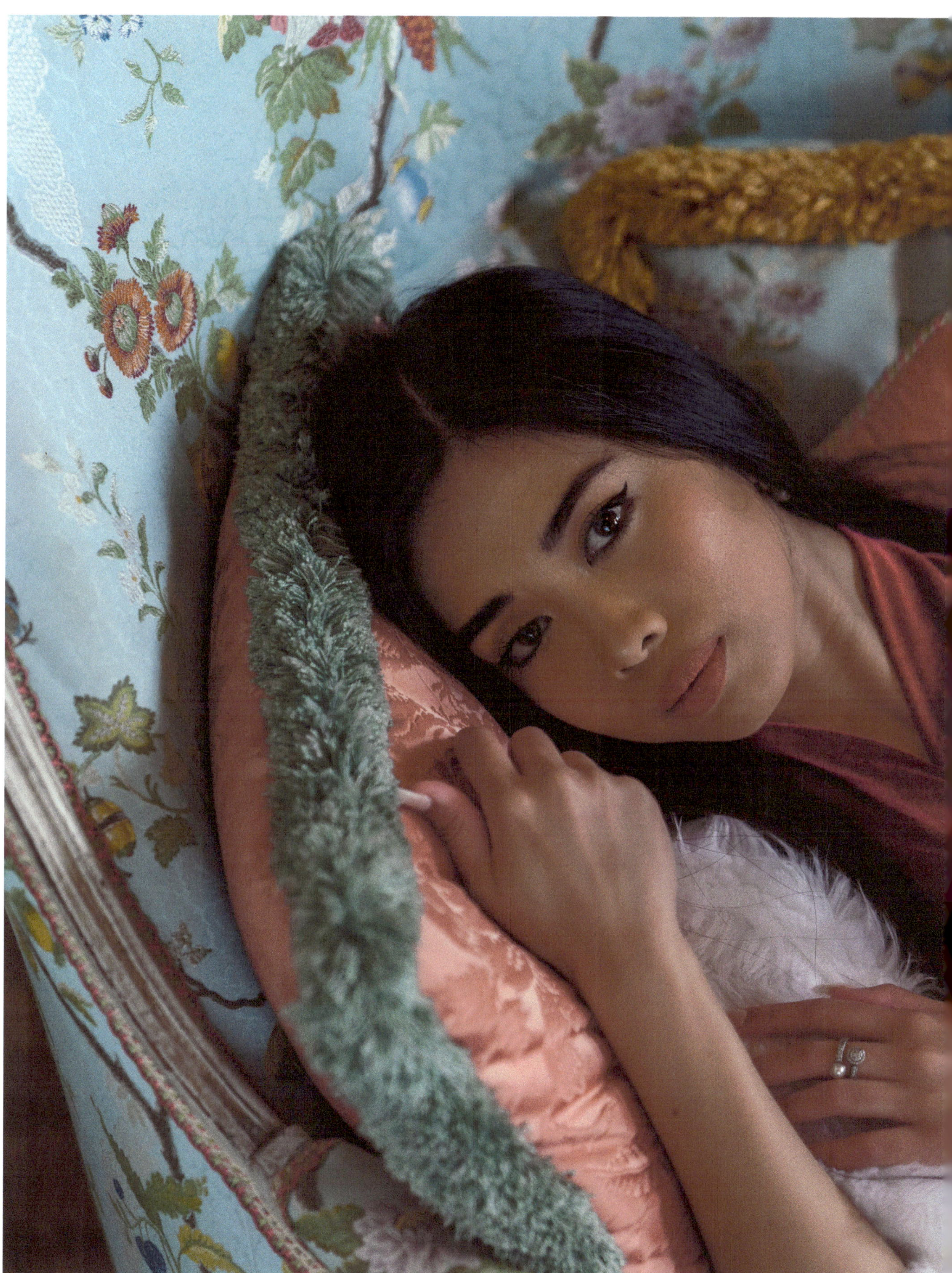

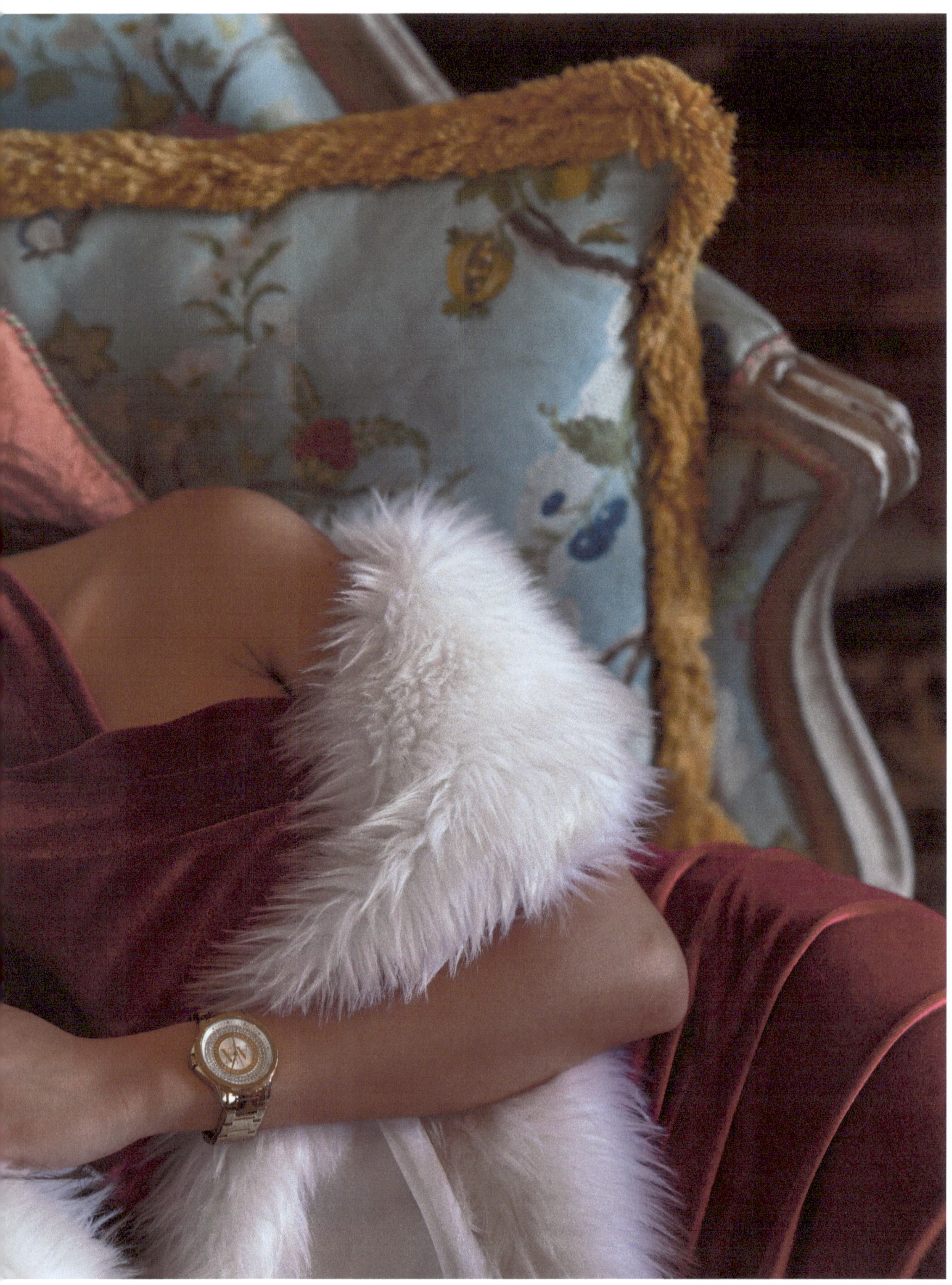

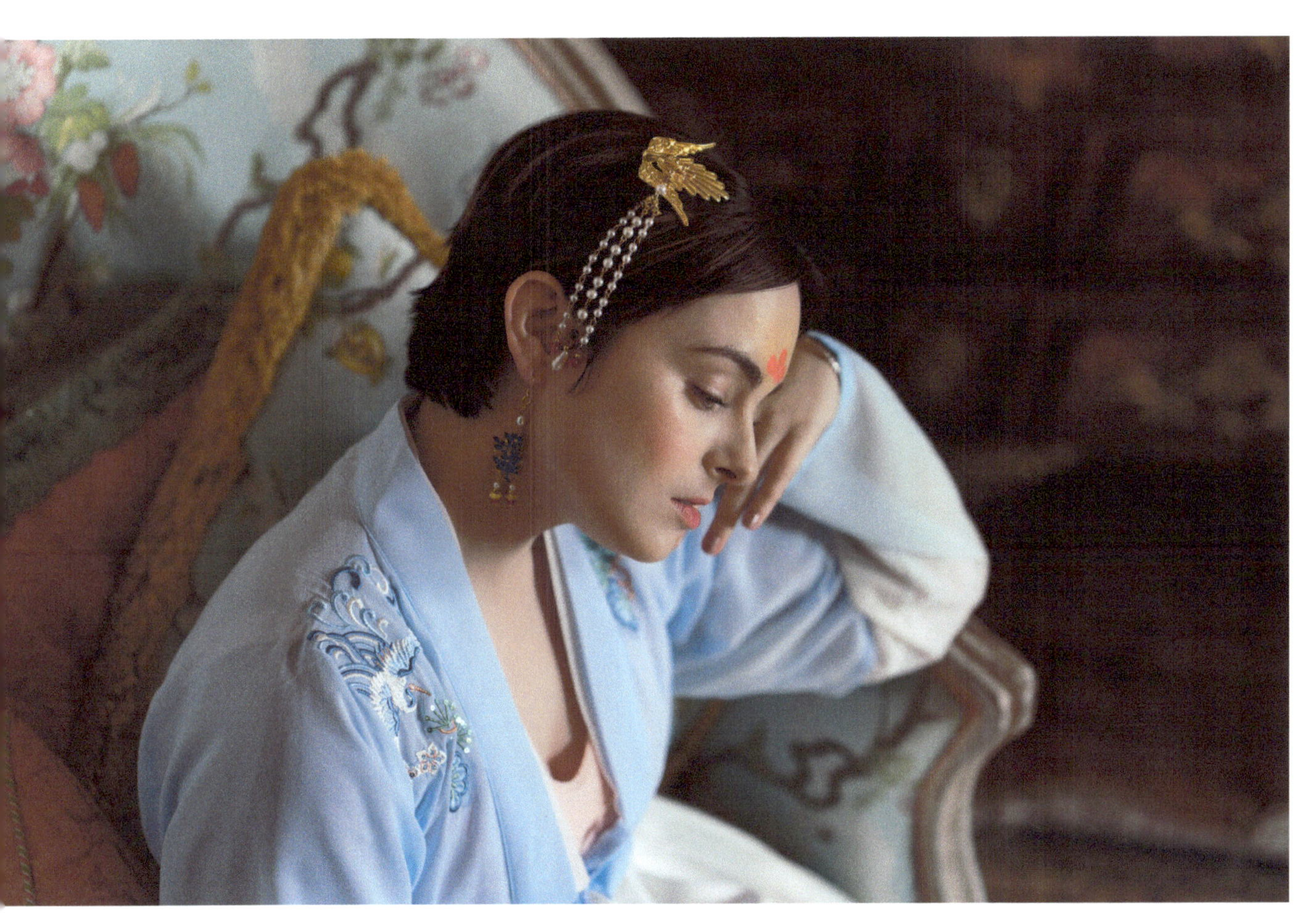

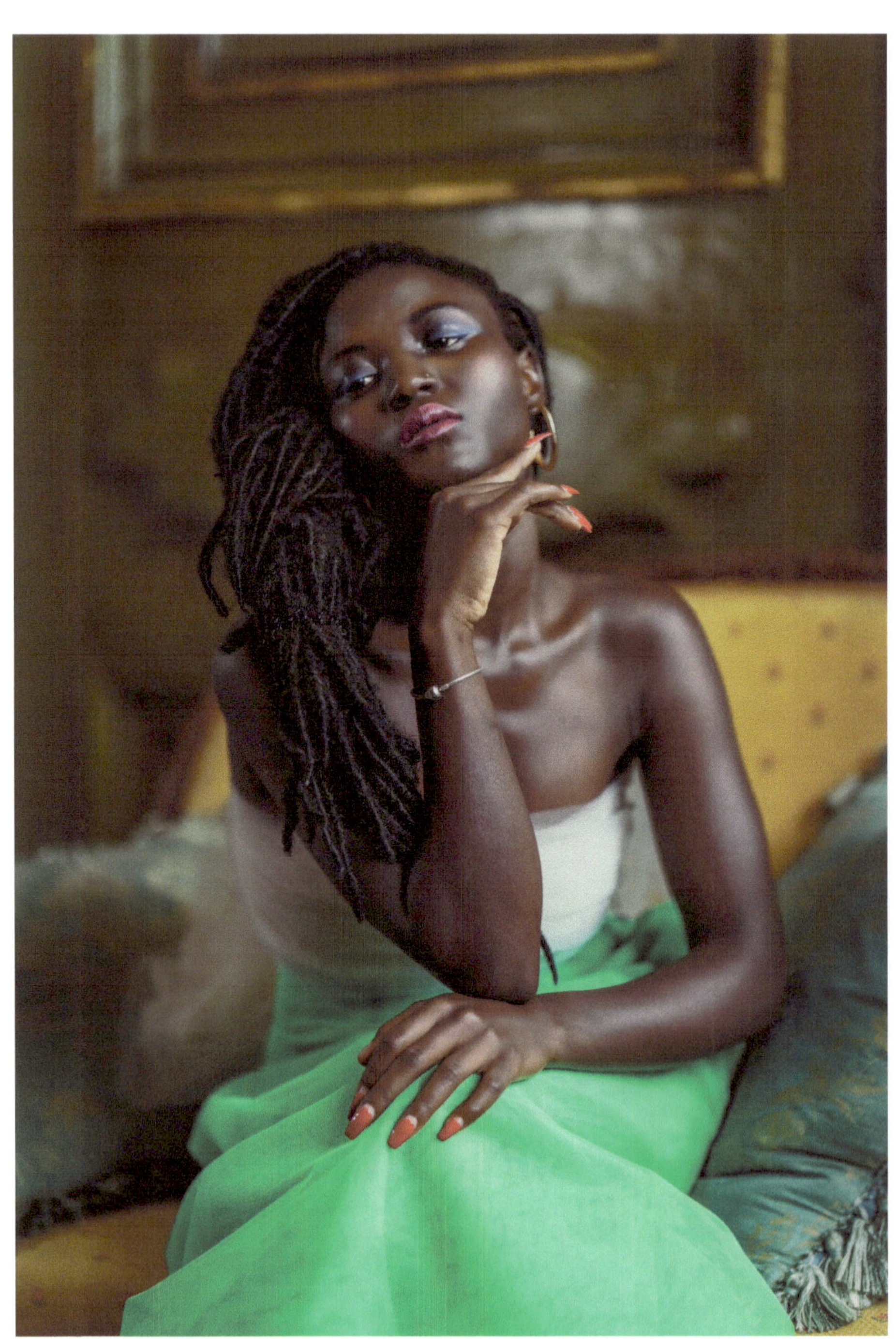

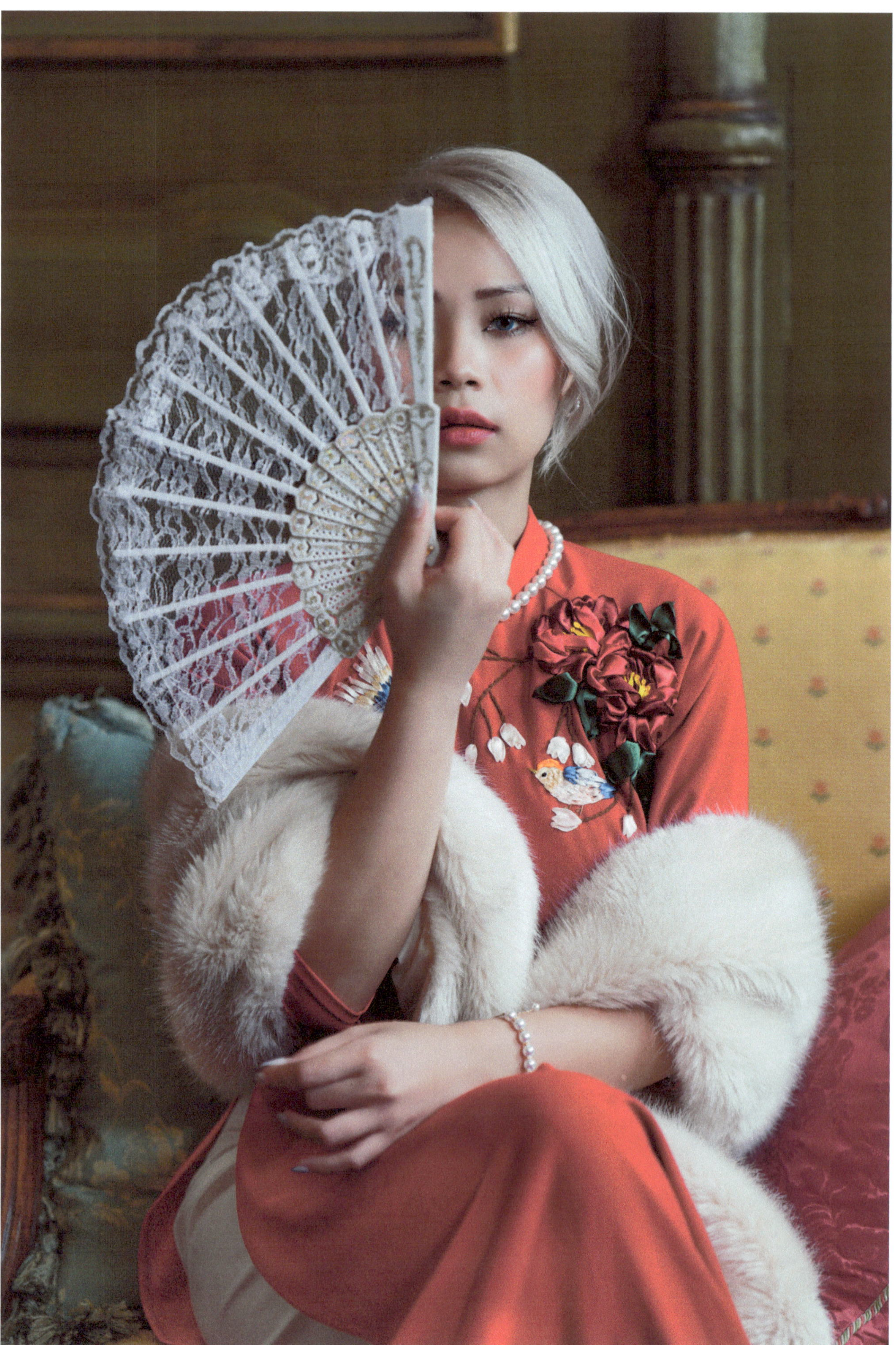

Chapter 12

Graffiti Lane

"To find the light,
seek the art."

Lillith "Painter" Fox

Graffiti Lane

Street art is raw, bold, and unapologetic, providing a powerful foundation for portraits that embody the same energy. In this chapter, graffiti-covered walls and laneways burst with color and creativity, infusing each image with an undeniable edge. The rebellion and freedom expressed through street art mirror the spirit of those featured, capturing a connection between the environment and the vibrant personalities within it.

Melbourne's laneways are renowned for their ever-changing street art, where each wall becomes a canvas for expression. This setting elevates the portraits, creating a dynamic interplay between fashion, gesture, and art. The mix of colors, textures, and layers that graffiti offers adds a sense of unpredictability and rawness, allowing each moment to feel spontaneous and alive.

While these lanes are uniquely Melbourne, every city holds its own version of creative, untamed spaces. Discovering these spots brings a sense of adventure, inviting everyone involved to be bolder and dream bigger. It's in these spaces where art becomes part of the story being told, and both sides of the camera are challenged to embrace experimentation and fearlessness.

In these portraits, the graffiti doesn't simply exist in the background—it actively engages with the individuals, enhancing the emotions and narratives they convey. This chapter is a celebration of the creative spirit that thrives in the streets, where art, identity, and environment come together in a powerful visual collaboration.

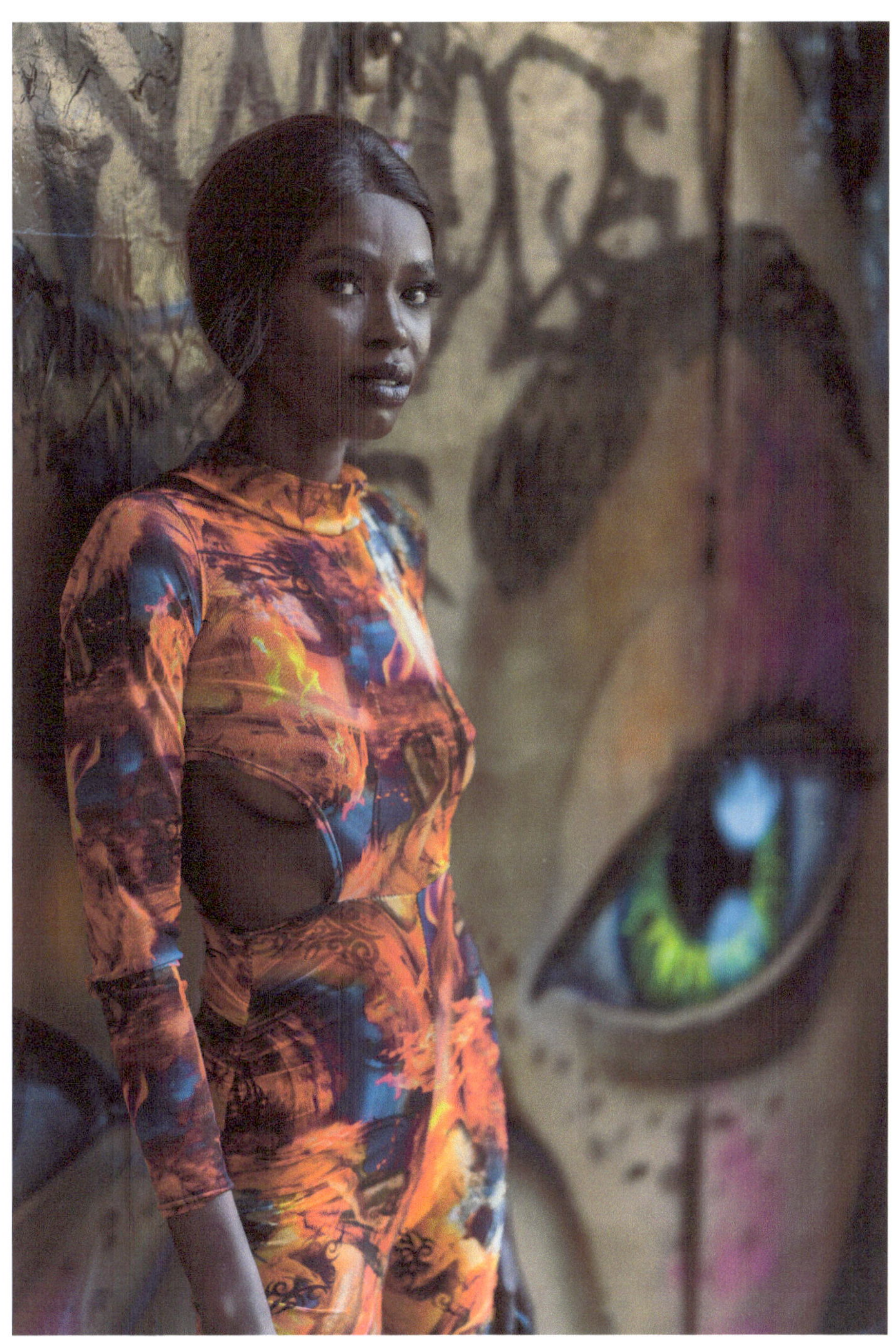

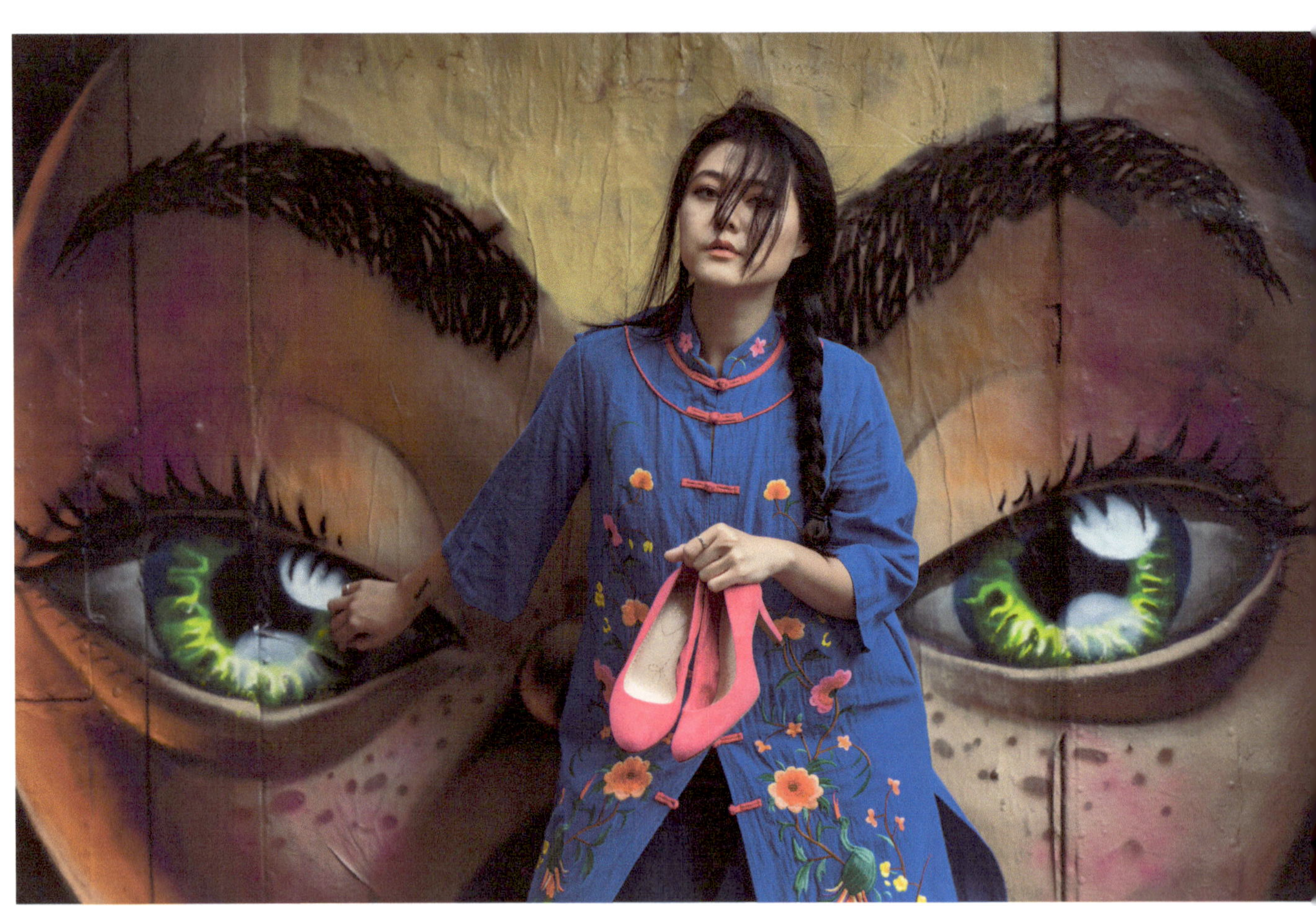

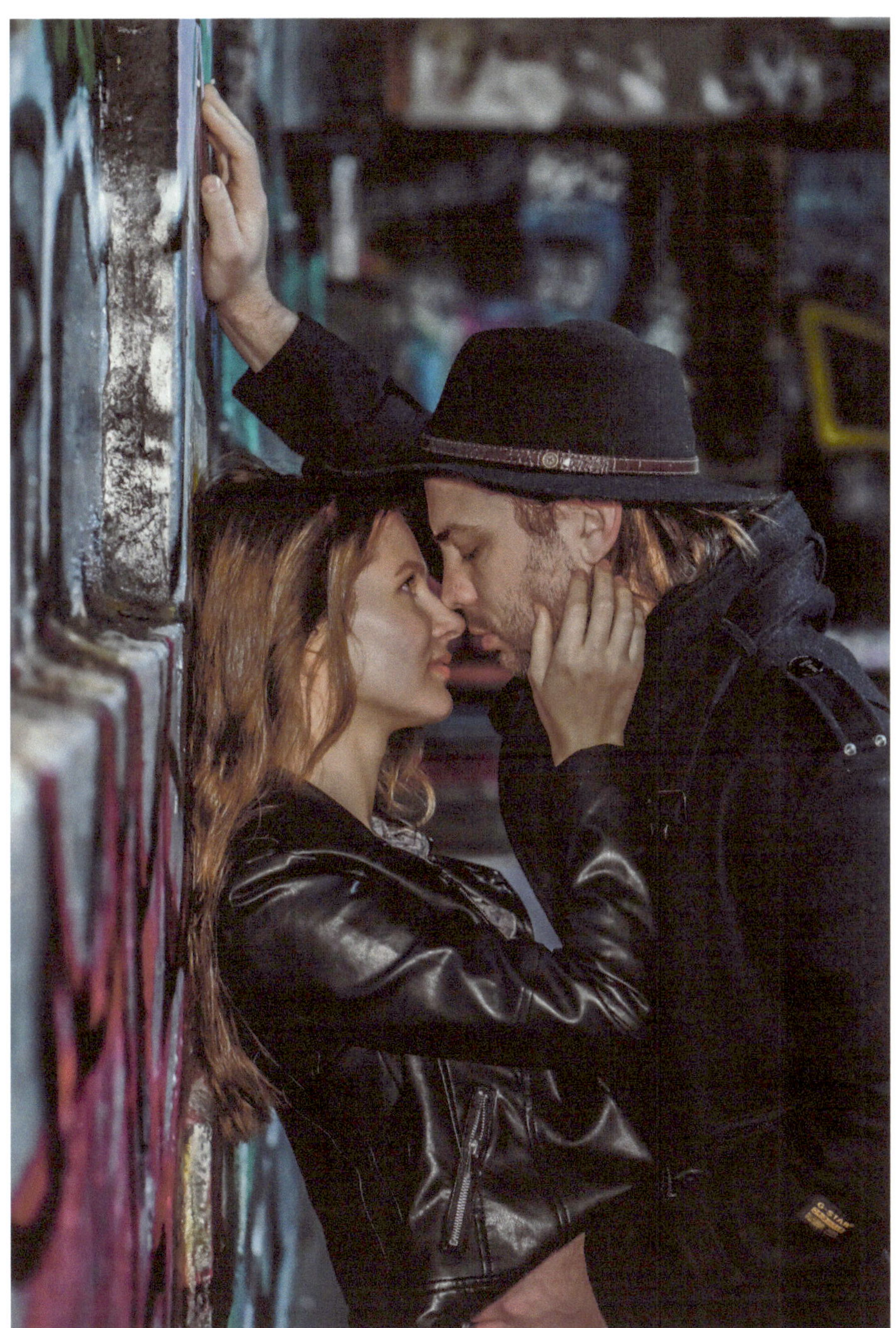

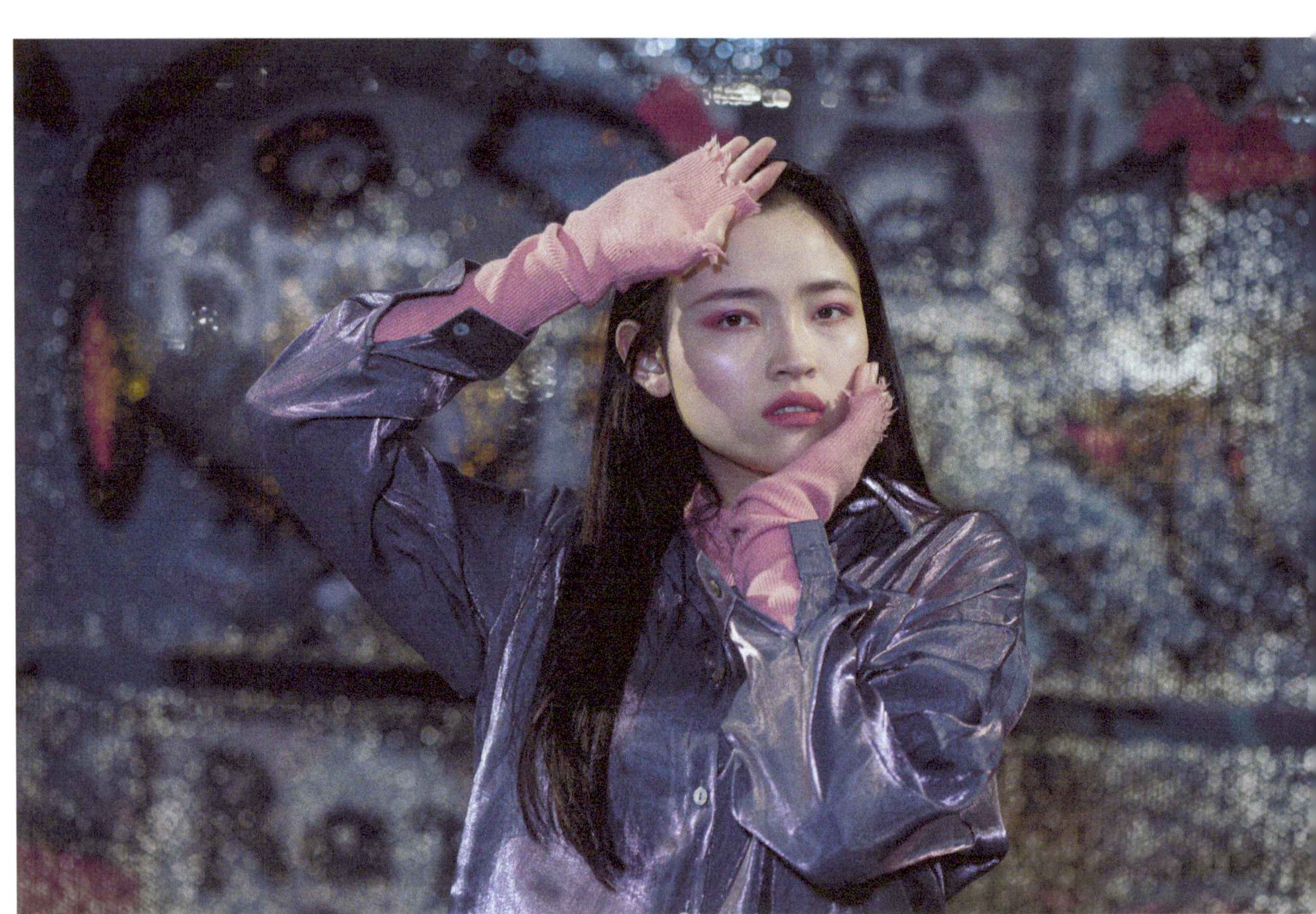

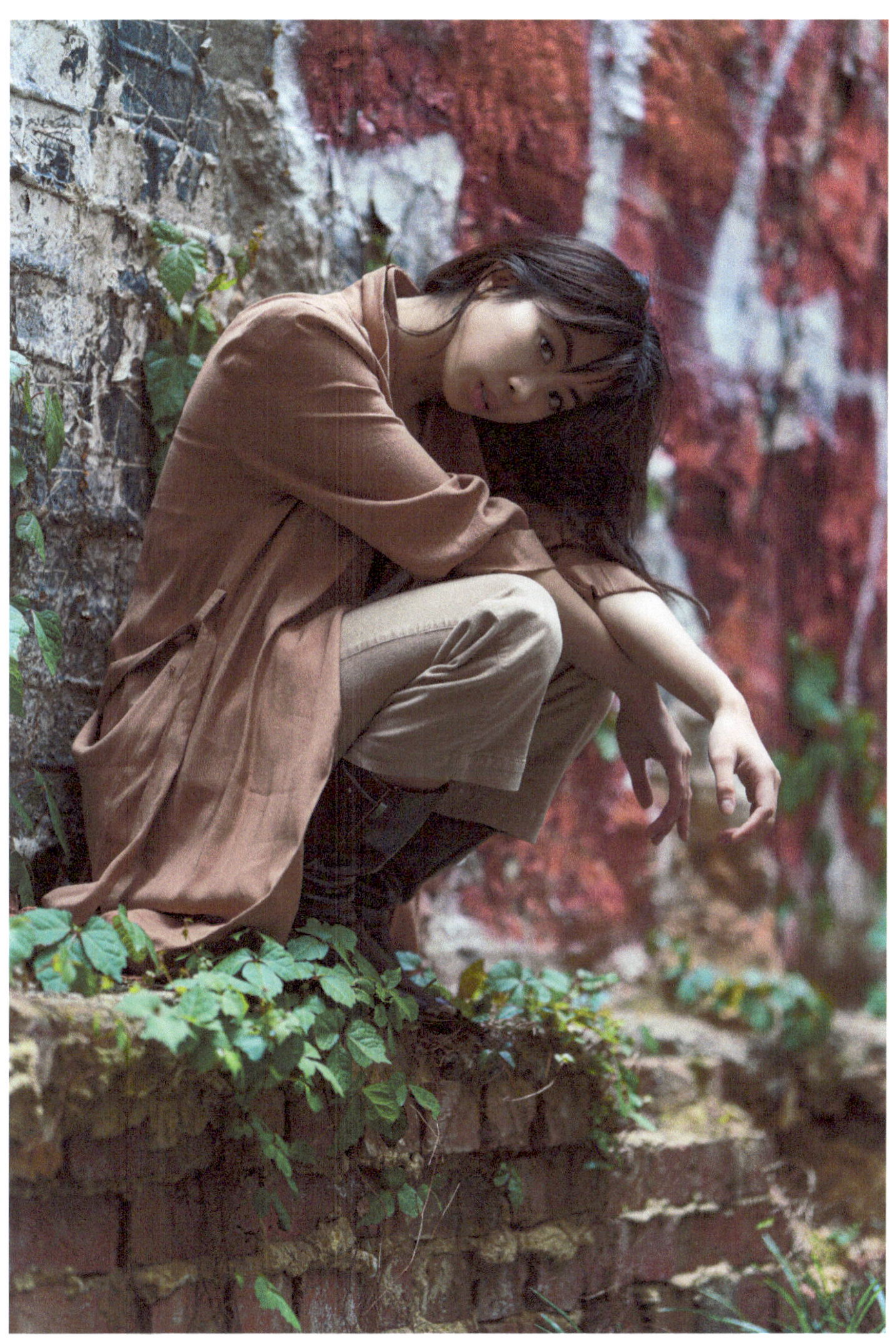

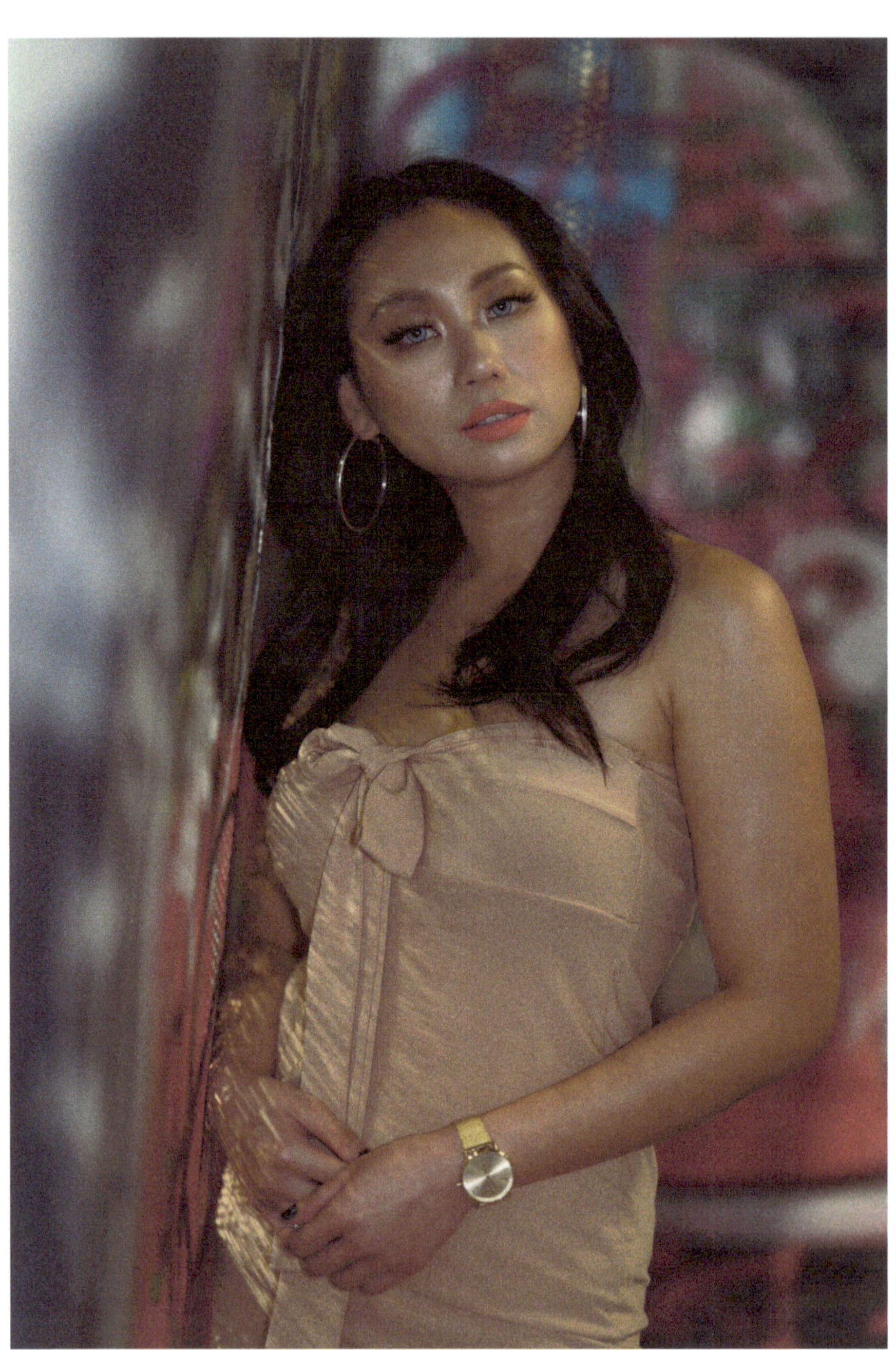

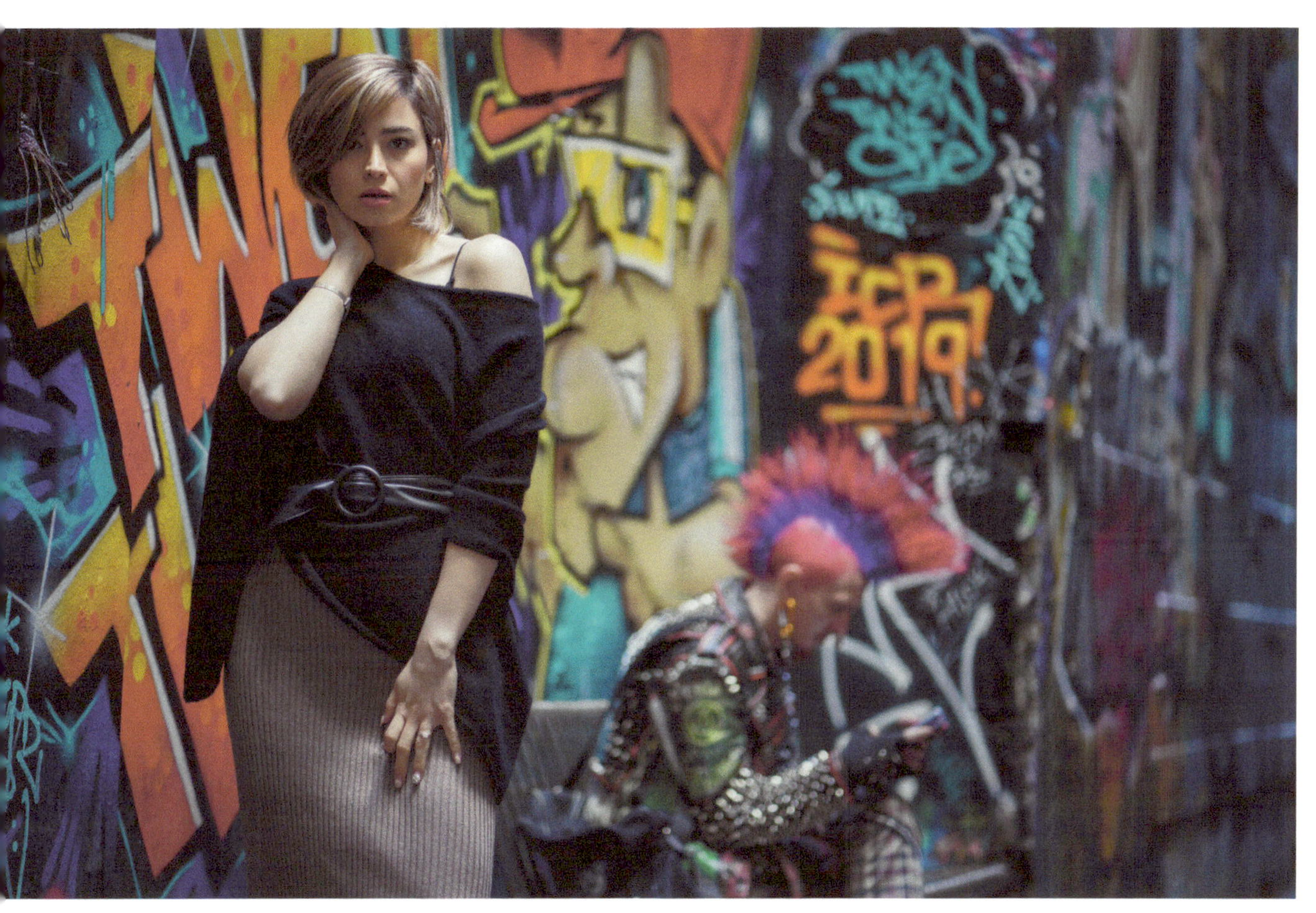

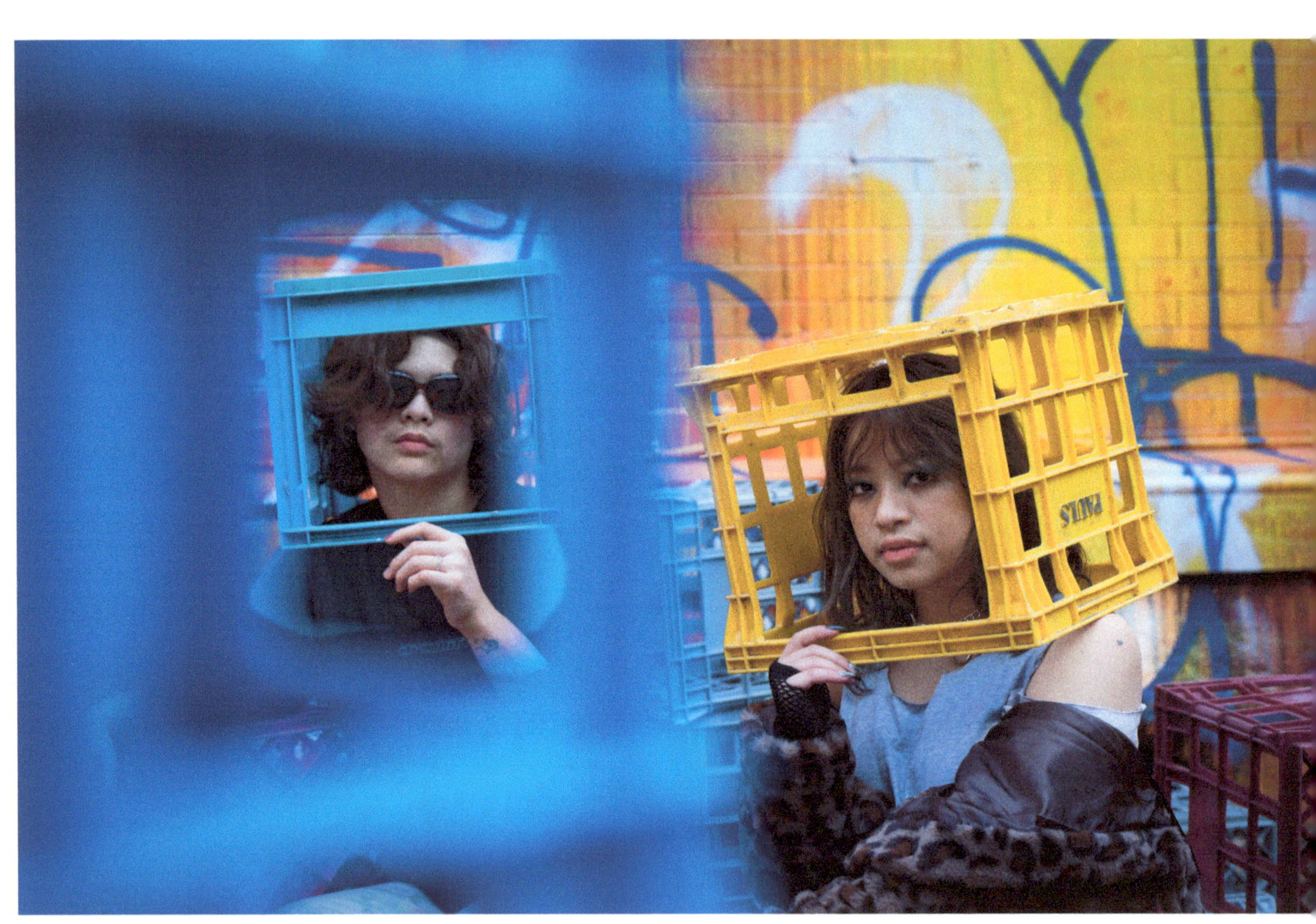

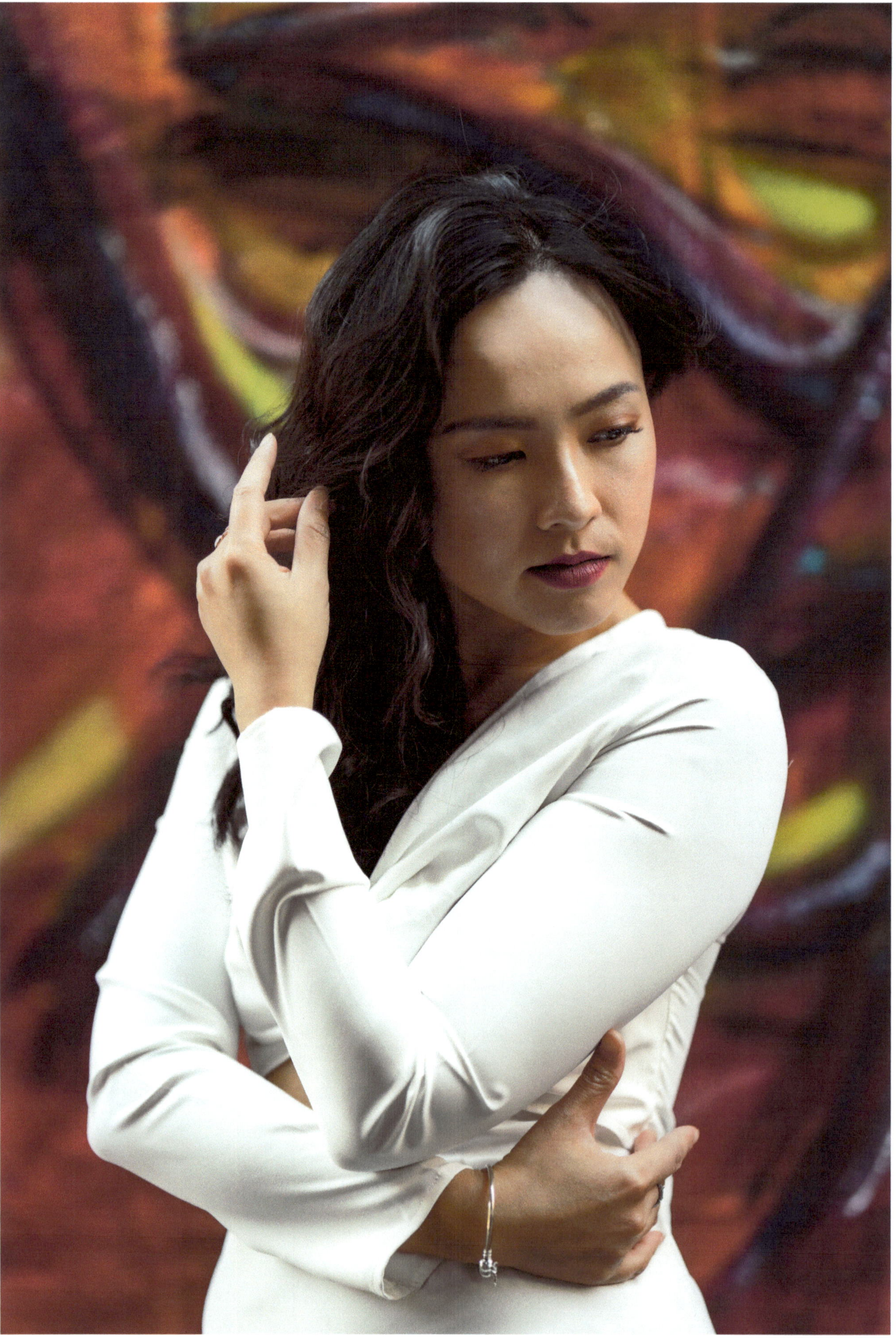

Behind The Lens

"Be Bolder.
Dream Bigger."

Paul Tocatlian

Behind The Lens

Hi, I'm Paul Tocatlian, and photography is how I celebrate what makes us bold and what inspires us to dream bigger. Based in the San Francisco Bay Area, my camera has taken me across five continents, collaborating with incredible creatives from all corners of the globe. Home? It's wherever inspiration hits—whether I'm in the vibrant streets of Melbourne, navigating the fast-paced fashion scenes of New York and Paris, or discovering something unexpected, I'm always chasing that next spark of creativity.

What really drives me is the connection with those I work alongside—brands, designers, models, and creatives alike. I'm drawn to more than just capturing what's in front of the lens; it's about the stories, the emotions, and the authenticity that come to life. Fashion, style, and personality all blend into a larger journey—a moment in time that feels alive, unique, and powerful. Every image becomes part of a bigger narrative, celebrating individuality and self-expression.

The most exciting part of this journey is the collaborative spirit behind every project. Photography isn't a solo act—it's a partnership where everyone, from designers and stylists to models, works together to create something unforgettable. Whether it's the pulse of runway coverage at New York Fashion Week or the creative direction of an editorial shoot, each experience has its own rhythm. I thrive in this balance of spontaneity and intention, where the most authentic stories come to life.

At the end of the day, my mission is simple: to connect, to inspire, and to remind everyone I work with that they're capable of being bold and dreaming bigger. Whether capturing the rush of a runway or shaping an editorial narrative, my goal is always to create something meaningful that resonates beyond the moment. I'd love to collaborate on your next project—feel free to reach out and let's bring your vision to life together.

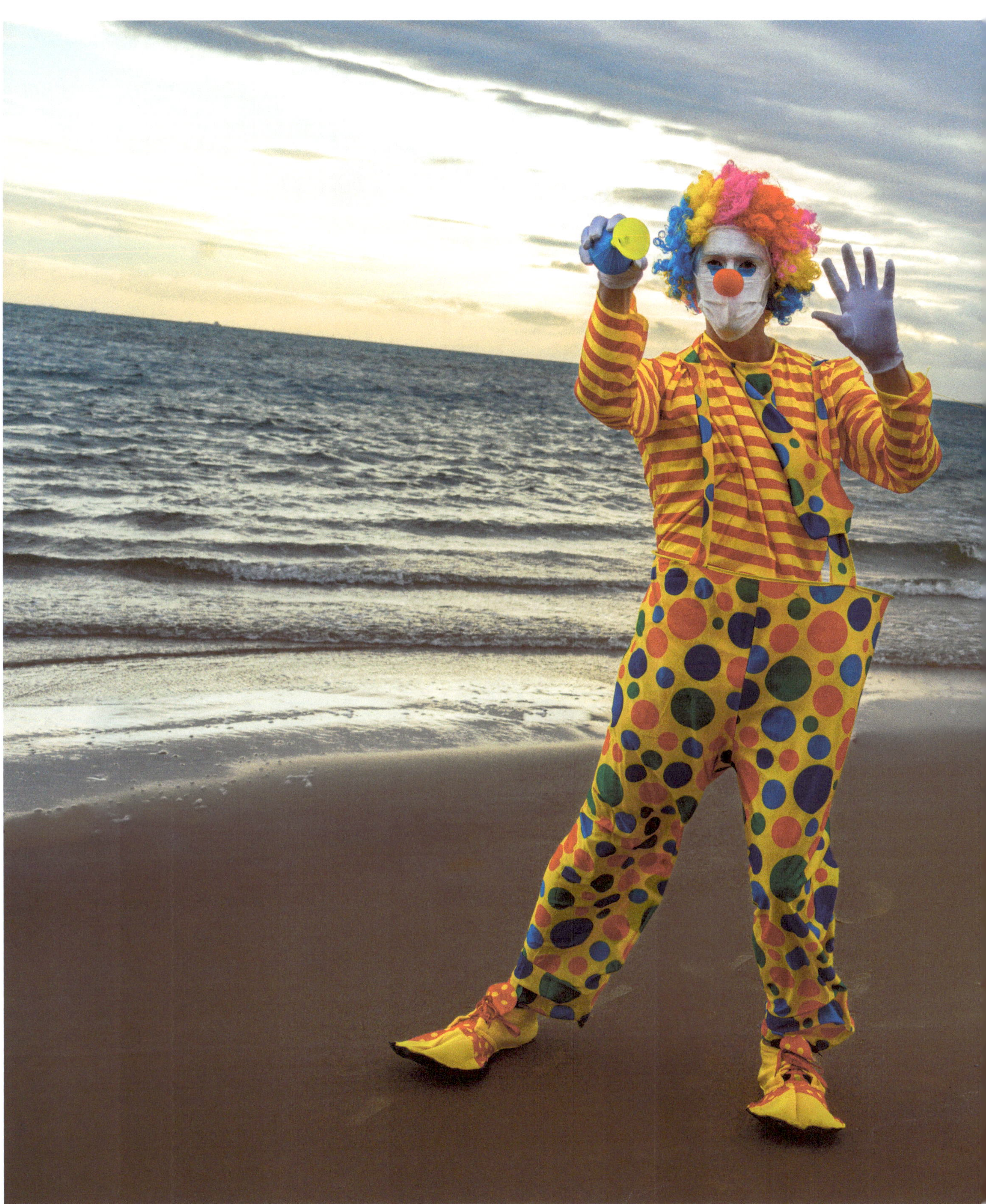

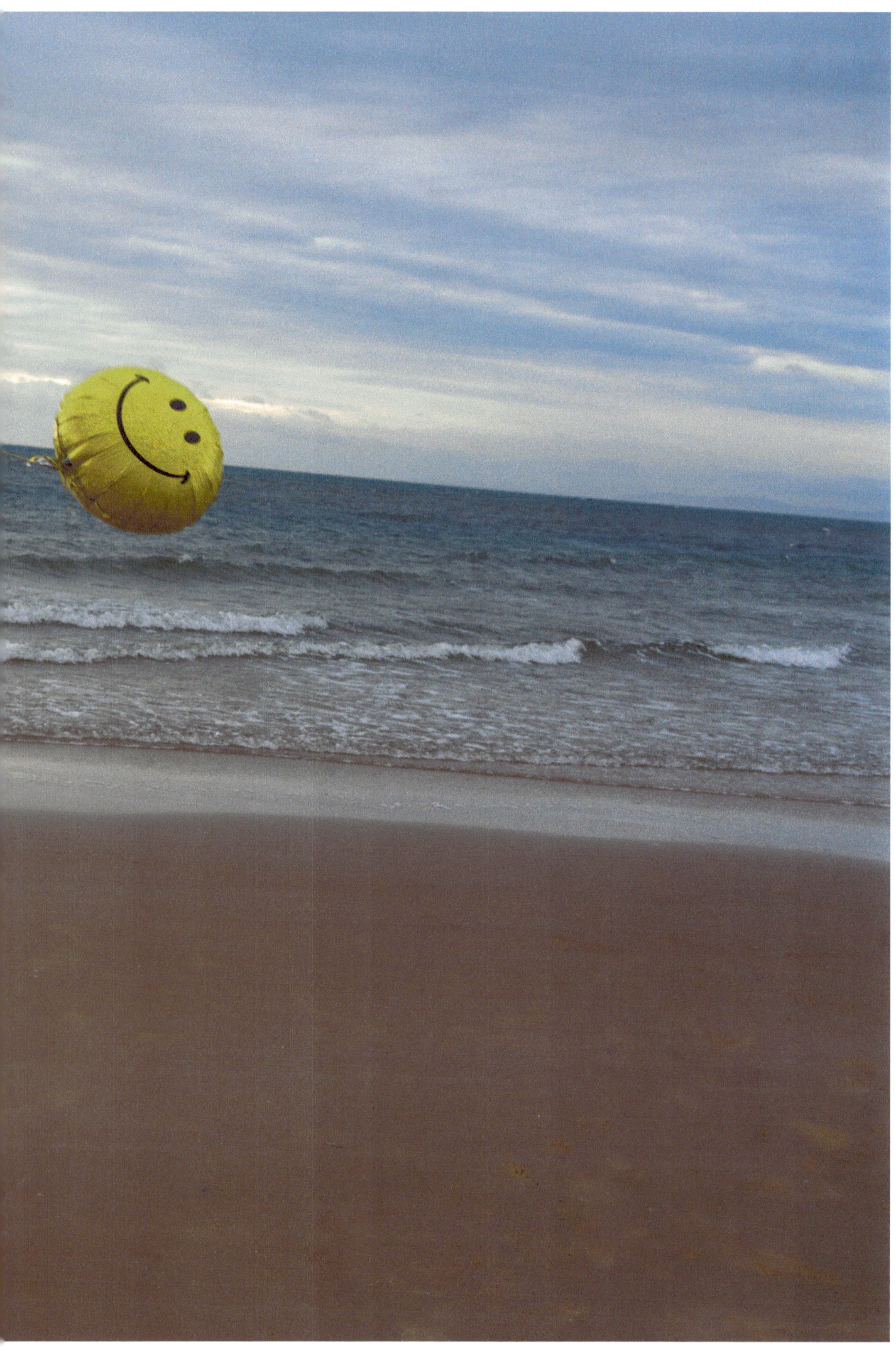